Venture into Cultures

A Resource Book of Multicultural Materials and Programs

Edited by Carla D. Hayden

American Library Association
Chicago and London 1992

Cover and text designed by Ray Machura
Composed by Publishing Services, Inc.,
   in Melior on a Xyvision/Cg 8600
Printed on 50-pound Glatfelter Thor, a pH-neutral
   stock, and bound in 10-point C1S cover stock by
   McNaughton & Gunn, Inc.

The paper used in this publication meets the
minimum requirements of American National
Standard for Information Sciences—Permanence of
Paper for Printed Library Materials, ANSI
Z39.48-1984.∞

Illustrations in Chapter 1 from *African Designs of
Nigeria and the Cameroons,* © by Caren Caraway.
Reprinted courtesy of Stemmer House, Inc.,
Publishers, Owings-Miller, Maryland.

Cover: *clockwise, beginning top left,* Merlin mask
(p.74); Adinkra symbol for unity (p.13); African
mask (p.11); and two characters in the Chinese New
Year's wish, May you prosper (p.63)

**Library of Congress Cataloging-in-Publication
Data**
Venture into cultures : a resource book of
   multicultural materials and programs / edited by
   Carla D. Hayden.
        p.   cm.
   Includes bibliographical references and index.
   ISBN 0-8389-0579-X
   1. Children's literature—Bibliography. 2. United
States—Ethnic relations—Juvenile literature—
Bibliography. 3. Minorities—United States—
Juvenile literature—Bibliography. 4. Pluralism
(Social sciences) in literature—Bibliography.
5. Ethnic groups in literature—Bibliography.
6. Minorities in literature—Bibliography.
I. Hayden, Carla Diane, 1952–
Z1037.9.V46   1992
[PN1009.A1]
011.62—dc20   91-43373

Printed in the United States of America.

96 95 94 93   5 4 3 2

Contents

Contents

Preface

As changing world events challenge perceptions and emotions, the authors of this resource book invite you to venture into the cultural aspects of children's literature and programming. The contributors to the book are librarians, educators, and American Library Association members who have more than an academic interest in the subject. In 1987, members of the Children's Services Task Force of ALA's Ethnic Materials and Information Exchange Round Table (EMIERT) began to discuss the needs of librarians and others who work with children in the presentation of culturally authentic materials and programs. Many of the discussions focused on the lack of resources that covered several ethnic groups and included more than just lists of books. The group decided to sponsor a resource guide that would present basic titles and practical program ideas. This book is the direct result of those spirited and sometimes heated discussions.

BACKGROUND

There is currently a great deal of interest in multiculturalism on all educational and societal levels. The growing number of programs to enhance diversity in the workplace and cultural awareness in schools reflect a corresponding increase in recognition of the changing ethnic composition of the United States. James Banks, noted educator and author (see the Selected Bibliography), asserts that multiculturalism is more than the content of materials and programs. It is a way of viewing the world and its people. Multiculturalism is a process that can

become a regular part of everyday programming activities.

A concern for ethnic diversity in children's books once was addressed as an aspect of promoting better world relations, particularly after World War II. In fact, the International Youth Library in Munich was founded after that war in the belief that if children could read about and, it was hoped, understand others, there might not be a need for warfare in the future. Further concern about ethnic representation in books for youth grew with the development of children's book publishing and changes in social conditions. In 1965, Nancy Larrick's landmark article "The All-White World of Children's Books" sounded a cry that signaled a subsequent flood of new ethnic titles, particularly about African Americans. During the remainder of the decade, attention was drawn to the portrayals of minorities in all types of materials for children, most notably textbooks.

In the 1970s, resources for adults promoting children's multiethnic literature appeared in significant quantities, with some distinctions made between world cultures and ethnic groups within the United States (see Selected Bibliography). Despite a decrease in the production of ethnic children's books during the next decade, a renewed interest in cultural representation in literature for youth has recently spurred more efforts in this area. There has been a notable increase in professional literature, special conference sessions, and local programming activities. Yet, there is still a need for additional guides, youth literature, and professional information. In an attempt to alleviate that need, *Venture into Cultures* identifies key and notable resources for children and adults and presents ideas for programs about seven cultural groups as aids for helping children gain an appreciation and understanding of their own and other cultures.

CRITERIA FOR INCLUSION

The emphasis in this book is on groups found in significant numbers in the United States, some involved in the migrations of the world wars and others who are native or more recent immigrants. Groups from Eastern Europe are thoroughly covered in a recently published book by Frances Povsic (see the Selected Bibliography).

Although each chapter of this book is individual in tone and content, all of the authors attempted to select items that were primarily accurate in cultural representation. The chapter on Hispanic cultures gives guidelines regarding selection that are worth elaborating on for general consideration in selecting materials with ethnic content or characters:

- Look for a quality of reality that gives the reader a chance to experience something.
- Try to determine the author's commitment to portray cultural groups accurately.
- Avoid materials that sensationalize, enumerate unusual customs, or practice reversed stereotyping.
- Be sensitive to emphasis on cultural differences at the expense of similarities.
- Whenever possible, use the same critical criteria appropriate for all types of literature—distinctive language and appropriate dialogue, style, relevance and potential interest, clear-cut plots, and believable characterizations.

ARRANGEMENT AND ORGANIZATION

Like the cultures they represent, each chapter is unique, reflecting the cultural orientation and background of the author, and making this effort rather like a cultural mosaic. Readers can often get a sense of those variations in the brief introductions to chapters. The numbers of materials in each section also reflect the varying bibliographic and publishing bases of the groups. An effort was made to include materials published by small or alternate presses that are often not easily identifiable. The annotated lists within each chapter include fiction, picture books, folklore, and nonfiction as well as media and materials for adults who work with children. Complete bibliographic information is given whenever possible; however, some titles may not have ISBN numbers because of the nature of the material. In other instances, prices may not be available or are variable. A few out-of-print titles are included (clearly marked o.p.) in cases where little else exists or the authors believe the value warrants inclusion. This work does not of course include everything written about the cultures represented but does give basic tools for learning and appreciation.

Thanks to the many librarians, educators, and interested others who contributed throughout the process and especially ALA Books editor Bettina MacAyeal for her guidance and patience and Bonnie J. Smothers for taking the project through the final stages. My personal appreciation is extended to the staff of the Department of Library Science at the University of Pittsburgh for their cheerful and careful assistance with the manuscript preparation.

Carla D. Hayden

CHAPTER 1

African-American Materials and Programs

by Martha R. Ruff

African Americans make up one of the largest ethnic groups in the United States. American society has been heavily influenced by the culture and personalities of this group. The resources and programs in this section highlight the culture and contributions of African Americans. Reclaiming their African heritage is a prominent issue among African Americans today. Consequently, recommended materials about Africa and the Caribbean are included as an integral part of this section. This bibliography presents only a small portion of the materials that are available. Other bibliographies are available through large public libraries, such as New York Public Library and Los Angeles Public Library.

A knowledge of the history of African Americans is a prerequisite for anyone who shares materials and programs about them. The history of African Americans begins in ancient Africa where the kingdoms of Mali, Ghana, and Songhai left a legacy of literature, art, and music. While most African Americans cannot trace their family history to Africa, their historical roots stem from central and west Africa where these kingdoms flourished. The history of ancient Africa is very limited in children's literature. Adults can learn more about this period from such reference sources as *They Came Before Columbus* by Ivan Van Sertima (Random House, 1976), *From Slavery to Freedom* by John Hope Franklin (Knopf, 1987), and *Before the Mayflower* by Lerone Bennett (Viking Penguin, 1984). To present the period of captivity in proper perspective, an understanding of ancient African history is essential.

Even though Africans were with the Europeans who explored America, many materials present slaves as the first blacks in America. African Americans were held in captivity in the United States for over two hundred years and yet they developed a culture and community spirit that thrived. The myths that supported the African slave trade were expressly designed to create the false impression that Africans were inhuman and lacked the structures of European civilization. Children's materials about this period should realistically relate the fact that all peoples of the world at some point in their history were slaves. This viewpoint is documented by Milton Meltzer in *All Times, All Peoples: A World History of Slavery* (HarperCollins, 1980).

Other aspects of African-American culture were formed during the periods that followed: the Civil War, Reconstruction, the Harlem Renaissance, segregation, and the civil rights movement. Knowledge of these events will provide a background for some of the themes prevalent in African-American literature for children. All of the books of Mildred Taylor, for example (*Roll of Thunder, Hear My Cry* and others in the series), require an understanding of segregation and the civil rights movement. Some highlights of African-American history are outlined in *Teaching Strategies for Ethnic Studies* by James A. Banks (Allyn and Bacon, 1991). In addition, Banks has included a synopsis of many of the aforementioned periods. This general background in African-American history is fundamental for planning programs and choosing materials that are historically and culturally accurate.

The following bibliography of recommended children's materials is presented in five sections: picture books, fiction, folktales, the arts, and history. Some materials that are out-of-print yet still available in libraries have been included. Books that are especially suited to reading aloud have that information included in their annotation, with the exception of picture books, most of which are designed for reading aloud. The sections vary in length but most contain at least ten selections.

BIBLIOGRAPHY

PICTURE BOOKS

K–3. Brenner, Barbara. *Wagon Wheels.* New York: HarperCollins, 1978. 64pp. $10.95. ISBN: 0-06-020668-3.

A father and his three sons travel west at the end of the Civil War. The beginning-reader format presents a solid story of life in developing Kansas and one family's adventures. Based on a historical incident, this novel is very realistic.

K–3. Bryan, Ashley. *The Cat's Purr.* New York: Atheneum, 1985. 48pp. $10.95. ISBN: 0-689-31086-2.

This Caribbean tale explains why cats purr. Rat and Cat are friends until Rat plays Cat's special drum. When Cat tries to punish Rat, he has an accident that causes him to purr. The text is rhythmic and has a West Indies flavor. Great for storytelling.

K–2. Caines, Jeannette. *Just Us Women.* New York: HarperCollins, 1982. 32pp. $14.95. ISBN: 0-06-020941-0.

A car ride to the South is a special occasion for Aunt Martha and her niece. The story lovingly portrays the bond between an African-American woman and her young relative. This story could be shared in a big brother/big sister program.

K–3. Clifton, Lucille. *Everett Anderson's Goodbye.* New York: Holt, 1983. 32pp. $10.95. ISBN: 0-8050-0235-9.

The story conveys the grief felt by Everett Anderson upon the death of his father. The love and support of an African-American family are portrayed as Everett is consoled by his mother and stepfather. Bold black-and-white drawings add power to the story.

P–2. Cummings, Pat. *Jimmy Lee Did It.* New York: Lothrop, 1985. 32pp. $13.95. ISBN: 0-688-04632-0.

A little girl tries to find the mystery boy who creates mischief around their house. Only her brother knows when Jimmy Lee is around. The fun of this deception is clearly illustrated with vibrant paintings and a catchy, rhyming text.

P–3. De Veaux, Alexis. *An Enchanted Hair Tale.* New York: HarperCollins, 1987. 40pp. $12.95. ISBN: 0-06-021623-9.

Sudan's dredlock hairstyle causes other people to make fun of him. He finds comfort with people who also have dredlocks. The poetic text and bold illustrations create fantastic images. This is the only book that addresses an increasingly popular hairstyle.

1–3. Feelings, Muriel. *Jambo Means Hello: Swahili Alphabet Book.* New York: Dial, 1974. 56pp. $13.95. ISBN: 0-8037-4346-7.

Using the alphabet, twenty-six Swahili words are defined and illustrated. Phonetic spelling is included along with a map of Africa showing the countries where Swahili is spoken. The dramatic black-and-white drawings clearly present traditional African life.

2–4. Flournoy, Valerie. *The Patchwork Quilt.* New York: Dial, 1985. 32pp. $13.95. ISBN: 0-8037-0097-0.

A young girl discovers the importance of family and her heritage as she helps her grandmother work on a patchwork memory quilt. This African-American family shows the tradition of support and love for elderly family members.

1–3. Greenfield, Eloise. *Africa Dream*. New York: Crowell, 1989. 32pp. $13.89. ISBN: 0-690-04776-2.

A girl's dream about Africa is told in a poetic style with dreamy pencil drawings. She is welcomed and finds comfort in her heritage. This book can help children begin to understand the relationship between Africans and African Americans.

P–1. Hayes, Sarah. *Happy Christmas Gemma*. New York: Lothrop, 1986. 32pp. $13.95. ISBN: 0-688-06508-2.

A British Jamaican family celebrates Christmas with the well-intentioned help of the young brother and baby sister. Baby Gemma gives readers a realistic view of a toddler's world. This story provides a glimpse of black life in Europe.

P–2. Lewin, Hugh. *Jafta and the Wedding*. Minneapolis: Carolrhoda, 1983. 24pp. $9.95. ISBN: 0-87614-210-2.

A South African boy describes the week-long celebration of his sister's wedding. The bold two-tone drawings illustrate the joyous emotions of the people who participate in this village ceremony. This book is one of a series about Jafta and his life in South Africa.

K–3. McKissack, Patricia. *Mirandy and Brother Wind*. New York: Knopf, 1988. 32pp. $13.95. ISBN: 0-394-88765-4.

Mirandy is led on a wild-goose chase for her partner in the cakewalk dance. In the end, Brother Wind and clumsy Ezell help her shine at her first dance contest. This lively story brings dignity to an African-American dance style that was once ridiculed.

1–3. Yarbrough, Camille. *Cornrows*. New York: Coward, 1981. 48pp. $7.95. ISBN: 0-698-20462-X.

This story relates the sense of community that is passed on from Africans to African Americans. Two children hear their grandmother and mother share the story of their heritage. A rhyme in the story presents several prominent historical figures, including Paul Robeson, Queen Nzinga, and Richard Wright.

FICTION

5–8. Boyd, Candy Dawson. *Breadsticks and Blessing Places*. New York: Macmillan, 1985. 216pp. $14.95. ISBN: 0-02-709290-9.

Toni studies to raise her math scores on the exam for the King Academy. Her loyalty to two girlfriends is also tested during this time. Toni learns to handle guilt and grief when one friend dies. The author skillfully presents meaningful relationships.

1–3. Cameron, Ann. *The Stories Julian Tells*. New York: Pantheon Books, 1981. 96pp. $8.95. ISBN: 0-394-84301-0.

Julian's imagination keeps his younger brother entertained and makes his father stay on his toes. A colloquial style and creative pencil drawings give a special touch to stories about catalog cats and cooking pudding like a night on the sea.

3–6. Hamilton, Virginia. *Bells of Christmas*. New York: Harcourt Brace Jovanovich, 1989. 60pp. $16.95. ISBN: 0-15-206450-8.

During Christmas in 1890, young Jason waits for his relatives, for the bells, and for the holiday festivities to begin. A heartwarming story is created by the loving African-American family whose roots and traditions are a memorable part of nineteenth-century Ohio.

5–8. _____. *The House of Dies Drear*. New York: Macmillan, 1968. 256pp. $14.95. ISBN: 0-02-742500-2.

Thomas and his family move into a house in Ohio that was once a stop on the Underground Railroad. Through mysterious events, he and a friend discover the house's secrets. A sequel, *The Mystery of Drear House*, also shows how modern children find their relationship to the past.

3–5. _____. *Zeely*. New York: Macmillan, 1967. 128pp. $13.95. ISBN: 0-02-742470-7.

Summer in the South allows Elizabeth and her brother a chance to be imaginative and meet a strange woman who looks like an African princess. Powerful characters and a descriptive story combine to reveal the emotions of growing up and developing self-esteem.

6–8.   Lester, Julius. *This Strange New Feeling.* New York: Dial, 1982. 160pp. $14.95. ISBN: 0-8037-8491-0.

Three love stories recreate the emotion and drama of three slave couples who gain their freedom. This sensitive and realistic portrayal presents these African Americans as fully developed personalities. The harsh realities of the period are fully described.

3–7.   Myers, Walter Dean. *Me, Mop, and the Moondance Kid.* New York: Delacorte, 1988. 128pp. $13.95. ISBN: 0-440-50065-6.

T. J. and his younger brother Moondance are adopted and have a chance to leave the orphanage. They are unhappy about leaving Mop (Miss Olivia Parrish) and their winning Little League team. These memorable characters show the love that is possible among children who are not relatives.

4–8.   Naidoo, Beverley. *Journey to Jo'burg: A South African Story.* Philadelphia: Lippincott, 1986. 96pp. $11.95. ISBN: 0-397-32168-6.

Two children travel from their small village to the big city of Johannesburg to tell their mother of an illness in the family. These black South African children experience the effects of apartheid during their trip.

4–6.   Tate, Eleanora. *Just an Overnight Guest.* New York: Dial, 1980. 182pp. o.p.

Nine-year-old Maggie is outraged when an unruly four-year-old white girl comes to live with her family. Maggie discovers that this racially mixed girl is her uncle's child. The sensitive issues are presented in a realistic and appropriate manner.

5–8.   _____. *The Secret of Gumbo Grove.* New York: Watts, 1987. 256pp. $12.95. ISBN: 0-531-15051-8.

Cleaning a neglected cemetery with an elderly woman in the community leads Raisin to some local African-American history.

She learns the importance of her heritage and of respect for senior citizens. This mystery includes well-developed characters.

5–8.   Taylor, Mildred D. *Roll of Thunder, Hear My Cry.* New York: Dial, 1976. 276pp. $14.95. ISBN: 0-8037-7473-7.

Young Cassie and her brothers discover what it means to grow up in the segregated South. The scenes in this novel provide powerful images of the forces of racism facing a strong black family. This Newbery Award-winning book has several sequels.

3–6.   Walter, Mildred P. *Have a Happy . . .* New York: Lothrop, 1989. 144pp. $10.95. ISBN: 0-688-06923-1.

Because his father is laid off, Chris is worried about getting a bicycle for his birthday, which is on Christmas Day. His family's celebration of Kwanzaa helps him understand the importance of his family and heritage. The characters and plot are realistic.

2–5.   _____. *Justin and the Best Biscuits in the World.* New York: Lothrop, 1986. 128pp. $12.95. ISBN: 0-688-06645-3.

Justin's grandfather helps him understand what it means to be a man and teaches him about blacks in the Old West. This novel creates sensitive images of black men and introduces historical black cowboys, such as Bill Pickett and Nat Love.

5–8.   Yarbrough, Camille. *The Shimmershine Queens.* New York: Putnam, 1989. 128pp. $13.95. ISBN: 0-399-21465-8.

Ten-year-old Angie learns to handle being teased about her dark skin and to calm her fears about her parents' separation. Finding the "shimmershine" feeling makes her feel good about herself. A colloquial style warmly conveys this story's message.

FOLKTALES

K–3.   Aardema, Verna. *Bringing the Rain to Kapiti Plain.* New York: Dial, 1981. 32pp. $14.95. ISBN: 0-8037-0809-2.

This cumulative poetic folktale from East Africa shows how a cow herder ends a drought with a mighty shot from a bow and arrow. A faithful rendering of an old tale, the story also shows how folktales developed in reaction to some of the harsh realities of life.

1–3. _____. *Rabbit Makes a Monkey of Lion.* New York: Dial, 1989. 32pp. $11.95. ISBN: 0-8037-0297-3.

Rabbit and her friends Turtle and Bush-rat outwit the Lion and eat the honey from Lion's calabash tree. The story introduces another African trickster and shows small creatures overcoming large ones. Vibrant illustrations bring the story alive.

1–3. _____. *Who's in Rabbit's House.* New York: Dial, 1977. 32pp. $14.95. ISBN: 0-8037-9550-5.

A scary animal is in Rabbit's house and tricks the other animals who come to help. The illustrations reveal how the Masai people of eastern Africa might act out this story with animal masks. Audience members wear traditional Masai dress.

1–3. _____. *Why Mosquitoes Buzz in People's Ears.* New York: Dial, 1975. 32pp. $14.95. ISBN: 0-8037-6089-2.

A mosquito's comment to an iguana causes a chain reaction that keeps the jungle in darkness. This African folktale gives an imaginative explanation of a very common event. This Caldecott Award-winning book could be used for storytelling and dramatics.

1–3. Dee, Ruby. *Two Ways to Count to Ten.* New York: Holt, 1988. 32pp. $12.95. ISBN: 0-8050-0407-6.

This west African folktale is about the leopard, king of the animals, who sets a test to choose the new king. Only the antelope is able to discover a way to win. The moral of brains beating brawn is clearly shown. The writing style is suitable for storytelling.

1–3. Haley, Gail. *A Story, a Story.* New York: Atheneum, 1970. 32pp. $14.95. ISBN: 0-689-20511-2.

This folktale explains how Ananse, the spiderman trickster, receives stories from the sky god Nyame. By completing a seemingly impossible task, Ananse brings stories into the world. Caldecott Award-winning woodcut illustrations present African customs.

3–5. Hooks, William H. *The Ballad of Belle Dorcas.* New York: Knopf, 1990. 48pp. $13.95. ISBN: 0-394-84645-1.

Belle Dorcas is free but chooses to marry the man she loves, Joshua, who is a slave. When Joshua is to be sold, Belle uses conjure magic that turns him into a tree. This magical tale gives glimpses of slavery and has provocative illustrations.

4–8. Lester, Julius. *The Tales of Uncle Remus: The Adventures of Brer Rabbit.* New York: Dial, 1987. 154pp. $16.95. ISBN: 0-8037-0271-X.

This collection of African-American animal stories features Brer Rabbit and other animals who have adventures with him. Many of the tales illustrate how the small rabbit outwits the larger animals. This collection and two others are written in modern language.

4–8. Rollins, Charlemae. *Christmas Gif'.* Chicago: Follett, 1963. 119pp. o.p.

A classic collection, this book presents African-American Christmas traditions in story, song, poetry, and food. It includes a west African version of the Christmas story. Rollins included recipes from her grandmother, who was a slave. The book is a good source for programs.

3–5. San Souci, Robert D. *Talking Eggs.* New York: Dial, 1989. 32pp. $13.95. ISBN: 0-8037-0619-7.

This African-American tale is based on a familiar theme. When the mistreated sister in a family receives riches, the older girl tries unsuccessfully to follow the same method. Bright watercolor illustrations add life to this humorous tale.

1–3. Steptoe, John. *Mufaro's Beautiful Daughters: An African Tale.* New York: Lothrop, 1987. 32pp. $14.95. ISBN: 0-688-04045-4.

An award-winning retelling of an African folktale, the story is a Cinderella tale of two sisters who vie for the hand of the prince. The kind and generous sister is chosen over the mean and spiteful sister. Lush illustrations show the ancient kingdom of Zimbabwe.

THE ARTS

1–5. Bryan, Ashley. *All Night, All Day: A Child's First Book of African American Spirituals.* New York: Atheneum, 1991. 48pp. $14.95. ISBN: 0-689-31662-3.

This collection of black spirituals and illustrations reveals the experiences of African Americans during slavery. The words and music can be used by both children and adults. The author's notes help readers understand the inspiration and use of these songs.

5–8. Davis, Ossie. *Langston: A Play.* New York: Delacorte, 1982. 144pp. $11.95. ISBN: 0-385-28543-4.

Highlighting the life of Langston Hughes, African-American poet and playwright, this drama centers around Hughes's help for a theater group producing one of his plays. The play is suitable for young actors or reader's theater.

5–8. Dunbar, Paul L. *Complete Poems of Paul Laurence Dunbar.* New York: Dodd, 1980. o.p.

Using a variety of poetic forms (from sonnets to free verse), Dunbar expresses his feelings about the black experience during the early 1900s. This collection displays why Dunbar was considered an outstanding and prolific poet in his short lifetime.

1–5. Giovanni, Nikki. *Spin a Soft Black Song: Poems for Children.* New York: Hill and Wang, 1985. 57pp. $11.95. ISBN: 0-8090-8796-0.

Childhood times and feelings are described in free verse. The joyous poems are about playing, dancing, family, and friends in the black community. Black musicians and historical figures are included in some of the poems.

K–4. Greenfield, Eloise. *Honey, I Love and Other Love Poems.* New York: HarperCollins, 1986. 48pp. $3.50. ISBN: 0-06-443097-9.

These poems explore the many meanings of love that children understand. Poems like "Honey, I Love" and "Harriet Tubman" express the idea that love is more than kissing and hugging. Other poems share black rhythms that children use in jump rope and music.

1–5. _____. *Nathaniel Talking.* New York: Black Butterfly, 1989. 32pp. $11.95. ISBN: 0-86316-200-2.

These poems share the emotions and interests of a young African-American boy. Love of family and traditions are strong themes. The author includes notes on blues music and on making rhythms with "bones." The title poem gives a positive example of rapping.

6–8. Haskins, Jim. *Black Music in America; A History through Its People.* New York: Crowell, 1987. 224pp. $12.95. ISBN: 0-690-04460-7.

This succinct history of African-American music from fifteenth-century Africa to the present day includes chapters on blues, jazz, soul, and other kinds of music. The text and photographs clearly present this unique musical contribution.

3–6. Hughes, Langston. *Dream Keeper.* New York: Knopf, 1962. 78pp. $10.99. ISBN: 0-394-91096-6.

In selecting these poems with child appeal, Lee Bennett Hopkins has included some of Hughes's famous poems, such as "Mother to Son," "I've Known Rivers," and "I Too Sing America." This book is a good introduction to an important African-American writer.

4–8. Kuklin, Susan. *Reaching for Dreams: A Ballet from Rehearsal to Opening Night.* New York: Lothrop, 1987. 128pp. $12.95. ISBN: 0-688-06316-0.

The Alvin Ailey American Dance Theater is featured in this documentary of how a modern dance performance is produced. African Americans appear as dancers, choreographers, and managers. Black-and-white photographs are included.

P–5. Langstaff, John. *What a Morning! The Christmas Story in Black Spirituals.* New York: Macmillan, 1987. 32pp. $13.95. ISBN: 0-689-50422-5.

Biblical verses and black spirituals combine to relate the story of Christ's birth. Ashley Bryan's stunning paintings provide a perfect picture-book format for use in story hours and musical programs. Musical arrangements are included.

1–3. Little, Lessie Jones. *Children of Long Ago.* New York: Philomel, 1988. 32pp. $13.95. ISBN: 0-399-21473-9.

In this collection of poems about children during the early 1900s, rural life is described in scenes of chopping wood and getting water from a well. The poems reveal practical items, such as the clothing of the period, as well as the black community spirit.

K–5. Mattox, Cheryl Warren. *Shake It to the One that You Love the Best.* El Sobrante: Warren-Mattox Productions, 1989. 56pp. $25.00. ISBN: 0-962-3381-0-9.

This book-and-cassette of over thirty songs celebrates play songs and lullabies from black musical traditions. Included are such familiar rhymes as "Hambone" as well as songs from other countries, such as "Jump Shamador" from the Caribbean. Musical arrangements and game directions are provided in this colorful music book.

3–8. Walker, David A., and James Haskins. *Double Dutch.* Hillside, N.J.: Enslow, 1986. 64pp. $15.95. ISBN: 0-89490-096-X.

Double dutch, a jump-rope game popular among African Americans, has become an organized team sport. The text includes a history of double dutch, instructions for beginning and advanced players, and photographs of an official double dutch tournament.

HISTORY

K–5. Chocolate, Deborah Newton. *Kwanzaa.* Chicago: Children's Press, 1990. 32pp. $14.60. ISBN: 0-516-03991-1.

This colorful picture book presents the African-American holiday of Kwanzaa. After a short introduction, a young boy describes his family's celebration of the seven-day holiday. The illustrations add to the information about Kwanzaa.

1–4. Ellis, Veronica F. *Afrobets First Book about Africa.* Orange, N.J.: Just Us Books, 1990. 32pp. $13.95. ISBN: 0-940975-12-2.

This story relates how a class studies Africa and learns about many aspects of that continent's history and culture. The book sets a model that teachers could follow and can be used as a starting point for studying Africa. Colorful illustrations enhance the text.

5–8. Haskins, Jim. *Bill Cosby: America's Most Famous Father.* New York: Walker and Co., 1988. 128pp. $13.95. ISBN: 0-8027-6785-0.

As a comedian, actor, businessman, philanthropist, and doctor of education, Bill Cosby is a role model for young people. The major achievements of his career are highlighted. Black-and-white photographs are included.

1–5. Laird, Elizabeth. *The Road to Bethlehem: An Ethiopian Nativity.* New York: Holt, 1987. 32pp. $12.95. ISBN: 0-8050-0539-0.

Vibrant paintings show ancient Ethiopian versions of Christ's birth and reveal the heritage of one of the world's oldest sects of Christianity. Facts about the artist add to the reader's understanding of Ethiopia's role in Christianity.

1–3. Lowery, Linda. *Martin Luther King Day.* Minneapolis: Carolrhoda, 1987. 56pp. $9.95. ISBN: 0-87614-229-4.

Using an easy-to-read format, the author relates the life of Dr. King and the history of the holiday. The text is suitable for reading aloud and can be used to encourage children to think of appropriate activities for the holiday.

6–8. Magubane, Peter. *Black Child*. New York: Knopf, 1982. 112pp. o.p.

An award-winning black South African photographer documents the living conditions of black children in South Africa. The book includes a history of the apartheid system and how it affects the lifestyles of black South Africans.

5–8. McClester, Cedric. *Kwanzaa: Everything You Always Wanted to Know*. New York: Gumbs and Thomas, 1990. 48pp. $5.95. ISBN: 0936073-08-X.

This brief handbook includes information and activities for Kwanzaa. A short history of the holiday and how it is celebrated are presented in a question-and-answer format. The suggestions for decorations, food, and clothing can be used in programs.

K–3. McKissack, Patricia C. *Our Martin Luther King Book*. Chicago: Children's Press, 1986. 32pp. $11.97. ISBN: 0-89565-342-7.

This story describes a classroom celebration of Martin Luther King Day. Facts about Dr. King and the civil rights movement are included in the story line. Some of the activities are suitable for public library programs and the story can be replicated in classes.

6–8. McKissack, Patricia and Fredrick. *The Civil Rights Movement in America*. Chicago: Children's Press, 1987. 320pp. $39.93. ISBN: 0-516-00580-4.

This textbook format presents a comprehensive overview of the events that led to the civil rights movement from 1865 to the present. It includes photographs and information about the people and organizations that spearheaded the movement.

6–8. Meltzer, Milton. *Black Americans: A History in Their Own Words*. New York: Crowell, 1984. 320pp. $14.95. ISBN: 0-690-04419-4.

Using historic documents, the author creates an overview of African-American history from 1619 to 1983. Letters, speeches, and so forth provide a glimpse of the people and the times. Each document includes an introduction that summarizes the period.

2–5. Obadiah. *I Am a Rastafarian*. New York: Watts, 1987. 32pp. $10.90. ISBN: 0-531-10440-0.

A British Rastafarian family describes their religion and lifestyle. Young Petra, the narrator, shares information about the family's hairstyles, music, holidays, and language. Colorful photographs give a clear picture of the Rastafarian people.

4–8. Stanley, Diane, and Peter Vennema. *Shaka: King of the Zulus*. New York: Morrow, 1988. 40pp. $14.95. ISBN: 0-688-07343-3.

This succinct picture book documents the life of South Africa's nineteenth-century chief who conquered and led the Zulu people. Shaka's interaction with Europeans and his leadership qualities are highlighted. The dramatic illustrations clearly portray the events.

4–8. Turner, Glennette Tilley. *Take a Walk in Their Shoes*. New York: Dutton, 1989. 176pp. $14.95. ISBN: 0-525-65006-7.

This collection of biographies and skits about fourteen famous African Americans features some less common personalities, such as Oscar Micheaux, Maggie Lena Walker, Daniel "Chappie" James, Charles White, and Arthur Schomburg. Included are pencil sketches of each person.

K–5. Zaslavsky, Claudia. *Count on Your Fingers African Style*. New York: Crowell, 1980. 32pp. $12.89. ISBN: 0-690-03865-8.

The marketplace is the setting for this demonstration of the counting methods used by several West African ethnic groups. Detailed illustrations add to the information about Africa. This is a good source for counting games.

PROGRAMMING IDEAS

Most program formats (i.e., storytelling, films, arts and crafts) can be used to highlight African-American culture and history. Black history calendars are a resource for planning programs about the black experience. Some calendars are available through Pomegranate Calendars and

Books,*[1] or Pyramid Book Store.* Use the calendar to choose dates, events, and personalities that are suitable topics for children's programs. Contact African-American cultural groups in your community for program ideas. Create activities that encourage active audience participation.

The following activities are arranged in chronological order. Use these ideas as a springboard for creating other programs. For example, the activities in the Martin Luther King Day programs could be used for programs about other notable African Americans, such as Harriet Tubman, Malcolm X, Fannie Lou Hamer, or W. E. B. DuBois. Remember, no program is written in stone; make changes that are appropriate for your audience. Consider choosing an African-American theme for established programs, such as spring story hours, summer reading programs, or Christmas programs. Remember that African-American culture is an integral part of American culture.

MARTIN LUTHER KING DAY

On the third Monday in January, the United States celebrates the life of Dr. Martin Luther King Jr., an African-American civil rights leader who was born on January 15, 1929.

Arts and Crafts

Few commercial products are manufactured for this holiday, so children of all ages can create cards and gifts that reflect Dr. King's philosophy of peace, justice, and brotherhood. Greeting cards, bookmarks, posters, and stationery can be made with simple art supplies. Provide some examples of the crafts and encourage the children to create their own designs.

1. Gather and set up before the program: pictures of Dr. King and the civil rights movement, poster board, construction paper, plain stationery paper, envelopes, colored markers, watercolor paints, scissors, paste, and other art supplies.
2. Provide examples of the crafts, such as greeting cards with quotes by King, bookmarks that list books about Dr. King, posters that show events from King's life, or stationery with pictures of King. Contact the Martin Luther King Center* for items available in the gift shop.
3. Use a graphics software program to make cards, bookmarks, posters, and stationery that can be printed with a computer and decorated by the children.
4. Invite artists from the community to participate in the program by helping the children create artwork.
5. Allow the children to make several cards so they can exchange them or mail them to others.
6. Display some of the completed crafts along with books and other materials about King.

Story Hour

A story hour for elementary school children can help them understand the significance of Dr. King's contributions. This program highlights Dr. King's life, including the literature and music that he enjoyed. The following activities are suitable for a story hour at a public library or school.

1. Plan the program for a date near King's January 15 birthday. Distribute publicity about the story hour to the public and the media about three to four weeks in advance.
2. Gather and set up before the program: pictures, books, recordings, and other materials about Dr. King, his family, and the civil rights movement. Make arrangements for an adequate sound system.
3. Play gospel music softly as the audience gathers. One of King's favorite songs was "Precious Lord Take My Hand," which can be found on albums by such performers as Mahalia Jackson, Shirley Ceasar, or James Cleveland.
4. Welcome the audience and begin the program with a poem about King, such as "In Memory" by Ericka Northrop (*Jack and Jill,* Feb. 1989).
5. Ask a few children to share what they know about Dr. King's life. Point out any displays or materials that provide information about the event the child is sharing.

[1] Complete addresses for all sources marked with an asterisk (*) can be found in the Resources section at the end of this chapter.

6. Read or tell the story of Dr. King's life by using a short biography, such as *The Picture Life of Martin Luther King Jr.*, by David Adler (Holiday House, 1989).

7. Teach audience participation poems or songs. When he was a child, two of Dr. King's heroes were Frederick Douglass and Harriet Tubman. Share the poem "Harriet Tubman" by Eloise Greenfield in *Honey, I Love and Other Love Poems*.[†2] Practice the poem's refrain with the audience. Sing "Free At Last" from *Walk Together Children* by Ashley Bryan (Atheneum, 1974).

8. Tell protest stories, such as "Ole Sis Goose" from *The Book of Negro Folklore*, edited by Langston Hughes (Dodd, 1983), or "Brer Rabbit's Protest Meeting" from *The Days When the Animals Talked* by William Faulkner (Follett, 1977). Remind the children that these stories protested the segregation laws of that time.

9. Recite one of Langston Hughes's poems, such as "I Too Sing America," "The Dreamkeeper," or "My People." As a child, Dr. King enjoyed the poetry of Langston Hughes and had the opportunity to recite a poem when Hughes visited his school.

10. Read or recite excerpts about Dr. King from *Selma Lord Selma* by Sheyann Webb (Morrow, 1980) or "Daddy" by Yolanda King in *Talk That Talk*, edited by Linda Goss (Simon and Schuster, 1989). A child from the community could present one of these readings, which show that, as an adult, Dr. King was a friend to children.

11. Ask the audience to tell what gift they would give to honor the memory of Dr. King. End the program with a recording, such as Stevie Wonder's "Happy Birthday to Ya."

AFRICAN-AMERICAN HISTORY MONTH

Carter G. Woodson, an African-American historian and teacher, established February as a time to celebrate black history. During this month, plan programs that highlight the many facets of black history and black culture. Program topics can range from the achievements of blacks in ancient Africa to their contributions to the exploration of outer space. Programs during this month might include films about famous African Americans, storytelling programs by professional storytellers (for suggestions, contact the National Association of Black Storytellers*), talks by successful African Americans in the community, performances by cultural groups, or exhibits of artwork or other artifacts. Sponsoring a book fair that features African and African-American materials is another option for this celebration.

The following activities and storytelling program could be presented individually or as a series during the month of February. It cannot be stressed enough, however, that black history programs should be presented all year long, not just in February.

African Crafts

An increasing number of African Americans are wearing African clothing and accessories and showing that they are proud of their African heritage. Capitalize on this interest and create black history month programs that feature African artifacts. African artwork, such as wood carvings, metalwork, and fabric designs, was usually put to practical uses. Items were not made just to be exhibited.

The following crafts were chosen because children can usually complete them in one session. Also the completed craft can be put to practical use. If time permits, include a story, poem, or song during these sessions. Some appropriate books to use are: *Africa Dream*[†] by Eloise Greenfield, *Spin a Soft Black Song*[†] by Nikki Giovanni, and *I'm Going to Sing*[†] by Ashley Bryan. Other activities can be found in *Children Are Children* by Ann Cole (Little, Brown, 1977).

MASKS

African masks (see figures 1 and 2) are usually carved from wood and might be decorated with beads, shells, straw, or other objects. The masks are worn in religious ceremonies and represent spirits. They are carved in the shape of human faces or animal heads.

---

[2] Titles marked with a dagger (†) have complete annotations in the Bibliography for this chapter.

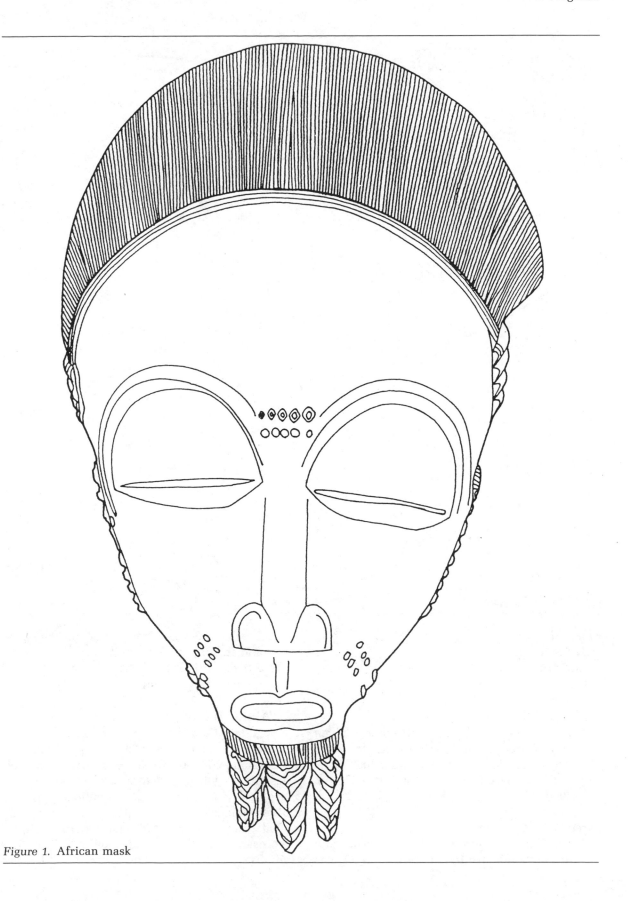

Figure 1. African mask

Figure 2. African mask

Materials
  Tag board
  Construction paper
  Crayons or markers
  String
  Scissors
  Examples of masks from different African ethnic groups, such as the ones found in *African Designs of Nigeria and the Cameroons* by Caren Caraway (Stemmer House, 1984).

Directions
  1. Display examples of African masks and discuss their use in ceremonies in Africa.

  2. Create face-sized masks with the tagboard and art supplies. Cut out the eyes and mouth.
  3. Attach string to the masks and let the children wear them.

FABRIC DESIGNS
Weaving, tie-dyeing, and stamping are some of the methods used for fabric designs in Africa. The Akan people of western Africa use symbolic designs on fabric, artwork, and woodcarvings (see figure 3). These Adinkra symbols represent different facets of Akan culture and folk sayings (God, drum, war horn). The ladder, for example, represents death in the saying "Everyone climbs death's ladder," and two crossed lizards

represent the saying "Sharing one stomach yet they fight over food." These symbols are carved on wood, dipped in dye, and stamped repeatedly on cotton fabric (see figure 4). The fabric is used for clothing, blankets, and household needs.

Materials

Cotton cloth cut in squares
Fabric paint
Brushes
Examples of Adinkra symbols (found in *Shining Legacy* by Nkechi Taifa, House of Songhay, 1983).

Directions

1. Create stencils of the Adinkra symbols before the program. Young children can use stencils, while older children (eight and older) can draw the designs freehand.
2. Cover the tables with newspaper. Display examples of the Adinkra symbols and a completed design painted on a cloth square.
3. Allow the children to use a stencil or to paint a symbol freehand on a square of cloth. After the paint dries, the square can be sewn onto such items as blue jeans, a T-shirt, or a pot holder.

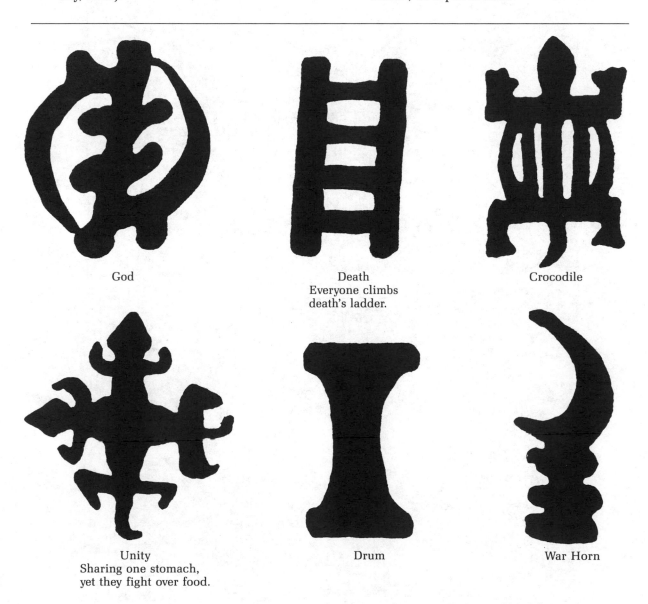

God

Death
Everyone climbs
death's ladder.

Crocodile

Unity
Sharing one stomach,
yet they fight over food.

Drum

War Horn

Figure 3. Adinkra symbols

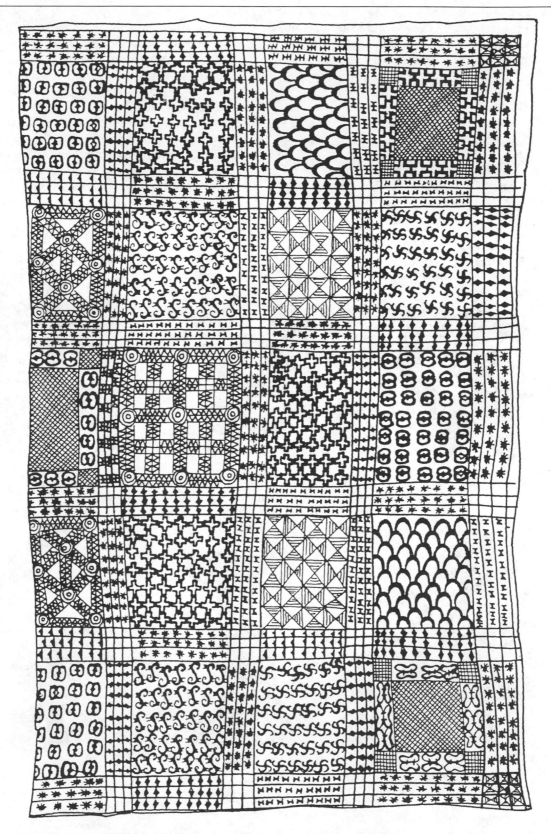

Figure 4. Adinkra cloth

WARI GAME

Sometimes called *African checkers*, wari is one version of the Mancala games, which originated in north Africa. This game is usually played on a wooden carved game board that has twelve cups. Unless you have woodcarving skills or an artisan is invited, the children will just get a glimpse of African woodcarving. Display pictures of wari game boards in African art books or acquire a game board from an African cultural shop. Encourage the children to decorate their game boards to resemble the carvings on the displayed game boards. Instructions for this game are also found in *The World of Games* by Jack Botermans, et al. (Facts on File, 1989).

Materials
Egg cartons (one for each child)
Game pieces (pebbles, marbles, acorns), 48 for each child
Paint
Markers
Construction paper
Glue
A copy of the rules for each child

Directions
1. Decorate the egg cartons with African symbols using paint, markers, or construction paper.
2. Practice playing the game with the following rules:

Wari Rules

There are two players. Each player owns the six cups on one lengthwise side of the game board. Fill every cup with four game pieces. One player chooses a cup on her side of the board. Taking all the pieces in that cup, the player drops one piece at a time into the next cups in a counterclockwise direction. The opponent chooses a cup from her side and plays in the same manner. They take turns alternately.

Winning: If the last piece dropped results in two or three pieces in a cup on the opponent's side, the player wins those pieces. The player also wins the pieces in any cups on the opponent's side that have two or three pieces and are consecutively behind the winning cup. The captured pieces are taken out and kept aside. The playing continues alternately until it is impossible to win the remaining game pieces. The player who captures the most game pieces is the winner.

Storytelling

Storytelling programs are an entertaining and instructive activity to present during black history month. Folktales, true stories, and legends provide insight to African-American culture. A thirty- to forty-minute program of stories is appropriate for elementary age children and their families. Remember to include poetry, songs, or games that will allow the audience to participate and add variety to the program. Announce the program to the public and the media three to four weeks in advance. Choose a performance space that has few distractions, comfortable seating, and good acoustics. The following suggestions are guidelines for planning a storytelling program.

1. In a brief introduction, explain that folktales are an expression of cultural experiences. Stories, songs, and dances provided relief to enslaved African Americans who had few recreational outlets. Some stories were humorous and were told simply to entertain, to eliminate boredom, or to help listeners forget their troubles. Other tales served an underlying purpose. Some were told to teach children how to behave. Many revealed a hatred of slavery and a desire to outwit the slaveowners and overthrow the system. Today we can enjoy these stories and share the wisdom that helped African Americans survive a dehumanizing experience.
2. Share three or four different types of African-American folktales. The following suggestions come from story collections that also have other storytelling choices.
   "The Comeuppance of Brer Wolf" in *Jump! The Adventures of Brer Rabbit*, adapted by Van Dyke Parks (Harcourt Brace Jovanovich, 1986).
   "The Fox and the Goose" in *The Book of Negro Folklore*, edited by Langston Hughes (Dodd, 1983).
   "Wiley and the Hairy Man" in *The People Could Fly*, retold by Virginia Hamilton (Knopf, 1985).
   "A Riddle for Freedom" in *The Days When the Animals Talked*, retold by William Faulkner (Follett, 1977).

3. Show a video of an African-American storyteller as another option for the program. Information about storytelling resources, such as audio tapes, records, and books, is available from N.A.P.P.S. (National Association for the Preservation and Perpetuation of Storytelling). The following are some of the most noteworthy videos by African-American storytellers:

"American Storytelling Series, Vol. 5," includes Mary Carter Smith (H. W. Wilson Co., 1986), $99.

"Hands Upon the Heart" by Ossie Davis and Ruby Dee (Cornerstone Films, 1990), $24.

"Two White Horses: A Mountain Tale" by Jackie Torrence (Weston Woods, 1986), $60.

KWANZAA

Kwanzaa is an African-American holiday that is celebrated for seven days from December 26 to January 1. In 1966, Maulana Karenga and the US organization created this holiday, which resembles African harvest festivals. In Swahili, *kwanza* means "first"; the word *Kwanzaa* (with two *a*'s) was created to mean "festival of the first fruits." Each day is a time for community members to remember the year's achievements and rededicate themselves to the Kwanzaa principles: unity, self-determination, collective work, cooperative economics, purpose, creativity, and faith. These principles are the foundation of Kwanzaa.

Arts and Crafts

Two of the goals of Kwanzaa are to avoid meaningless commercialism and to instill the principle of creativity. Creating Kwanzaa materials, such as decorations, gifts, poems, or stories, is strongly recommended. The color scheme for Kwanzaa uses the African liberation colors of red, black, and green. These colors and the use of African artifacts and clothing make Kwanzaa a festive occasion. Choose crafts that can be used during the Kwanzaa ceremony. Adapt some of the ideas in these activity booklets:

Kwanzaa Coloring Book by Valerie J. R. Banks (Sala Enterprises,* 1985)

Let's Celebrate Kwanzaa by Helen Thompson (Gumbs and Thomas,* 1989)

My Kwanzaa Book by Carolyn Coxfield (Sea Island Information,* 1990)

The following crafts are suitable for elementary age children and can be used for decorations during the Kwanzaa ceremony.

POSTERS

Materials
Poster board
Lettering supplies
Colored markers
Paint
Other art supplies

Directions
1. Write the Kwanzaa principles in large letters. Decorate the poster with pictures that relate to Kwanzaa (e.g., map of Africa, liberation flag, candles).
2. Create three-dimensional posters by decorating them with small objects, such as cowrie shells, beads, or pieces of African cloth.
3. Use the posters during the Kwanzaa ceremony.

TABLE DECORATION

Materials
Blank index cards
Red, black, and green colored markers or crayons
Plastic drinking straws
Modeling clay
Other art supplies

Directions
1. Divide each side of the index cards into thirds horizontally. Color the rectangles on each side red, black, and green (in that order from top to bottom). Add variety by writing one of the Kwanzaa principles on the flag or by drawing on it one of the Kwanzaa symbols (e.g., candles, fruit, corn).
2. Attach a drinking straw to the short side of each index card. Stick the free end of the drinking straw into a small portion of modeling clay.

3. Decorate tables with the liberation flags during the Kwanzaa ceremony.

Kwanzaa Ceremony

The procedure for celebrating the holiday is described in several books, including *The African American Holiday of Kwanzaa* by Maulana Karenga (Univ. of Sankore Press,* 1988). Because Kwanzaa is not a religious holiday, more people from all segments of the African-American community are participating in Kwanzaa celebrations. The following program can be held before or during Kwanzaa. Although there is nothing religious about Kwanzaa, it is helpful to have a participant who is familiar with Kwanzaa celebrations. The objects for the Kwanzaa table can be made or purchased. They are usually available at African-American bookstores, at African cultural stores, and by mail order.

Ki-Swahili, an east African language (usually shortened to *Swahili*), is used in the Kwanzaa ceremony. Swahili words are easy to pronounce because Swahili has consistent phonetic sounds. Nevertheless, the Swahili words should be practiced ahead of time.

1. Announce the program to the public and the media three to four weeks in advance.
2. Create or purchase posters of the seven principles of Kwanzaa: *Umoja* (unity), *Kujichagulia* (self-determination), *Ujima* (collective work), *Ujamaa* (cooperative economics), *Nia* (purpose), *Kuumba* (creativity), *Imani* (faith).
3. Gather supplies: Kwanzaa posters; African cloth to cover the table; a *kinara* (candleholder) with red, black, and green candles; a basket of fruit; a few ears of corn; a small straw mat for the table; a libation cup; a potted plant; a red, black, and green flag; recordings of African music; an adequate sound system; and a display of books and other materials about Kwanzaa.
4. Play African music as the audience assembles. The Kwanzaa table is decorated; the libation cup has water in it; matches are available for the candles and decorations; the flag, posters, and books are displayed.
5. Welcome the audience with the Kwanzaa greeting *"Habari Gani?"* ("What's the news?"). Teach the audience to reply with one of the Kwanzaa principles.
6. Give an explanation of pouring libation, which is a way of honoring the ancestors. Recite a libation statement. Ask the audience to call out the names of black heros and heroines as the water in the libation cup is poured into the potted plant.

Libation Statement

For them who gave so much, we give in return. May our eyes be the eagle, our strength be the elephant, and the boldness of our life be like the lion. May we remember and honor our ancestors and the legacy they left us for as long as the sun shines and the water flows (paraphased from *The African American Holiday of Kwanzaa*).

7. Explain the Kwanzaa symbols that are on the table. The candles represent the seven principles. The corn symbolizes the children in the community. Fruit is a reminder of the harvest. Explain the seven principles. Choose children to repeat the principles and light the candles.
8. Highlight one of the Kwanzaa principles with a cultural presentation, such as storytelling, dance, poetry, or music. Show a filmstrip, such as "Kwanzaa: A New Afro-American Holiday" (SVE*).
9. End the program with a unity song (e.g., "Lift Every Voice and Sing" or a song about the Kwanzaa principles) and a farewell statement.

Farewell Statement

Strive for discipline, dedication, and achievement in all we do. Practice daily Umoja, Kujichagulia, Ujima, Ujamaa, Nia, Kuumba, and Imani. May the wisdom of the ancestors always walk with us. May the year's end meet us laughing and stronger. May our children honor us by following our example in love and struggle. At the end of next year, may we sit together again with greater achievements and a stronger community (paraphrased from *The African American Holiday of Kwanzaa*).

10. Provide a reception with African and African-American food as an optional activity. Allow time for informal discussion and answering questions about Kwanzaa.

RESOURCES

Africa World Press/Red Sea Press
15 Industry Court
Trenton, NJ 08638

Association of Black Storytellers
P.O. Box 67722
Baltimore, MD 21215
(410) 664–9204

Gumbs and Thomas
142 West 72nd Street
Suite 9
New York, NY 10023

Just Us Books
301 Main Street
Suite 22–44
Orange, NJ 07055

Martin Luther King Center
449 Auburn Ave. N.E.
Atlanta, GA 30312
(404) 524–1956

N.A.P.P.S. (National Association for the Preservation and Perpetuation of Storytelling)
P.O. Box 309
Jonesborough, TN 37659
(615) 753–2171

Pomegranate Calendars and Books
P.O. Box 808022
Petaluma, CA 94975

Pyramid Book Store
2849 Georgia Ave. N.W.
Washington, DC 20001
(202) 328–0190

Sala Enterprises
P.O. Box 76122
Los Angeles, CA 90076

Sea Island Information
P.O. Box 10628
Silver Spring, MD 20914

SVE (Society for Visual Education)
1345 Diversey Parkway
Chicago, IL 60614

Third World Press
7524 S. Cottage Grove Ave.
Chicago, IL 60619–1999

University of Sankore Press
2560 West 54th Street
Los Angeles, CA 90043

CHAPTER 2

Arabic Materials and Programs

by Julie Corsaro

There is probably no cultural group today that arouses more passion or prejudice in Western countries than the Arabs. These feelings are partially understandable because of volatile events in the Arab nations that often involve violence. The conflict between Arabs and Western countries, however, is not a modern one. It is evident in the centuries-old division between Christianity and Islam. In the twentieth century, the major source of contention has been Western support of Israel, to which the Arab nations have been traditionally and bitterly opposed. The conflicts have been debated in the Western media and continue to occupy a prominent place in the world order.

It is, therefore, not a surprise to find that distorted perceptions and negative stereotypes of Arabs abound. Gun-toting terrorists, greedy oil barons, salacious sheiks with their harems, and pitiful refugees are the images often perpetuated. To gain an accurate understanding of who the Arabs really are and introduce them to children through books, it is essential to know more about their culture and history.

The term *Arab* originally referred to some of the nomadic or Bedouin peoples of the Arabian peninsula before the time of Mohammed. Although the Bedouins today account for only about 10 percent of the population of the Arab world, their values of hospitality, generosity, courage, honor, and self-respect are basic components of the Arab personality. The prophet Mohammed (founder of the Islamic religion) was born in Mecca in Arabia about A.D. 570 and during his lifetime saw Islam become the foremost religion in the region. After his death, Mohammed's followers set out from their homeland to conquer a region that stretched across northern Africa and the entire Arabian peninsula into southwest Asia as far north as the Caucasus Mountains and west into India. Spain and several Mediterranean islands were also part of this empire.

At its height, the Arab Empire was notable for its artistic and intellectual brilliance (contributions in mathematics and science are particularly noteworthy). This second group, or "new" Arabs, were people who, after having converted to Islam, gave up their native tongue and adopted Arabic instead. However, not all conquered peoples were "Arabized." For instance, although the Persians (today's Iranians) became followers of the faith, they retained their ancestral language and national identity. Although 90 percent of all Arabs today are Muslims, they account for only one-sixth of the world's Islamic population. However, as the originators of the faith, Arabs consider themselves at its core, and seldom distinguish between the two.

The major part of a vast geographical region in northern Africa and southwest Asia known as the Middle East is home for the contemporary Arab world, which comprises a group of nations in which Arabic is the official state language and Arab people or an Arab ideology is dominant. Bahrain, Kuwait, North Yemen, Oman, Qatar, Saudi Arabia, South Yemen, and the United Arab Emirates constitute the arid peninsula of Arabia. Iraq, Jordan, Lebanon, Syria, and Palestine make up most of the Fertile Crescent, a region commonly introduced to students as "the cradle of civilization." The Nile Valley includes Egypt and Sudan, the latter not always identified with the Arab world. Here, Arabs live largely in the north and constitute, according to various estimates, anywhere from one-half to three-quarters of the population. A variety of African peoples live in the south. The northern African nations of Algeria, Libya, Morocco, and Tunisia were originally the territory of the Berbers, who have never been totally assimilated. That French is still spoken in Algeria, Tunisia, and Morocco (Spanish is also spoken here) has created the impression that these three nations are more in line with Western thought than are other Arab countries. Mauritania is an Arab Islamic republic in northwestern Africa.

Arabs have migrated to neighboring (non-Arabized) countries in Africa and Asia and also reside in areas that are geographically separate from this core region. The most substantial populations are found in Argentina, Brazil, Canada, and the United States (Detroit, Michigan, has the largest concentration of Arabs in North America).

For additional background information about Arabic culture, Jules Archer's *Legacy of the Desert: Understanding the Arabs*[†][1] is the best place to start. Juanita Will Saghikian's *Land, Peoples and Communities of the Middle East*[†] also provides a quick overview of the culture. Those seeking more sophisticated analysis have several choices among books written for adults. British journalist Peter Mansfield's *The Arabs* (New York: Penguin, 1985. 537pp. $7.95. ISBN: 0-14-022561-7) is similar in scope to Archer's book, but more detailed. It contains a comprehensive history in chronological sequence, an analysis of each modern Arab state, and an assessment of the future. In *The Arab Mind* (New York: Scribner's, 1983. 435pp. $15.95. ISBN: 0-684-17810-9), Middle East scholar Raphael Patai builds a strong case for a distinctive Arab personality by examining such elements as child-rearing practices, language acquisition, the impact of European colonialism, and "pre-Islamic and Islamic components." French scholar Maxime Rodinson's *The Arabs* (Chicago: Univ. of Chicago Press, 1981. 188pp. $6.95. ISBN: 9-226-72356-9) is a brief but dense book that provides an extended definition of the group.

Although the quantity and quality of Arab culture books for children are still relatively low, there was a substantial increase in their numbers in the 1980s. This was largely due to the efforts of curriculum-oriented publishers who responded to a vacuum in the marketplace, as well as to many revised social studies programs. While the efforts of these publishers should be applauded, many of the books have certain drawbacks. Because publishers targeted the school library market, the books are very similar. The books are usually published and marketed in series rather than individually, with substantial discounts given for buying entire sets. These series books are usually formulaic and are often written by free-lance or staff writers with little or no expertise (e.g., most of the country books in Watts's *Take a Trip To* series are written by the same individual).

Most of the books currently being published about Arabic culture are nonfiction. Unfortunately, there is very little fiction available for children about Arabs and none at all about Arab Americans. The majority of available titles are informational books and biographies about Arab countries and leaders, as opposed to Arab Americans (until 1988 there were no nonfiction books about Arab Americans). While some nonfiction books are being published for primary graders and still more for middle graders, most are directed toward children in the upper elementary grades and middle school. There is still very little folklore being produced, with only a few anthologies available. No single picture-book versions of popular stories are in print or available. A few words about the Arabian Nights are in order at this point.

Scholars generally agree that the core of the collection of nearly two hundred tales known as *The Thousand and One Nights* were of Indo-Persian origin. However, these appealing stories reflect the life and attitudes of medieval Arabs and actually reinforce the colorful and exotic image of the culture. Although these magical tales deserve to be as well known as Grimm's Fairy Tales, they should be balanced with works that portray the modern Arab experience (which may be somewhat difficult to find as well). In addition to the need for more fiction and folklore, books that examine Arab-Israeli relationships objectively, analyze the status of women, and focus on artistic and intellectual achievements would be welcome indeed.

Locating materials for review and purchase can be especially problematic. Only a few titles are listed in the *Subject Guide to Children's*

---

[1] Titles marked with a dagger (†) have complete annotations in the Bibliography for this chapter.

Books in Print, and many titles identified in publishers' catalogs are available in local libraries or through interlibrary loan. In compiling information for this chapter, I found the publishers' catalogs (which are sometimes hard to identify) to be the best and most efficient sources. Recommended out-of-print titles may be available in public or school libraries.

BIBLIOGRAPHY

FICTION

K–2. Alexander, Sue. *Nadia the Willful.* Illus. by Lloyd Bloom. New York: Pantheon, 1983. 48pp. $12.99. ISBN: 0-394-95265-0.

That often-used theme—the struggle to accept the death of a loved one—is given unique and perceptive treatment in this modern story about a spunky Bedouin girl who loses her brother to the desert. When Nadia's father, the sheik, refuses to acknowledge his grief, he is challenged by her defiant wisdom. Soft pencil drawings convey the harsh beauty and the natural as well as human-made patterns of the environment.

4–6. Ashabranner, Brent. *Gavriel and Jemal: Two Boys of Jerusalem.* New York: Putnam, 1984. 96pp. $11.95. ISBN: 0-396-08455-9.

Two boys living in Jerusalem's Old City—the Palestinian Jemal and the Israeli Gavriel—share a dedication to family, learning, and religion—and a heritage of suspicion and violence. This timely book features expressive black-and-white photographs and distinguished writing.

5–adult. Atil, Esin. *Kalila wa Dimna: Fables from a Fourteenth-Century Arabic Manuscript.* Washington, D.C.: Smithsonian, 1981. 96pp. $24.95. ISBN: 0-87474-216-1.

A brief introduction precedes eight selected stories about the wily jackal Dimna and his honorable brother Kalila. Included are a history of this popular Islamic work, detailed notes on the manuscript text and illustrations, and a multilingual bibliography. The clear-cut scholarship will attract adults, while the fables will strike a responsive note in children.

K–2. Berson, Harold, adapter. *Kassim's Shoes.* Illus. by the author. New York: Crown, 1977. o.p.

Berson's energetic line drawings are well-suited to this humorous Moroccan folktale about a likable merchant whose attempts to dispose of an old pair of shoes are met with repeated failure and, even worse, fines.

K–2. Brown, Marcia. *The Flying Carpet.* Illus. by the author. New York: Scribner's, 1956. o.p.

The Arab admiration for generosity is given a splendid forum in this picture-book version of a favorite (yet little known) story about three brothers who unselfishly band together to save the life of the woman each hopes to marry. Retold from Sir Richard Burton's translation, Brown's prose is simple yet lyrical, while her vivid paintings have an appropriate Middle-Eastern quality.

5–adult. Bushnaq, Inea, ed. and tr. *Arab Folktales.* New York: Pantheon, 1987. 386pp. pap. $14.00. ISBN: 0-394-75179-5.

Elegant and engaging prose, beautiful book design, and fastidious research of printed sources highlight this definitive collection for older children and teens as well as adult students of folklore. Each group of tales is preceded by an informative and detailed introduction. Bedouin tales, *Djinn* (spirit) tales, *Djuha* (fools) tales, religious tales, and tales of magic, wit, and guile are all included.

6–8. Cohen, Barbara, and Bahija Lovejoy. *Seven Daughters and Seven Sons.* New York: Atheneum, 1982. 216pp. o.p.

Based on a traditional Iraqi folktale, this is the story of Buran, an educated and intelligent young woman who dresses as a man in order to secure bride wealth for her sisters. Disguised as a merchant, she succeeds in acquiring a fortune as well as a handsome and understanding prince. Details about life in the medieval Arab world emerge naturally in this engaging feminist offering.

5–9. Davis, Russell, and Brent Ashabranner. *Ten Thousand Desert Swords: The Epic Story of a Great Bedouin Tribe.* Illus. by Leonard Everett Fisher. Boston: Little, Brown, 1960. 158pp. o.p.

The marvelous stories of the Bani-Hillel, the great desert warriors of Arabia, constitute one of the great epics of Arabic folk literature. Gracefully retold with dignity, romance, and verve, these tales provide an entertaining introduction to the Arab ideals of loyalty, courage, and honor.

6–adult. El-Shamy, Hasan M., ed. *Folktales of Egypt.* Folktales of the World. Chicago: Univ. of Chicago Press, 1982. 347pp. $10.95. ISBN: 0-226-20624-6; pap. $12.95. ISBN: 0-226-20625-4.

Part of an outstanding series, this anthology of seventy recently collected Egyptian folktales (each one annotated) includes both traditional characters—ghosts, tricksters, wizards—and contemporary actors—chauffeurs, government bureaucrats, construction workers, and so on. Three indexes aid access: motif, type of tale, and general.

6–9. Harris, Rosemary. *Zed.* London: Faber and Faber, 1990. 185pp. pap. $4.95. ISBN: 0-571-12922-6.

Cultural stereotypes are challenged in this compelling and complex novel about a teenage boy's coming to terms with his captivity by Arab terrorists when he was seven. His experiences include witnessing a great act of cowardice committed by his father as well as the murder of his Lebanese uncle.

K–3. Heide, Florence Parry, and Judith Heide Gilliland. *The Day of Ahmed's Secret.* Illus. by Ted Lewin. New York: Lothrop, 1990. $13.95. ISBN: 0-688-08894-5.

Beautiful, detailed watercolor paintings capture the bustle of Cairo's busy streets and the excitement of a young boy as he looks forward to the end of his workday when he can share with his family the achievement of learning to write his name.

2–5. Lang, Andrew, adapter. *Aladdin and His Wonderful Lamp.* Illus. by Errol LeCain. New York: Puffin, 1983. 32pp. pap. $4.95. ISBN: 0-14-050389-7.

This smooth abridgement of a traditional tale from *The Arabian Nights Entertainments*† is stunningly illustrated in an oversized format. The full-color paintings, done in pen with watercolor inks, are intricately and ornately patterned on parchment paper and surrounded by multiple, decorative borders.

5–8. _____. *The Arabian Nights Entertainments.* Illus. by Vera Block. Mattituck, N.Y.: Amereon, 1969. $20.95. ISBN: 0-89190-085-3; Illus. by H. J. Ford. New York: Dover, 1969. 424pp. pap. $6.95. ISBN: 0-486-22289-6.

Aladdin, Ali Baba, and Sinbad the Sailor, along with other appealing but lesser-known adventurers, crown this treasure chest of dramatic, timeless, and beautifully written tales that are complemented by highly stylized, black line drawings. Although Lang's insensitive remarks in the introduction detract, enlightened readers should say "Open sesame" to this definitive work.

3–5. Mayer, Marianna, adapter. *Aladdin and the Enchanted Lamp.* Illus. by Gerald McDermott. New York: Macmillan, 1985. 96pp. $15.95. ISBN: 0-02-765360-9.

By adding details, dialogue, and characterization to this classic rags-to-riches tale, Mayer has created a lively mininovel. The highly stylized, softly colored illustrations by the Caldecott medalist are done in colored pencils and watercolors. Surrounded by borders, the full-page renderings as well as the smaller drawings are reminiscent of Persian miniatures.

1–5. McVitty, Walter, adapter. *Ali Baba and the Forty Thieves.* Illus. by Margaret Early. $14.95. New York: Abrams, 1989. ISBN: 0-8109-1888-9.

The wise and faithful woman servant Morgiana is the heroic figure in a welcome picture-book version of the famous fairy tale. Like Islamic miniatures from the Middle Ages, the sumptuous artwork features dominant settings composed of intricate and detailed patterns; flat, abstract characters; and rich colors.

K–2. Moxley, Susan. *Abdul's Treasure*. London: Hodder and Stoughton, 1988. 28pp. $15.95. ISBN: 0-340-38918-4.

The Arab value of generosity is highlighted in this funny folklore-inspired tale of a fisherman who finds a royal diamond and chooses the opening of the palace gates to all as his reward. Geometric designs dominate the brightly colored, stylized illustrations that blend Islamic and postmodern imagery.

5–9. Riordan, James, ed. *Tales from the Arabian Nights*. Illus. by Victor Ambrus. Chicago: Checkerboard Pr., 1985. $11.95. 128pp. ISBN: 0-528-82672-7.

Although Lang's prose is clearly better, Riordan has restored the earthy quality that made Scheherazade's tales inappropriate for polite society by adding details (notably the characters' motivations) to basic plot lines. Ambrus's illustrations are lusty as well, vibrantly colored, vigorously lined, and sparked with humor.

7–10. Schami, Rafik. *A Hand Full of Stars*. Translated from the German by Rika Lesser. New York: Dutton, 1990. $14.95. ISBN: 0-525-44535-8.

Encouraged by the vivid stories of his warm, elderly mentor, a Syrian teenager writes in his diary about school, friends, family, love, and the terror that leads him to become an underground journalist.

K–3. Scott, Sally, adapter. *The Magic Horse*. Illus. by the author. New York: Greenwillow, 1986. 32pp. o.p.

Competently simplified from Sir Richard Burton's ten-volume *The Arabian Nights*, this core tale chronicles the glittering adventures of a flying black steed, a handsome royal couple, and a scheming magician. The gorgeous, full-page acrylic paintings, evocative of traditional Islamic art, are distinguished by vivid colors and geometric patterns.

3–5. Travers, Pamela L., ed. *Two Pairs of Shoes*. Illus. by Leo and Diane Dillon. New York: Viking, 1980. o.p.

Graceful, cadenced prose and striking paintings in the tradition of Persian miniatures make these two folktales, the poignant "The Sandals of Azar" and the humorous "Abu Kassem's Slippers," wonderful for both storytelling and reading aloud.

K–2. Wells, Rosemary. *Abdul*. New York: Dial, 1986. 40pp. $3.50. ISBN: 0-8037-0281-7.

That mainstay of Bedouin life—the camel—is given humorous treatment in this pint-sized book that packs a punch line. When Geisel's beloved mother camel gives birth to a (gasp!) horse, the trio are abandoned by the tribe. Suddenly, baby Abdul is gone too, but with a secret in tow. . . . Attractive drawings in desert hues complement the text.

5–8. Wiggin, Kate Douglas, and Nora Smith, eds. *Arabian Nights: Their Best Known Tales*. Illus. by Maxfield Parrish. New York: Scribner's, 1909. o.p.

The "best-known tales" about Sinbad, Ali Baba, and Aladdin have an ethereal quality thanks to Parrish's beautiful color paintings. A classic book, but it may be hard to find.

NONFICTION

6–adult. Abodaher, David J. *Youth in the Middle East: Voices of Despair*. New York: Watts, 1990. 58pp. $12.40. ISBN: 0-531-1096-5.

Although poorly written, Abodaher's even-handed, sympathetic analysis of the history of violence in the Arab world should help readers gain insight into the tragic lives of several contemporary Egyptian, Lebanese, and Palestinian teenagers.

6–10, younger with supervision. Amari, Suad. *Cooking the Lebanese Way*. Easy Menu Ethnic Cookbooks. Minneapolis: Lerner, 1985. 48pp. $10.95. ISBN: 0-8225-0913-X.

Both fresh and canned foods are called for in these twenty recipes, most of them simplified, for such popular and tasty dishes as *hommos*, *baba ghannouj*, and *tabbouleh*. A list of special ingredients and sample menus with pronunciation guides will be helpful for classroom feasts.

7–9. Archer, Jules. *Legacy of the Desert: Understanding the Arabs*. Boston: Little, Brown, 1976. 214pp. o.p.

Archer writes skillfully and provides a comprehensive, cogent history of the Arab world. The text, well organized and sympathetic, also analyzes the causes of anti-Arab prejudice in the West; the sharp national, cultural, religious, and gender differences that divide the Arab people; and the primary forces for change in the potentially explosive region. The bibliography is extensive and scholarly.

5–9. Ashabranner, Brent. *An Ancient Heritage: The Arab-American Minority.* Illus. by Paul Conklin. New York: HarperCollins, 1991. 160pp. $14.95. ISBN: 0-06-020048-0; lib ed. $14.89. ISBN: 0-06-020049-9.

Based on a series of interviews with a wide variety of American Arabs who exhibit qualities worthy of respect, this handsome photo-essay rebuffs negative stereotypes that have damaged the reputation of the group.

5–7. Beshore, George. *Science in Early Islamic Culture.* First Book. New York: Watts, 1988. 72pp. $10.40. ISBN: 0-531-10596-2.

Throughout this straightforward and clearly written book, Beshore emphasizes the role of Islamic scientists (Arab and non-Arab) in building upon the intellectual heritage of the Greeks and in developing the scientific method. Original, often brilliant, contributions in astronomy, mathematics, medicine, geography, physics, and optics are duly noted.

4–6. Cross, Wilbur. *Egypt.* Enchantment of the World Series. Chicago: Children's Press, 1982. 128pp. $25.27. ISBN: 0-516-02672-X.

In keeping with the general format of this handsomely photographed series, the data highlight geography, history, cities, religion, economy, and culture. Little attention is paid to Egypt's overwhelming contemporary problems, including overcrowding, food shortages, and extensive illiteracy.

6–9. DeChancie, John. *Gamal Abdel Nasser.* World Leaders Past and Present. New York: Chelsea House, 1988. 112pp. $15.95. ISBN: 0-87754-542-1.

The triumphs and defeats of Nasser's long political career are given top billing in this even-handed biography. Giving little personal information, DeChancie points out the prominent Egyptian's competing roles as revolutionary leader, president, warmonger, and peace negotiator.

3–5. Families the World Over Series. Minneapolis: Lerner. 32pp. $9.95.

Bennett, Olivia. *A Family in Egypt.* 1985. ISBN: 0-8225-1652-7.
Dutton, Roderic. *An Arab Family.* 1985. ISBN: 0-8225-1660-8.
Stewart, Judy. *A Family in Morocco.* 1986. ISBN: 0-8225-1682-9.

Fascinating details in the text and color photographs add to the sense of immediacy in these three award winners. Highlighted are ten-year-old Ezzat, who lives with his extended clan in a farming village on the banks of the Nile; Mohammed, an agriculturist in oil-rich Oman, and his relatives; and twelve-year-old Malika, whose large nuclear family is supported by her father's handwoven crafts.

7–adult. Goldston, Robert C. *The Sword of the Prophet: A History of the Arab World from the Time of Mohammed to the Present Day.* New York: Dial, 1979. o.p.

Although out of date, this well-written book provides an in-depth, political history of the Arab world through the Israeli-Egyptian peace talks.

6–9. Gordon, Matthew S. *Gemayels.* World Leaders Past and Present. New York: Chelsea House, 1988. 111pp. $17.95. ISBN: 1-5546-834-9.

In this blunt biography of Lebanon's influential Gemayel family—father Pierre and presidential sons Bashir and Amin—Gordon exposes their controversial methods, including assassination and genocide, for maintaining the Maronite Christian community's dominance over their Muslim countrymen. Numerous black-and-white photographs and annotations in broad margins extend the sobering text.

5–8. Harik, Elsa Marston. *The Lebanese in America.* In America. Minneapolis: Lerner,

1988. 95pp. $8.95. ISBN: 0-8225-0234-8; pap. $3.95. ISBN: 0-8225-1032-4.

Ninety percent of Arab Americans, including the author, are of Lebanese descent. This well-rounded portrait examines immigration and early settlement, typical values, outstanding contributions, the unique relationship with the motherland, the role of women, and recent problems with discrimination. The historical photographs and artwork are a definite bonus.

4–6. Hintz, Martin. *Morocco*. Enchantment of the World Series. Chicago: Children's Press, 1985. 128pp. $25.27. ISBN: 0-516-02774-3.

Covering the basics of geography, history, religion, language, art, and so forth, this straightforward colorfully illustrated account also takes note of the ethnic and cultural diversity within this fringe Arab nation.

6–10. Kyle, Benjamin. *Muammar El-Qaddafi*. World Leaders Past and Present. New York: Chelsea House, 1987. 112pp. $15.95. ISBN: 0-877-54598-7.

In this fairly thorough, somewhat stereotyped profile, the author downplays Qaddafi's good works at home and focuses on the statesman's worldwide terrorist activities, his alienation from other Arab leaders, and his erratic, often contradictory behavior. Like Lawson's *Libya and Qaddafi*,[†] this book is relatively current and heavily illustrated.

6–8. Lawson, Don. *Libya and Qaddafi*. Rev. ed. Impact. New York: Watts, 1987. 128pp, o.p.

Lawson's account of this historically colorful nation and its controversial leader is well balanced and lucid. He explores Qaddafi's ties to international terrorism, the roots of his xenophobia, his involvement with the Arab unity movement, and his redistribution of oil wealth among the common people.

Living Here series. New York: Watts/Bookwright Press. 60pp.

   3–6. Al Hoad, Abdul Latif. *We Live in Saudi Arabia*. 1987.
   4–8. Kristensen, Preben, and Frona Cameron. *We Live in Egypt*. 1987. o.p.

Individuals from different social levels reveal each country's culture and customs, as well as details of their daily lives, through engaging first-person accounts. Voices (fifty-two in all) include those of a camel breeder, falconer, belly dancer, carpet weaver, royal astronaut, and Bedouin sheik. Illustrated with color photographs that extend the familiar tone. Includes an index and a glossary.

4–7. McCarthy, Kevin. *Saudi Arabia: A Desert Kingdom*. Discovering Our Heritage. New York: Dillon, 1986. 128pp. $14.95. ISBN: 0-87518-295-X.

Hats off to McCarthy for addressing the problem of Arab bashing in the United States. By focusing on the Saudis' positive values, including their love of country, religion, and family, their spirit of generosity, their admiration for literary expression, and their delight in games and sport, the author presents a humanized picture.

6–9. Messenger, Charles. *The Middle East*. Conflict in the Twentieth Century. New York: Watts, 1988. 62pp. $10.29. ISBN: 0-531-10539-3.

Although hampered by its British viewpoint, this large-format, densely illustrated survey provides solid coverage of regional politics since the Second World War. Information highlights the Arab-Israeli conflict, the role of extra-regional forces (the United States, the Soviet Union, and Western Europe), and the rise of Islamic fundamentalism.

6–9. Naff, Alixa. *The Arab Americans*. The Peoples of North America. New York: Chelsea House, 1988. 112pp. $17.95. ISBN: 0-87754-861-7.

Focusing on the experiences of Arab immigrants who came to the United States between 1870 and World War I for economic reasons, this unique history also provides coverage of post–World War II political refugees. Written by an Arab American and Middle East scholar who interviewed second-generation Arab Americans, this treatment suffers from a lack of documentation and some insufficiently defined terms.

4–6. Percefull, Aaron W. *Nile.* First Books. New York: Watts, 1984. 72pp. $10.40. ISBN: 0-531-04828-4.

The interdependence between Egypt and the world's longest, most mysterious river is emphasized in this informative and intriguing book. Focusing on the past three hundred years, Percefull examines Napoleon's influential conquest of the region in the late 1700s, nineteenth-century British exploration and colonialism, and modern water storage projects.

7–10. Regan, Geoffrey. *Israel and the Arabs.* Cambridge Topic Books. Minneapolis: Lerner, 1986. 52pp. $8.95. ISBN: 0-8225-1234-3.

Initially published by Cambridge University Press, this concise yet detailed study focuses on Great Britain's pivotal role in the notorious conflict, from the late nineteenth century through the Suez War in 1956. Although the profusely illustrated format (black-and-white maps, charts, diagrams, etc.) suggests a younger audience, this is most suitable for middle schoolers with previous knowledge.

4–6. Rosen, Deborah. *Anwar el-Sadat: A Man of Peace.* People of Distinction Series. Chicago: Children's Press, 1986. 152pp. $17.27. ISBN: 0-516-03214-3.

Like Sullivan in *Sadat: The Man Who Changed Mid-East History,*[†] Rosen chronicles the controversial areas of Sadat's life. This treatment is more complete and up-to-date; it draws heavily on Sadat's own writings and is bolstered by the inclusion of footnotes.

3–5. Saghikian, Juanita Will. *Lands, Peoples and Communities of the Middle East: A Cultural Region in Southwest Asia and North Africa.* Middle East Gateway. Illus. by Penny Williams Yaqub. Detroit: International Book Centre, dist.*[2] 74pp. o.p.

Although librarians may be discouraged by the workbook format, this is a very good survey of an influential area. The text, well organized, clearly written, and enhanced by effective illustrations, emphasizes the relationship between people, landforms, and the development of culture. Suitable for middle graders as well as adults looking for introductory material.

7–9. Shapiro, William. *Lebanon.* Impact Books. New York: Watts, 1984. 88pp. o.p.

A brief overview of Lebanon's complex political history precedes Shapiro's competent discussion of the shattering events that have overtaken the nation since World War II, including terrible internal wars, the Israeli invasion, and the destruction of Beirut. The book was published before the hostage crisis and the emergence of non-Arab Iran as a key player in regional affairs.

6–9. Stefoff, Rebecca. *Yasir Arafat.* World Leaders Past and Present. New York: Chelsea House, 1989. 111pp. $15.95. ISBN: 1-55546-826-8; pap. $9.95. ISBN: 0-7910-0554-2, 0-685-18936-8.

Readers will acquire reliable information through a direct, chronological text and abundant illustrations in a biography that treats the life and political career of one of the Middle East's most controversial figures in the context of modern Arab-Israeli relations. Although the book was published relatively recently, the intifada—the Palestinian uprising in the Occupied Territories—is not covered. A brief bibliography, a chronology, and an index are included, but no footnotes.

5–8. Sullivan, George. *Sadat: The Man Who Changed Mid-East History.* New York: Walker, 1981. 99pp. $9.85. ISBN: 0-8027-6435-5.

In an objective and honest manner, Sullivan examines Sadat's life—from his humble beginnings in a close-knit peasant village and his revolutionary activity against the British—including terrorism and collaboration with the Nazis—through his daring as the first Arab statesman to openly seek peace with Israel.

---

[2]Complete addresses for all sources marked with an asterisk (*) can be found in the Resources section at the end of this chapter.

2–3. Take a Trip to Series. New York: Watts. 32pp. $7.99.

> Lye, Keith. *Take a Trip to Egypt.* 1983. ISBN: 0-531-03758-4.
> _____. *Take a Trip to Morocco.* 1988. ISBN: 0-531-10467-2.
> _____. *Take a Trip to Saudi Arabia.* 1984. ISBN: 0-531-04872-1.
> _____. *Take a Trip to Syria.* 1988. o.p.

There is no comparable source of information on the government, land and climate, people, economy, religion, and history of these countries for this age group. The text of each is simply written with large print and sufficient white space. The full-color photographs, including child-oriented pictures of stamps and money, are generally clear and handsome.

> Tames, Richard. *Libya.* 1989. ISBN: 0-531-10653-5.

Several improvements distinguish this latest addition to the familiar, easy-to-read series, including an expert author, a more informative text, and close-up color photographs that enhance immediacy. Modern controversies are objectively noted.

6–8. Tames, Richard. *The Muslim World.* Morristown, N.J.: Silver Burdett, 1985. 48pp. o.p.

First published in England, this oversized, generously illustrated book provides an excellent introduction to the religious faith of most Arabs. Information is concisely conveyed about such essentials as history, education, marriage, scientific and artistic contributions, and Islamic sects. The bibliography includes juvenile as well as adult sources, and the book has a useful glossary and index.

5–7. Visual Geography Series. Minneapolis: Lerner. 64pp. $12.95.

> *Egypt in Pictures.* 1989. ISBN: 0-8225-1840-6.
> *Jordan in Pictures.* 1988. ISBN: 0-8225-1834-1.
> *Lebanon in Pictures.* 1988. ISBN: 0-8225-1832-5.
> *Morocco in Pictures.* 1989. ISBN: 0-8225-1843-0.

Diverse black-and-white and color photographs of varying quality help create a balanced portrait of each country. These entries in the Visual Geography series cover much the same ground as the Enchantment of the World books but devote more attention to modern politics and problems. The book about Lebanon, for example, covers not only internal religious rivalries and dilemmas with neighboring countries but also the illegal drug trade.

3–5. Wright, David K., ed. *Jordan.* Children of the World. Milwaukee: Gareth Stevens, 1988. 64pp. $14.95. ISBN: 1-55532-224-7.

Jordan. Children of the World. Clearvue.* 1987. One filmstrip (50 fr., 13 min.), one cassette, one guide. $29.95. #G3-16.

Differences in living conditions and experiences are examined in an easily read photo essay and sound filmstrip that contrast the life of Ali, a twelve-year-old boy who resides with his middle-class family in the capital city of Amman, with that of his rural relatives. Information about day-to-day activities, culture and customs, and contemporary politics, particularly the Palestinian question, is sound. The audiovisual version extends the historical presentation.

PROGRAMMING IDEAS

Most of the holidays in the Arab world are of a religious nature, although some are national or political. One of the biggest holidays is the Islamic Festival of Eid ul-Fitr (it goes by other names as well), which comes at the end of Ramadan, the month of fasting. Similarly to Christmas, children receive gifts and sweets on this day. The other important religious holiday is Eid ul-Adha, the festival of sacrifice, which commemorates Abraham's willingness to sacrifice his only son Eshmael on God's command. On this day, children wear new clothes and a lamb is sacrificed. The celebration of these two holidays is determined by the Muslim lunar calendar.

St. Barbara's Day, a Christian Lebanese holiday celebrated in November, will be of special interest to children. Similarly to Halloween, the young people dress up in costumes and masks and go begging for treats. The anniversary of the establishment of the Arab League (an organization created to promote Arab unity) on March 22 is a political holiday observed in many Arab nations. Of course, there are also civic holidays distinct to each country that will not be elaborated on here.

In several of the art activities in this section, the terms *Islamic art* and *Arabic art* are used interchangeably. As the Arab-Islamic Empire spread, it drew something from each of the many cultures with which it came into contact. This assimilation, along with the Islamic prohibition of the realistic portrayal of the human figure (less strictly adhered to in the non-Arab countries of Persia and Turkey), resulted in distinctive art forms that are most commonly referred to as *Islamic*.

Special thanks are extended to Annie Downes Catterson, Philip Matsikas, and Sandra Newbury of the Fine Arts Department of the University of Chicago Laboratory Schools for their help with these art programs.

> *Art attempts to find in the universe in matter as well as in facts of life, what is fundamental, enduring, essential.*

These words, spoken by Saul Bellow upon receiving the Nobel Prize for Literature in 1976, support the notion that children should be exposed to the rich and impressive culture of a people in order to gain an accurate understanding of them. This is especially important when introducing the Arabic cultures because of possible misconceptions and prejudices and because of the lack of literary works, particularly fiction and folklore, for young readers.

The following activities involve ancient superstitions, the visual arts, food, games, music, and dance and are intended to enhance children's appreciation of Arabic cultures. To help ensure success, work through the activities before presenting them to children, share your own artwork, and provide pieces of art and reproductions as models.

Acknowledging the potential expense of the latter suggestion, there are ways to economize. Instead of purchasing art books, for instance, which are notoriously costly, take advantage of local public and academic libraries. Many libraries also have collections of artwork and reproductions that can be checked out. Other alternatives are poster and postcard reproductions, which can be obtained in museum gift shops. The most substantial collections of Arab and Islamic art in the United States are those of the Museum of Fine Arts* in Boston; the Fogg Art Museum* at Harvard; the Sackler Gallery* in Washington, D.C.; the Los Angeles County Museum of Art*; and The Metropolitan Museum of Art* in New York City. In addition, museum libraries will often produce slides and photographs for educational use at a minimal cost.

If funds are available, the books and curricular materials in this section (except where noted) can be purchased from the International Book Centre.* Materials for art projects can be obtained from art and craft supply stores. Specialty shops are a potential source for food items, recordings, clothing, and so forth.

These activities are suitable for both schools and libraries.

AMULETS

The belief that harm can be caused by a malevolent glance is universal in all Arab countries and can be traced to the Bedouins of pre-Islamic Arabia. Protective devices for these people included seashells painted with red, white, and green spots and carried in a cloth or animal-skin pouch, and a blue and white bead-laden string, wrapped behind the index finger and then tied around the wrist.

Another common practice was the wearing of silver amulets, or ornaments, around the neck. It was believed that the first glance of an evil eye was the most destructive, so any object worn in full view caught the venom intended for the wearer. Amulets are still worn today, although their significance now holds somewhat less importance for the more sophisticated.

These three objects can be easily reproduced by children in the upper elementary grades and middle school in an artistic, literary, and philosophical program concerning this superstition.

Two brief folktales can be used to introduce this magical concept and illustrate its continued acceptance in the villages. "The Stone in the Bed" and "The New Car" in *Folktales of Egypt*[†] illustrate envy for a new baby and a new car, respectively. In a follow-up discussion, children

Figure 1. Arabic geometric motifs can be used to make beautiful stencils

extensive literature and of the Koran, the holy book of Islam. Some of the most beautiful examples of calligraphy appear in illuminated Koranic manuscripts.

Children are naturally interested in other languages. Activities involving both spoken and written Arabic can be easily incorporated into both school and library settings.

Full-color plates of manuscripts and other art objects featuring linear designs can be found in Martin Ling's *The Quaranic Art of Calligraphy and Illumination* (Brooklyn, N.Y.: Interlink, 1990. 244pp. $49.95) or in similar books. Discuss these pictures with children before the following activity. Note the appearance of the scripts (Kufic is angular and large, Nakshi is round), the use of dominant colors and geometric patterns, and the flat, abstract quality of humans and beasts.

Arabic Name Designs

An excellent way to introduce this activity is to read aloud Florence Parry Heide and Judith Heide Gilliland's *The Day of Ahmed's Secret.*[†] Then help children select an Arabic name. A useful book is M. A. Qazi's *What's in a Muslim Name?* (Chicago: Kazi Publications, 1974. 54pp. $4.95. ISBN: 0-86685-1858), an alphabetical listing in both Arabic and English that includes definitions. Then, on a piece of construction paper folded in half lengthwise, write the Arabic name of each child in script along the fold (see figure 2).

Materials
Construction paper in varied colors
Crayons
Scissors
Paste or glue (always use nontoxic)

Directions
1. Using a crayon, draw around the top side of your name.
2. Cut on the line you just drew.
3. Discard the cutout and open up the paper. You now have an Arabic name design.
4. Paste your name design on a piece of colored paper.
5. Illustrate the meaning of your Arabic name, using geometric designs, manuscript-style drawings, etc.

If children (or adults for that matter) are interested in learning Arabic, James Peters'

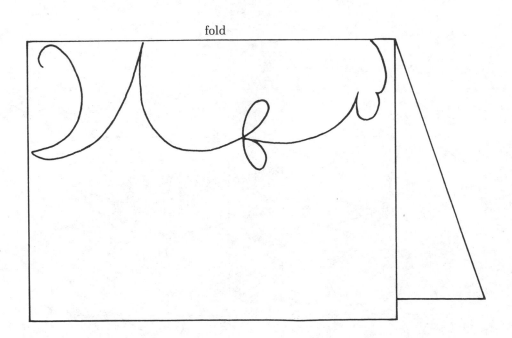

Figure 2. Arabic name stencil design

Figure 2—continued

Very Simple Arabic (Kent, England: Norbury, 1988, o.p.) is written in illuminated script and features such basic terms as greetings, days of the week, and numbers as well as simple grammar and a pronunciation guide. Alphabet wall cards and tapes are also available from the International Book Centre.

LEBANESE FOOD

One of Lebanon's greatest exports to the West has been its delicious and healthy cuisine. Much use is made of grains, especially wheat and barley; cheese; yogurt; fresh vegetables; fresh and dried fruits, especially dates, figs, and oranges; nuts; and legumes. Lamb and veal are the meats most often used. Pastries are very sweet and are often made to accompany religious and family celebrations. Ice water is the most popular beverage in Lebanon. Many Lebanese dishes are now available in restaurants in the United States, especially in larger cities.

Arab generosity and hospitality are legendary. A visitor to an Arab or Arab-American home will never go away feeling hungry or unappreciated. A wonderful story that introduces both of these values is "The Lost Camel of Emir Hamad" in *Arab Folktales,*[†] edited by Inea Bushnaq. In this Bedouin story, a sheik who sacrifices his last camel in order to feed his guest—a sultan in disguise—is lavishly rewarded.

Middle-Eastern cooking is sophisticated, but with the proper selection and supervision, it can be enjoyed by children as early as the middle elementary grades.

Hommos b' Tahini
(Tart Chick-pea Dip)

Hommos is a staple of the Lebanese diet. I collected this recipe from Albert Mokhiber, an American of Lebanese descent, who is a vegetarian. Mr. Mokhiber is the president of the American Arab Anti-Discrimination Committee.

1 12-oz. can chick-peas
2 cloves garlic
juice of one lemon
3/4 cup tahini
olive oil
paprika and parsley to garnish

1. Bring the chick-peas to a boil in a saucepan using the liquid from the can. Remove from heat and let cool. Puree the garlic, lemon juice, and tahini in a food processor or blender. (Tahini is a white, sesame-seed paste. It can be purchased in health food stores, Greek food shops, and Continental delis. If a food processor or blender is not available, the ingredients can be prepared by hand. Raw peas can also be used.)
2. Set aside some peas for garnish. Blend the rest into the puree.
3. Serve dip on a platter. Sprinkle with olive oil for taste. Garnish with paprika and parsley.
4. Eat with Arabic bread (also called pita or pocket bread) or raw vegetables.
5. For a spicier taste, cayenne pepper can be substituted for the paprika.

Laban
(Yogurt)

Yogurt is a staple of the Arab diet—there is always a bowl of fresh yogurt waiting to be served in Arab and Arab-American homes. It is easy to make but the right conditions are essential. Yogurt is served with rice, vegetables, and meat. If you don't want to do more cooking, however, you can serve it with fruit (apricots, peaches, citrus fruits) and chopped mint.

1 quart whole milk
2–3 tablespoons plain yogurt (it must have an active culture to work)

1. Place the milk in a heavy pot. Boil until it is ready to spill over.
2. Turn the heat off. Let the milk cool slightly (to about 100° F.). Test it by immersing your finger for a count of ten. A skin is likely to form on the top of the milk.
3. Place several tablespoons of the warm milk in a bowl. Mix in the yogurt. When the yogurt is thoroughly dissolved, add the mixture to the rest of the milk.
4. Mix well and place in a large glass or metal bowl.
5. Cover the bowl with a dish or plastic wrap. Carefully wrap three or four towels or a woolen blanket around the bowl. Let it sit for eight hours in a draft-free place. Store in a refrigerator.

Making laban can also be incorporated into a science unit on culturing milk, that is, letting carefully selected bacteria grow in the milk.

What is known and understood about this process is clearly and simply explained in the popular vegetarian cookbook *The New Laurel's Cookbook* (Berkeley, Calif.: Ten Speed Press, 1986. $16.95. ISBN: 0-89815-166-X).

Biskout Bi Mish Mish Wa Lowz
(Apricot and Walnut Cookies)

Children, of course, love to bake and eat cookies. This is one of the simplest recipes for Arab sweets.

1/3 cup sugar
1/2 cup oil
1 egg
1/2 teaspoon vanilla
1 cup flour
1/2 teaspoon salt
3 egg whites, slightly beaten
1 cup chopped walnuts
1/2 cup apricot jam

1. Preheat the oven to 350° F. (180° C). Grease cookie sheets.
2. Mix the sugar and oil. Add the egg and vanilla, blending thoroughly. Mix the flour and salt together and add to the first mixture. Blend thoroughly.
3. Shape with the fingers into small (1-inch) balls. Dip in the egg whites, then roll in the chopped almonds.
4. Place on the cookie sheets, about 1½ inches apart. Indent each in the center with your finger. Bake for 20 minutes. Cool, then fill indentations with apricot jam. Makes 1½ dozen cookies.

Foods eaten throughout the Middle East are quite similar, although their names may differ. To locate other recipes, check your library or the culinary section of a large bookstore. Several guides to Middle Eastern cooking are available from the International Book Centre. Strongly recommended are *Sahtain, Middle East Cookbook* (Detroit: Arab Women's Union, 1976. 321pp. $15.00. ISBN: 0-86685-036-8) prepared with a Western audience in mind, and Sima Osman Yassine's *Middle Eastern Cuisine* (Detroit: International Book Centre, 1984. 120pp. $20.00. ISBN: 0-86685-360-X), which features appetizing full-color illustrations.

Some basic rules concerning the etiquette of serving and eating food are included in *Very Simple Arabic*. It is interesting to note the order in which diners are served—males from the eldest to the youngest, followed by females. This can be explained to children or can be a fun sequencing exercise to accompany the serving of food for those not offended by this ritual.

CHILDREN'S GAMES

Georgette Sesi, supervisor in the Bilingual Department, Detroit Public Schools, fondly recalls these two games from her own youth in Baghdad.

The Fox

The original significance of this game has been lost; however, it probably grew out of the concern of shepherds about animals dangerous to their flocks. This is a large-group activity suitable for grades K–2.

Materials
A cloth handkerchief knotted into a ball

Location
Gym or large indoor space or an outdoor playground

Directions
1. Select a player to be the fox.
2. The remaining players make a big circle sitting or standing at arm's length.
3. Holding the hanky, the fox runs around the outside of the circle several times, calling (the louder the better!): "The fox goes round and round."
4. In turn, the other players respond, "And on his/her tail there are several knots."
5. With the hanky, the fox hits a player who then must chase the fox once around the circle.
6. If the fox is tagged before reaching the starting point, the chaser becomes the next fox. If not, the chaser returns to the circle and the fox continues.

Variations
1. Instead of running outside the circle, the fox weaves in and out between each player. The chaser must do the same.
2. The fox can invent a pattern, running in and out between some players, leapfrogging over others, etc. The chaser must do the same. If the chaser misses an action, he or she is automatically out.

3. An Egyptian version of this game, along with the Arabic words, English translation, and music, can be found in *Sing, Children, Sing* (New York: U.S. Committee for UNICEF, 1972. 72pp. $3.50. ISBN: 0-935738-05-3).
4. A small, soft ball (like a nerf ball) can be used instead of a hanky.

The Bead Game

The "trickster" element involved in this game appeals to children everywhere. This is a small-group activity suitable for grades 2–4.

Materials
Sand
Plastic water pitcher (*never use glass*)
Plastic or glass colored beads

Location
Outdoor playground

Directions
1. Select a captain.
2. With the other players watching, the captain arranges the sand in a semicircle and then wets it enough so it can be molded later.
3. The captain next arranges some beads on the sand semicircle.
4. The other players close their eyes. The captain *rearranges* the beads on the semicircle and then forms sand hills of varying sizes containing varying amounts of beads (of course, the biggest hills do not necessarily have to contain the greatest number of beads!). There should be one hill for each player.
5. When the captain is finished, he or she signals to the other children to open their eyes.
6. Each player quickly claims a mound. The players uncover their beads and count them.
7. Rotate until each player has served as captain. A running tally should be kept. The player with the most beads at the end is the winner.

Although out-of-print, the well-indexed *Folkway's Omnibus of Children's Games* (Harrisburg, Penn.: Stackpole Books, 1970, 320pp.) is useful as a source of the play ways of the Bedouins, Yemenites, and Iraqis as well as non-Arab groups. Another out-of-print but excellent resource is UNICEF's multicultural Hi Neighbor Series (published from 1958 to 1965 and still available in many public libraries), which includes a number of children's games and songs from several Arab countries.

Popular Middle Eastern board games that American children also enjoy are chess and *taawila* (backgammon). Soccer is the most popular Middle Eastern spectator sport.

FOLK DANCE AND MUSIC

The *Debka*, as it is called in Lebanon and Syria, is the traditional Arab folk dance that involves all members of the community. It is a row dance that moves in a semicircle to the right. The dancer farthest to the right is the leader and waves a hanky. The other dancers link arms or hold their hands upraised.

Like all traditional Arab folk music, debka music has strong rhythms that are repeated many times. The main instruments (other than the human voice) are the guitarlike *uud*, the *darabukkas*, *duffs*, and *zummara*. Recordings can be purchased from the International Book Centre or found in the international music sections of large record stores.

There are literally hundreds of variants of this dance. This is the one I learned from members of a Lebanese-Greek community in Niagara Falls, N.Y. It can be easily learned by children as well.

The Debka

Step One: Slide your right foot to the right.

Step Two: Swing your left foot in front of your right.

Step Three: Slide your right foot to the right again.

Step Four: Swing your left foot *back* behind your right foot. Stamp your left foot.

Step Five: At the same time, kick with your right foot and hop with your left.

REPEAT

RESOURCES

Arthur M. Sackler Gallery
Smithsonian Institution
1000 Jefferson Dr. S.W.
Washington, DC 20560
Mailing address:
900 Jefferson Dr. S.W.
Room 241C
Washington, DC 20560
(202) 357-2700
FAX: (202) 786-2515

Claudia's Caravan
P.O. Box 1582
Alameda, CA 94501

Clearvue
5711 N. Milwaukee Ave.
Chicago, IL 60646

Fogg Art Museum
32 Quincy Street
Harvard University
Cambridge, MA 02138
(617) 495-9400
FAX: (617) 495-9936

Imported Books
P.O. Box 4414
2025 W. Clarendon
Dallas, TX 75208

International Book Centre
Attn.: Claudette Mukala
P.O. Box 295
Troy, MI 48099
(313) 879-8436

Los Angeles County Museum of Art
5905 Wilshire Blvd.
Los Angeles, CA 90036
(213) 857-6111
FAX: (213) 931-7347

The Metropolitan Museum of Art
5th Avenue at 82nd Street
New York, NY 10028
Mailing address:
1000 Fifth Avenue
New York, NY 10028-0198
(212) 879-5500
FAX: (212) 570-3879

Museum of Fine Arts
465 Huntington Avenue
Boston, MA 02115
(617) 267-9300
FAX: (617) 267-0280

Rashid Sales
191 Atlantic Avenue
Brooklyn, NY 11201

CHAPTER 3

Asian Materials and Programs

by Ginny Lee, Suzanne Lo, and Susan Ma

For most of Western history, Asia has been thought of as mysterious, fabulous, and inscrutable. A myriad of stereotypes has characterized and defined Asia. Only in the past decade or so have these stereotypes been challenged and Asia redefined on its own terms.

Although the term *Asia* has been used to include everything from what is now referred to as the Middle East to the Pacific Islands and from Siberia to the borders of the "down under" countries, for the purposes of this bibliography, only a fraction of that great part of the globe will be included. The concentration will be on those countries known as East Asia (China, Japan, and Korea) and those comprising Southeast Asia (Vietnam, Laos, Thailand, Cambodia, Burma, Malaysia, Indonesia, and the Philippines). Minority groups, such as the Hmong, have been included within those countries. We have also included several entries about India, although we did not examine South Asian materials in depth.

There has also been a tendency, mainly in Western countries, to artificially lump together a number of Asian countries that can conveniently be referred to as one group (e.g., Indochina). However, Indochina is actually made up of very distinct, separate countries that are not Chinese. In fact, Asians view themselves as members of ethnic groups from specific countries and take great pride in their heritage. In an article in *Asian Week* (Dec. 16, 1988) about New York City's population changes, Betty Sung commented on this aspect of Asian cultures:

Each of these groups has its own languages, its own culture, its own religions, and its own ethnic identity. In other words, Asian Americans are not homogeneous and they cannot be treated as such. From the city bureaucracy's point of view, it is more convenient and more economical to lump Asian Americans together, but their diversity demands differential consideration. Unlike Hispanics with a common language, Spanish, a common religion, Catholicism, and similar cultural backgrounds, Asians are unlike in many ways. For example, the Chinese may be Confucianist-Taoist ancestor worshippers; the Japanese may be Buddhist; . . . Filipinos may be Catholic. . . . Each country has its own national tongue and perhaps its own unique history. In its dealings with, in its provisions for, and in its delivery of services to these newcomers, attention must be given to the background of each group.

The books in this chapter were written for or about Asian or Asian-American children through junior high school. Although most of the books are in English, some are bilingual and some are in various languages. Because there is much more material published for children about China than about other Asian countries, this chapter contains a great deal of material about that country. However, we have tried to include as much material as we could adequately examine on other Asian countries as well.

In addition to our own library collections, we have used three other annotated bibliographies: *Literature for Children about Asians and Asian Americans* by Esther C. Jenkins and Mary C. Austin (Greenwood Press, 1987), *Japan Through Children's Literature* by Yasuko Makino (Greenwood Press, 1985), and *Recommended Readings in Literature, Kindergarten through Grade Eight* (California State Department of Education, 1988). These bibliographies were useful in allowing us to identify the gaps in our lists and to follow certain trends in publishing in the past few decades.

The present bibliography includes only what we were able to examine. We decided to include material published in the 1980s or later. We included some material on Asian Americans even when the original country was not emphasized. Of prime importance was that the culture of each country be authentically described, free of stereotypes, and well and distinctly depicted. This led us to exclude some titles that have been popular for years, such as *The Five Chinese Brothers* and *Tikki Tikki Tembo*. Even though these are interesting stories, they do not accurately portray a particular culture, nor are they free of unpleasant stereotypes.

Many of the books we did select are based on folktales mainly because the materials are often connected with a particular festival. We also examined those materials for literary merit as well as cultural authenticity, but in some cases, as in those books published in China for export, a lack of literary merit did not always justify the exclusion of a rich tidbit of culture.

For years there were few books published about the Asian countries. Although there had been books on fairy tales and folktales and also many series books dealing with the history and cultures of the modern nations, there was not much quality literature. During the 1980s, however, beautiful new books on Asia, both from the West and from Asian countries, began to appear—it was a welcome trend. Currently, such authors as Laurence Yep, Yoshiko Uchida, Lensey Namioka, and Yoko Kawashima Watkins are contributing to a brand of insightful and universal literature that is not merely formulistic or token. There are also Western authors who were children of missionaries in Asia or had some other strong connection to Asian cultures and who have written wonderful novels dealing with their experiences.

We hope this bibliography will encourage you to fill in the gaps about Asia in your own collection. We also hope that this work will encourage other writers and publishers to continue the trend toward producing more literature that demystifies Asia.

BIBLIOGRAPHY

PICTURE BOOKS

K–4.   Baker, Keith. *The Magic Fan.* Illus. by the author. San Diego: Harcourt Brace Jovanovich, 1989. 18pp. $14.95. ISBN: 0-15-250750-7.

Yoshi the carpenter builds things for his village—until he runs out of practical ideas. He finds a fan that shows him what to build. When the fan shows him the earthquake fish (the mythical fish that causes earthquakes), he invites the people up onto the bridge that they had all thought useless. It saves their lives. Though Yoshi loses the fan, ideas still come to him. Here is the timeless and universal *Dumbo* theme: You don't need your magic feather to fly; the magic is within you.

The fan-shaped insert in every page turns separately, giving an added dimension of surprise to the story. The illustrations are within the fan shapes; the text is on the page. Illustrations are in the strong, muted colors of Japanese woodblock prints, and the style also owes something to Hiroshige's Fifty-three Stages of the Tokaido, a popular series of nineteenth-century woodcut prints. Baker does take liberties with the depiction of Japan in a way that is not Japanese. For example, the roofs of Japanese buildings are not floral and multicolored—clothing is. Houses are an earthy brown or gray and roofs might have been thatched.

1–4.   Birdseye, Tom. *A Song of Stars: An Asian Legend.* Illus. by Ju-Hong Chen. New York: Holiday House, 1990. 15pp. $14.95. ISBN: 0-8234-0790-X.

The herd boy and the weaving maid so enjoyed each other that they forgot their work and had to be separated as stars in the sky, able to meet only once a year across the Milky Way. The Emperor in this retelling of an old Chinese tale looks truly omnipotent. He has Buddha-like features, which imply his mercifulness. The illustrations are mosaiclike, flowing like a modern ballet yet still implying China. This tale is also the basis for the Japanese Tanabata festival, and in many places the celebration that surrounds this story is like Valentine's Day.

K–3.   Blia, Xiong. *Nine-in-One Grr! Grr! A Folktale from the Hmong People of Laos.* Adapted by Cathy Spagnoli. Illus. by Nancy Hom. San Francisco: Children's Book Press, 1989. 32pp. $12.95. ISBN: 0-89239-048-4.

This simple tale, reminiscent of Aesop, is from the mountains of Laos and has a clever ending in which Bird thinks of a way to keep the land from being filled with tigers. Traditional Hmong embroideries that tell stories inspire the authentic illustrations.

3–5.   Fisher, Leonard Everett. *The Great Wall of China.* New York: Macmillan, 1986. 32pp. $11.95. ISBN: 0-02-735220-X.

Large and powerful black-and-white drawings, reminiscent of the terra-cotta figures unearthed in Xian, along with titles in Chinese characters and red ink seals form the basis for this picture book about the building of the Great Wall—to "keep China safe from the Mongols forever"—and its cost in the lives of those who built it. The book has great impact and will be useful both for story hour or for prompting discussion in the middle grades.

P–2.   Friedman, Ina R. *How My Parents Learned to Eat.* Illus. by Allen Say. Boston: Houghton Mifflin, 1984. 32pp. $12.95. ISBN: 0-395-35379-3.

Here is a charming mixture of Japanese, American, and British eating styles seen in the attempts of a Japanese schoolgirl and an American sailor to impress each other. Told by their daughter, the story actually has an adult perspective, but this detracts very little. The motives of love, making room for cultural differences, and even going out of the way to embrace what is seen as important to the other make a touching little drama.

K–3.   Ginsberg, Mirra, adapter. *The Chinese Mirror.* Illus. by Margot Zemach. New York: Harcourt Brace Jovanovich, 1988. 26pp. $14.95. ISBN: 0-15-200420-3.

A country man goes off to China and comes back with an amazing new item: a mirror. Everyone sees something different in this "strange round shiny thing," and arguments ensue until the mirror is finally broken, putting an end to arguments, images, and the tale. This simple tale is illustrated with almost cartoonlike brush paintings, which still manage to give enough detail to identify the scene as Korea rather than another country.

3–6.   Godden, Rumer. *Fu-Dog.* Pictures by Valerie Littlewood. New York: Viking, 1990. 64pp. $14.95. ISBN: 0-670-82300-7.

Two British children who are part Caucasian and part Chinese go on a journey to find their Great Uncle in London's Chinatown. Malcolm looks and feels more British, while Li-la looks like and identifies more with her Chinese heritage. The leading character, a Fu-Dog doll sent to them by Great Uncle, takes on a life and a voice of its own and eggs them on, both on their journey and in their squabbles. There are a few mishaps—Fu-Dog is lost in the New Year's parade, and Malcolm is trampled and breaks his arm. In the end, however, all is well. Dad learns to enjoy a bit of the Chinese side of the family; Malcolm warms up a little to Fu-Dog; Li-la learns a lot about Chinese culture, though much of it seems quite dated (Chinese elders no longer expect their progeny to kneel before them and bang their forehead on the floor); and Great Uncle gives Li-la a real Fu-Dog—a Peking puppy of her own.

The writing style, though clear and quite readable, hails from an old school of writing for children that was popular several decades ago. The story idea, however, is quite relevant to the emerging mixture of cultures in our population.

2–6.   Gretchen, Sylvia, adapter. *Hero of the Land of Snow.* Adapted from the Tibetan Epic Tale of Gesar. Illus. by Julia Witwer. Berkeley, Calif.: Dharma Publishing, 1990. 33pp. pap. $6.95. ISBN: 0-89800-202-8.

In a predictable fairy tale format, this old Tibetan epic recounts the magical beginnings of Gesar, king of the land of Ling in Tibet, and the great horse race that made him king. The lord who has usurped the throne is blatantly evil, the girl destined to be queen is incomparably beautiful, the horse is wild and spirited—but docile for Gesar. When Gesar was a boy, the evil lord sent him away to the wild northlands, for even then his magic was powerful. When the time comes for Gesar to retake his throne, he tricks the lord into proclaiming that a horse race will determine who should be king. Broughmo, the beautiful young girl sent to fetch Gesar, learns that "beauty is a fine thing, but it will not make you a queen." Only her good deeds and a good heart are important. Disguised as a ragged beggar, Gesar approaches several people, who learn that "appearances are not always what they seem." Gesar wins the race and the kingdom, and goes on to many other adventures to be related in successive books.

The terse style, common to comic books, leads us to expect a cartoon illustration above each brief paragraph. However, the illustrations are full-page pencil drawings in vivid colors depicting Tibetan costume in detail. A sketchy map of the mountains, a note on the Gesar epic, and a Tibetan pronunciation guide are helpful.

1–4. Hearn, Lafcadio. *The Voice of the Great Bell*. Retold by Margaret Hodges. Illus. by Ed Young. Boston: Little, Brown, 1989. 28pp. $14.95. ISBN: 0-316-36791-5.

A famous bell maker is commissioned to make a special, gigantic bell but cannot get the metals to mix. The emperor threatens his life if the bell is not completed. The bell maker's beautiful and devoted daughter visits an astrologer who explains that a pure maiden must be sacrificed. The willing sacrifice of the child for the good of the parent illustrates the importance of filial piety in the moral code of many Asian cultures. The daughter complies, but as she jumps into the molten metal, a servant grasps her shoe. Now the sound of the perfect bell echoes her name, Ko Ngai, who is said to be seeking her lost shoe. This ancient story is illustrated with dreamlike pastel chalks in just enough detail to evoke an image of old China.

3–5. Laurin, Anne. *Perfect Crane*. Illus. by Charles Mikolaycak. New York: Harper and Row, 1981. 31pp. $11.89. ISBN: 0-06-023743-0; 0-06-023744-0.

Black-and-white and gold ochre wash drawings reminiscent of old Japanese woodcut prints and full of details of Japanese life add to the charm of this simple folktale about a lonely magician whose paper foldings begin to come alive. His prize piece, a perfect crane, comes to life to keep him company. When the bird has to fly away in the fall, the magician turns to helping others and begins to lead a full life. Suitable for storytelling for grades three and up.

2–5. Leaf, Margaret. *Eyes of the Dragon*. Illus. by Ed Young. New York: Lothrop, 1987. 29pp. $11.75. ISBN: 0-688-06155-9; 0-688-06156-7.

This popular tale, embellished in the retelling and illustrated in glowing, flowing, brilliant watercolors, is the story of Ch'en Jung, who painted dragons so lifelike that the mere addition of a spot of light in the eyes was enough to make them come to life. Ch'en Jung accepts a request to paint a dragon on the wall that surrounds a village. He asks only two things—one, that a sum of money be donated to a Taoist temple, and two, that the dragon be left as painted (without eyes). This second request, however, is not understood and therefore not heeded—with disastrous results.

K–4. Levinson, Riki. *Our Home Is the Sea*. Paintings by Dennis Luzak. New York: Dutton, 1988. 30pp. $13.95. ISBN: 0-525-44406-8.

A child walks home from school, thinking about what he wants his life to be and noticing things in his environment as he passes. The story is set in Hong Kong, and the illustrator has obviously spent time there. Every beautifully detailed and lifelike painting rings true. Through the illustrations, the reader eventually realizes that the boy lives not in a house (common here, but uncommon in Hong Kong) nor in a big apartment or tall housing complex (the common way to live in Hong Kong), but on a boat. The story is more stream of consciousness than real plot, but it has a valid punch line: "I don't want to be a schoolteacher. I want to be a fisherman like my father."

2–5. Li, Zeru. *The Cowherd and the Girl Weaver*. Illus. by Liu Yi. Beijing: 1987, $4.00.

This traditional Chinese folktale tells of the love between a beautiful fairy maiden called Girl Weaver and a cowherd. Girl Weaver, the granddaughter of the Heavenly King, offended the law of the heavens and married an ordinary mortal. The couple were forever separated by the Milky Way and are allowed to meet each other briefly only on July 7 of the lunar calendar each year.

3–6. Louie, Ai-Ling. *Yeh-Shen: A Cinderella Story from China.* Illus. by Ed Young. New York: Philomel Books, 1982. 29pp. $12.95. ISBN: 0-399-20900-X.

Almost every country has its Cinderella story. This one from China is illustrated with the flavor of a minority group from the Southwest, just north of Indochina. A page recording the story, taken originally from a Tang dynasty (A.D. 618–907) book, is reproduced at the beginning. The story includes Cinderella, the mean stepmother and her greedy daughter, the prince who holds a ball to look for a bride, and the slippers whose tiny-footed owner must be found. The "fairy godmother" is a fish, which the stepmother finds and kills, but the bones continue to grant "Cinderella's" wishes.

1–4. Mahy, Margaret. *The Seven Chinese Brothers.* Illus. by Jean and Mou-sien Tseng. New York: Scholastic, 1990. 36pp. $12.95. ISBN: 0-590-42055-0.

Happily, the old story of multiple brothers who all look alike has been reillustrated and retitled. The great merit of this story lies in the new illustrations, which are so much more representative of China. Details of attire and site, possibly based on ancient Chinese drawing manuals and done in realistic watercolors, take us back to the time of the first emperor. Each of seven brothers, all of whom fall one by one into disfavor with the emperor, has a special power that he calls upon to save his life, changing places with the brother just before him.

1–4. Mui, Y. T. *The Magic Brush.* Adapted from the original folktale by Robert B. Goodman and Robert A. Spicer. Edited by Ruth Tabrah. Honolulu: Island Heritage, 1974. 58pp. $5.95. ISBN: 0-8348-3032-9.

This is an ancient Chinese tale that has been retold several times in Western picture

books, but the paintings in this version mark it as one of the best. Chinese ink paintings with a modern perspective give a tremendous amount of detail about life in ancient China and are full of both humor and compassion. The story is about a poor boy who studies painting so diligently that his works come to life—with the help of a magic brush. Mui's expressive paintings capture the awesomeness of the magic and bring the reader right into the heart of the Chinese countryside.

There have been several other versions of this story. One of them, *Liang and His Magic Brush* by Demi (Holt, 1980), is worth mentioning because her illustrations, though dainty, well drawn, and wonderfully Chinese, do almost nothing to enhance the text. They give the feeling of having been selected from Chinese scrolls and placed at random in the book. Some have nothing at all to do with the story.

P–3. Okawa, Essei. *Urashima Taro: The Fisherman and the Grateful Turtle.* Illus. by Koichi Murakami. Union City, Calif.: Heian International, 1985. 32pp. $9.95. ISBN: 0-89346-257-8.

In this version of one of the most popular and most ancient of Japanese tales, a fisher boy, Urashima Taro, befriends a turtle and is taken to visit the Sea King. The boy falls in love with the Sea King's daughter and stays for three hundred years, believing it to be merely three. Finally he becomes homesick for his own life, though he was very poor. He is given a box, which he is not to open, to take home with him. Astonished to find that three hundred years have passed, he opens the box and becomes as old as he is. The Rip Van Winkle and Pandora's Box motifs are key elements in many Asian folk stories. The illustrations provide some Japanese flavor, but do not offer much detail about the Japanese way of life.

2–6. Paterson, Katherine. *The Tale of the Mandarin Ducks.* Illus. by Leo and Diane Dillon. New York: Dutton, 1990. 32pp. $14.95. ISBN: 0-525-67283-4.

This is a classic tale of good and evil, or rather, of generosity and greed. Greedy is the emperor who cannot bear anything that is not beautiful. He captures a beautiful drake, but it pines away in captivity and becomes ugly. Generous is the servant who frees the drake, though it brings him trouble. "It is never foolish to help another living creature," he tells his wife. But trouble comes because of it. "Trouble can be borne if it is shared," he says. And the drake and his duck repay his kindness. The striking and original illustrations seem lifted from Japanese woodcut prints. The strong flowing lines, the muted colors, and the intricately patterned details of plumage and robe all blend to evoke a beautiful tale from ancient Japan.

K–3. Say, Allen. *The Bicycle Man.* Illus. by Allen Say. Oakland, Calif.: Parnassus Press; Boston: Houghton Mifflin, 1982. 18pp. $12.45. ISBN: 0-395-32254-5.

Detailed pen-and-ink drawings with color washes capture the character of a Japanese country village. In this simple story of a school sports day, two American servicemen perform bicycle tricks for the open-mouthed schoolchildren. The amusing, heartwarming, almost cartoonlike characters make this a good attempt to help the twain meet. Good read-aloud.

K–3. Snyder, Diane. *The Boy of the Three Year Nap.* Illus. by Allen Say. Boston: Houghton Mifflin, 1988. 32pp. $14.95. ISBN: 0-395-44090-4.

Exquisite watercolors reminiscent of ancient Japanese woodcut prints with their delicate color, flowing line, and intricate detail add much to this old Japanese folktale. A clever but lazy boy outwits himself while trying to obtain a desirable bride and avoid work at the same time. The former he manages with a bit of self-styled drama. As for the latter, well, by the end of the book we see that he was really more clever than lazy after all. This one is likely to survive for a long time.

1–4. Stamm, Claus. *Three Strong Women: A Tall Tale from Japan.* Pictures by Jean and Mou-sien Tseng. New York: Viking, 1990. 30pp. $12.95. ISBN: 0-670-83323-1.

A proud and powerful man who likes himself very much meets a girl who has more power than meets the eye. She takes him home (literally and forcibly) to meet her even more powerful mother and grandmother. After some time living with them, our hero develops not only superhuman strength but also a sense of humility. The illustrations have an element of cartoon buffoonishness that works quite well.

P–3. Surat, Michelle Maria. *Angel Child, Dragon Child.* Illus. by Vo-Dinh Mai. Milwaukee: Raintree, 1983. 35pp. $14.65. ISBN: 0-940742-12-8.

A charming Vietnamese girl and her sisters brave the cruel taunts of the American children at their new school. In the girl's imagination, however, her mother, left behind in Vietnam, encourages her to be an "angel child." A wise principal demands that one of the young ruffians talk to the girl and write down all that has happened to her. The resulting poignant story incites the schoolchildren to raise the money to bring the girl's mother to America. By the time she arrives, the girls have traded their *ao-dai* (Vietnamese dresses) for jeans but are still homesick for Vietnam. Suitable for storytelling.

1–3. Svend, Otto S. *Children of the Yangtze River.* London: Pelham, 1982, 1985. 30pp. $8.95. ISBN: 0-7207-1432-X.

A video camera could not have caught more vividly the daily life in this little village along the Yangtze and the time of the great flood that drove everyone from home, carrying along precious pigs, birds, and grandparents. The story is told through the eyes of two young children, which lends it further poignancy. The large format with only a few lines of print per page and the very detailed and true-to-life watercolors make this book good for storytelling.

P–1. Tsutsui, Yoriko. *Anna's Secret Friend.* Illus. by Akiko Hayashi. New York: Viking Kestrel, 1986, 1987. 32pp. $10.95. ISBN: 0-670-81670-1.

Here is an interesting twist on the difficulty of leaving friends and moving to a new neighborhood and a new school. The person who keeps leaving flowers and notes in Anna's mailbox is as shy as Anna, but the two little girls finally become good friends. The pen-and-ink watercolor drawings are a delight, and the English Japanese translation is very nicely done. The story, though illustrative of modern Japan, is quite universal.

P–K. _____. *Before the Picnic.* Illus. by Akiko Hayashi. New York: Philomel Books, 1987. 24pp. $10.95. ISBN: 0-399-21458-5.

Wonderful pen-and-ink watercolors capture the small child's good intentions to help get ready as she makes a mess of everything, to the eternally patient consternation of her parents. Nice touches, such as portraying the breakfast table with sushi and chopsticks, add a particularly Japanese flavor to this universally recognizable situation. The English translation is nicely done.

2–5. Yagawa, Sumiko. *The Crane Wife.* Translated by Katherine Paterson. Illus. by Suekichi Akaba. New York: William Morrow, 1981. 30pp. $9.95. ISBN: 0-688-00496-2.

One of the most beloved tales in Japan is that of the poor man whose kindness to an injured crane leads to his finding a wife as talented as she is beautiful. She weaves cloth so amazing it seems to be from another world. On disregarding her request to refrain from watching her weave, however, the poor man discovers, too late to keep her, that she is the very crane whose life he had saved. Splashy illustrations evoke a Japanese feeling. Good for story hour.

2–5. Young, Ed. *Lon Po Po: A Red-Riding-Hood Story from China.* Trans. and illus. by Ed Young. New York: Philomel Books, 1989. 30pp. $14.95. ISBN: 0-399-21619-7.

Here is a powerful story with almost too powerful illustrations. The children depicted in this 1990 Caldecott Award winner are very real and very frightened and the terror is sustained. Though not for the very young, this is a good scary story for a Halloween story hour. A wolf disguised as Grandmother gets into the house while Mother is away and designs to eat the children. In this version they escape but in an earlier retelling, the two younger children are actually eaten. The ded-

ication is just as powerful: "To all the wolves of the world, for lending their good name as a tangible symbol for our darkness."

From China

Many beautifully illustrated picture books of Chinese folk and fairy tales are now being published in English by Chinese publishing houses for export to Western countries. Some are also being translated into Spanish, French, German, Italian, and Esperanto. Some are in large format (8″ by 11″) with nearly full-page paintings using various Chinese styles with brush and ink and color washes, ranging from delicate to splashy, with a few lines of text below.

The stories, though briefly and simply related, are interesting for their revelation of the Chinese way of life and of thinking. Because of the large format, these books could be used with younger children, if the teacher is highly motivated.

Some of the books are in smaller format and some, such as the West Lake series of folktales, are grouped in boxes, but in all, the illustrations are striking.

The first few books discussed here come from a collection of ghost stories and strange tales from the early Qing dynasty (late seventeenth century) now known as the Tales of Liao Zhai. In these tales, there is often a fox or a snake who transforms itself into a human being either to help someone or to play mischief. Here also are stories of the soul leaving the body—which either remains inert as in a coma or is at least dull and spiritless—and going to inhabit another person or an animal in order to accomplish some powerful desire of the spirit.

Most of these retellings are a mere outline of the original story, adapted for the terse picture-book format, as popular in China as comic books are in the United States. The usually literal translations, inexpertly rendered, sound even worse in English than in Chinese, but the books are worth looking at nevertheless for their insight into the Chinese mind.

4–6. *Lu Ban Learns Carpentry.* Beijing: Foreign Languages Press, 1981.

Diligence, a kind heart, and a desire to serve people win a poor boy acceptance as apprentice to a mysterious master carpenter. Eagerly, the boy performs the impossibly tedious tasks set before him. After several years he is sent back home, a master carpenter himself, with the enjoinder to live up to the old master's reputation. Beautifully done.

5–up. Miao, Jie. *A Queer Cricket*. Based on a story in Tales of Liaozhai. Illus. by Huang Hongyi. Beijing: Morning Glory Press, 1987. 47pp. pbk: $3.65. 88-E-301.

During a time when the royal inclination was toward fighting crickets, a poor but honest scholar, in response to a royal decree, catches a cricket to present to the king. His little son inadvertently kills the cricket and is so mortified that he throws himself into the well. The parents mourn while the body of the boy lies inert in bed for many days. Meanwhile, another cricket is found. In spite of its diminutive size it proves to be a fierce fighter and wins all the matches for the boy's father. On waking, the boy reveals that he himself had entered the body of the cricket in order to win fights and redeem himself in his father's eyes.

5–up. Shu, Ying. *Daughter of a Fox Spirit*. Based on a story in Tales of Liaozhai. Illus. by Shen Qipeng. Beijing: Morning Glory Press, 1987. 30pp. $6.95. ISBN: 7-5054-0079-7/ L.0127.

Appropriate to the Tales of Liaozhai, there is in this story a fox spirit that has been transformed into a beautiful girl. A young man, until now interested only in his books, catches sight of her and falls irretrievably in love. An amusing change comes over him as he is mesmerized into neglecting his books in favor of moaning over his love. This is a simple tale of family etiquette and social propriety typical of China. This one has a happy ending, but many other fox stories end with the girl turning back into a fox and disappearing.

5–up. _____. *The Lotus Princess*. Based on a story in Tales of Liaozhai. Illus. by Pan Xiaoqing. Beijing: Morning Glory Press, 1987. 31pp. $6.95. ISBN: 7-5054-0065-7/L.0123.

Preparing for a nap one day, a young man receives a singular invitation to visit a nearby king. The estate proves to be "crisscrossed with roads and mansions. . . ." There, the young man falls in love with the king's daughter and marries her. Suddenly he finds himself back on his couch, just waking from his nap. At first he is disappointed to think it was only a dream. Then he realizes that he was visited by some bees in his dream and the king's mansion had been the beehive. Going outside, he discovers the very hive. He continues living his double life—a man while awake, a bee in his dream world.

From Japan[1]

1–4. Geijutsu Kyoiku Kenkyujo. *Warabeuta*. Edited by the author. Illus. by Haba Kazuo. Tokyo: Iwasaki Shoten, 1984. 24pp. $9.00.

The author presents Japanese nursery rhymes for the twelve months of the year. The book also introduces folk songs, such as grandmothers used to sing, as well as traditional Japanese customs and local festivals. This well-illustrated book brings back some old traditions that children of today have forgotten.

2–6. Komaniya, Rokuro. *Nippon no uta*. Illus. by the author. Tokyo: NHK (Nippon Hoso Kyokai), 1984. 59pp. $21.00. ISBN: 4-14-008356-5.

An established and internationally known artist, Komaniya here illustrates early-twentieth-century children's songs. Nostalgic children's songs were composed during this period by such well-known poets as Kitahara Hakushu and Noguchi Ujo, with music by Yamada Kosaku, Kirai Kosabura, Nakayam Shinpei, and others. The impressionistic illustrations, such as "The Rain in Josashima Island" and the silhouettelike picture of children against "The Moon," are especially beautiful. The poets, the composers, and the illustrator make this book a classic.

1–4. Sato, Satoru. *Nezumi to Yomeiri*. Illus. by Murakami Tsutomu. Tokyo: DoShin sha, 1984. 40pp. $13.00. ISBN: 4-494-01225-4.

---

[1] Annotations for this section were prepared by Sonoe K. Jitodai, Head, San Francisco Public Library Japanese Collection.

Shino, the village chieftain's daughter, looks sad standing alone in her garden in a remote village in Japan. Two mice in the house observe the scene and try to make the girl happy. They discover that she is in love with a young man who is poor and of lower status in the next village. Such things happened during feudal times in Japan. In this delightful story, the mice travel through the mountains to the next village where they succeed in arranging the marriage and, at the same time, find a suitable mate for their own son. The illustrations are sophisticated and breathtaking.

2–6. Sekiya, Toshitaka. *Jitensha tochan tabidayori.* Tokyo: DoShin sha, 1985. 40pp. $12.00. ISBN: 09-727010-9.

Intrigued by Hiroshige's "Fifty-three Stations on the Tokaido," a famous set of nineteenth-century Japanese woodblock prints, Toshitaka decided to cycle through Japan to sketch and describe the roadside scenes. He sent his work to his son along with letters as he traveled. This book is a collection of those letters together with rich information on Japanese history, customs, geography, food, and festivals. The ten days when the son joins the father in cycling are the highlight of this very colorful and well-written book.

1–4. Suzuki Kiyoharu. *Banzai, Machigai kin medaru.* Illus. by Meiko Inamoto. Tokyo: Obunsha, 1986. 48pp. $10.00. ISBN: 4-01-069129-8.

Yukari is a very shy first grader. Her teacher gives a homemade gold medal to students who make mistakes during reading class. Those who used to laugh at students who made a mistake gradually begin to want the gold medal and stop making fun. Yukari, who would never raise her hand before, now bravely stands in front of the class and reads. Instead of losing face, she now has a gold medal waiting for her. The teacher's imagination and sensitivity create a pleasant atmosphere.

K–3. Teramura, Teruo. *Sora made tondeke.* Illus. by Imoto Yoko. Tokyo: Akawa, 1983. 32pp. $9.00. ISBN: 4-251-00605-4.

For the Boy's Day Festival in Japan, all of the children try to make paper carp, which symbolize the festival, except Mineko, the little cat. Not only does she refuse to cooperate, she criticizes everybody else's work. Suddenly, a huge paper carp flies up into the sky, taking Mineko with it. The illustrations of the carp are breathtaking and the children's imagination and creativity are outstanding. Eventually, Mineko the cat cooperates in making the carp and everyone hoists their creations—skinny carp, fat carp, even a carp with ears and a funny nose.

1–4. Yoshizawa, Kazuo. *Kasan no omen.* Illus. by Kitajima Shinpei. Tokyo: Warohu, 1986. 32pp. $11.00. ISBN: 4-593-56224-4.

Derived from a folktale from the Iwate region in Japan, this entire story is told in an Iwate dialect. A poor girl named Osayo is sent away to a remote place to be a babysitter. One day at a festival she buys a mask that resembles her mother. Every day she greets the mask and asks how her mother is getting along. One day a servant plays a joke and switches the mask with that of a demon. When Osayo sees the mask, she fears that something is wrong with her mother. Running for home along a lonely mountain road, she is accosted by thieves, but the demon mask saves her life. She arrives home safely and finds her mother well. The village chieftain hears the story, and the thieves are caught. Osayo is given land, becomes rich, and lives happily with her family. This excellent story of both sadness and happiness has beautiful illustrations of Japanese festivals and of nature.

Written in Korean

4–6. So, Chung-Ae. *Hyonyo Simchong.* Seoul, Korea: Yearimdang Pub. Co., c1987. 94pp. $7.14.

In this well-known Korean folktale, a girl offers herself as a sacrifice to the sea-god so that her blind father might see again. Filial piety plays a major role in the moral structure of the family in many Asian countries. This is one of many stories exemplifying its importance. The girl is rescued by the dragon king who takes pity on her and sends her back to the world of the living. There, the emperor, taking her for a heavenly being, marries her. Only after she finds her father again does he regain his sight with a shock of joy. The illustrations, though accurate, give the impression of enlarged comic book drawings, which are very appealing to children.

4–6.   Sur, Kingsley C. *Korean Cinderella: Kongji wa patji*. Illus. by Lee Nam-gu. Korean Folk Stories for Children, series vol. 20. Seoul: Sam Seong Pub. Co., 1984. 32pp. $10.00.

One of Korea's most famous folk stories for children, this parallels the Cinderella story almost perfectly. A festival rather than a ball provides the setting for this version, which includes the added attraction of the attempted murder of Kongji (Cinderella) by Patji (the ugly and fat stepsister), and the utter generosity of Kongji in forgiving her. The bilingual format (English and Korean) adds to the usefulness of the book.

2–4.   Vorhees, Duance, and Mark Mueller. *Mr. Moon and Miss Sun*. Illus. by Kim Yon-kyong. Korean Folk Tales for Children, vol. 2. Seoul, Korea: Hollym International, 1990. 45pp. $10.00. ISBN: 0-930878-72-8.

The first of the two stories in this volume is a Little Red Riding Hood tale that is very similar to *Lon Po Po*.[†2] The events are nearly identical, except that the antagonist is a tiger instead of a wolf, and the two children, who have climbed into a tree for safety, are raised into heaven to become the sun and the moon.

The other story is about the Weaving Girl and the Herd Boy who fall in love but spend so much time playing that they forget about their work and are punished by being separated. They become stars in the sky, Vega and Deneib, and are reunited once a year by a bridge of magpies across the Milky Way. This story is common in many Asian countries and is one of the stories on which the Moon Festival is based.

This series is bilingual, with both Korean and English on one page and an illustration on the facing page. Each book has two stories.

The illustrations vary in style and depth, as does the literary quality, but the stories and the illustrations are both very Korean and nicely fill the need for Korean stories for children. Other titles in the series include *The Son of the Cinnamon Tree* and *The Woodcutter and the Heavenly Maiden*.

P–K.   Yun, Chong-guk. *Agi hangul kongbu*. Korea: 1987. 18pp. $8.00.

This picture book has heavy cardboard pages with three or four pictures of common items on each. The name of each item is printed in large Korean letters. Very young children would use this when they begin learning to read.

FOLK AND FAIRY TALE COLLECTIONS

6–up.   Carrison, Muriel Paskin. *Cambodian Folk Stories from the Gatiloke*. Trans. by the Venerable Kong Chhean. Rutland, Vt.: Tuttle, 1987. 139pp. $15.95. ISBN: 0-8048-1518-6.

This valuable collection of stories is taken from the ancient Cambodian literary classic, the Gatiloke (similar to Ireland's Mabinogian). Some of the tales are familiar stories of stupidity and cleverness; others are singularly Buddhist in that the rascal escapes with his loot, understood to be punished in a future lifetime but left enjoying the fruits of his crimes in this one. A seven-page introduction includes literary comment and historical and religious background, and a short moral or cultural comment follows each story. A twenty-page geographical and historical appendix, a glossary, and a bibliography make the volume even more useful. The book is also quite suitable for an adult collection.

6–up.   Chin, Yin-lien C., Yetta S. Center, and Mildred Ross. *Traditional Chinese Folk Tales*. Illus. by Lu Wang. An East Gate Book. Armonk, N.Y.: M. E. Sharpe, 1989. 180pp. $17.95. ISBN: 0-87332-507-9.

Some of these tales (for example, "The Cowherd and the Weaving Maid" or "Ma Liang and His Magic Brush") are often found

---

[2] Titles marked with a dagger (†) have complete annotations in the Bibliography for this chapter.

in other collections or in picture books while others, such as "Finding a Wife for the River God," a story from the Grand Historian Sz-Ma Chyan some 2,000 years ago, are rarely seen. Laced with humor and warmth, these stories take their place among those of Western traditions without sounding stilted or oddly foreign. The delightful new translations are a welcome relief after many near-literal ones. The illustrations are based on traditional Chinese line drawings and add to the authenticity of each tale with appropriate detail of dress and place.

He, Li Yi, translator. *Spring of Butterflies and Other Folktales of China's Minority Peoples.* Illus. by Pan Aiqing. New York: Lothrop, 1985. 144pp. ISBN: 0-688-06192-3.

An intriguing introduction by the editor and a touching and revealing biographical note on the translator add much to this worthwhile book. The delicate and beautiful illustrations reflect well the various minority cultures represented by these tales. The first tale, a retelling of the popular tale of the Zhuang Brocade, is also found in several picture books: Heyer's *The Weaving of a Dream*, San Souci's *The Enchanted Tapestry*, and Wei's *A Brocade of the Zhuang Nationality.* The stories are all charming and well rendered into English with just the right blend of strangeness and familiarity.

4–7. Hume, Lotta Carswell. *Favorite Children's Stories from China and Tibet.* Illus. by Lo Koon-chiu. Rutland, Vt., and Tokyo: Charles E. Tuttle, 1962, 1989. 119pp. $14.95. ISBN: 0-8048-1605-0.

These highly readable stories have been reissued in an attractive new format. The author, who lived for many years in China, retells these stories to be enjoyed in the West as much as they are in China. A fine touch with the brush and an eye for local color and cultural detail give the illustrations great appeal. They are based on traditional Chinese black-and-white brush illustrations, but are softly rounded out and highly polished. The stories, similar to those of Aesop and Grimm yet with a distinctly Chinese flavor, are good read-alouds for a group.

5–up. Jagendorf, M. A., and Virginia Weng. *The Magic Boat and Other Chinese Folk Stories.* Illus. by Wan-go Weng. New York: Vanguard, 1980. 236pp. ISBN: 0-8149-0823-3.

Amusing, well-told tales from China as well as from a number of minority cultures and such autonomous regions as Tibet, Sinkiang, and Mongolia grace this good-sized volume. Included are a few familiar stories, such as those of the Tibetan Envoy and the Zhuang Brocade, and a variety of stories about shooting the extra suns in the sky, as well as a number of fables from various parts of China. The illustrations, ink line drawings in the style of Chinese paintings, enhance the text throughout. Each story is introduced by the Chinese-language character that is the name of the ethnic group represented.

An introduction explaining why the Chinese are not all alike, notes about the stories and about the ethnic groups, and an extensive bibliography add a scholarly element to this book, which is appropriate for adult collections as well.

4–6. Sadler, Catherine Edwards. *Heaven's Reward: Fairy Tales from China.* Illustrated by Cheng Meng-yun. New York: Atheneum, 1985. 37pp. $12.95. ISBN: 0-689-31127-3.

China's literary history in miniature is contained in this slim volume of six fairy tales. The stories begin with early Confucianism and its emphasis on filial piety. The tales then reveal the social challenge of Taoism, which turned to the spiritual. The hardships of peasant life as well as the modern, morality stories of Communism are presented with literary taste. The book is illustrated with graceful pencil-and-pen drawings.

5–up. Terada, Alice M. *Under the Starfruit Tree: Folktales from Vietnam.* A Kolowalu Book. Illus. by Janet Larsen. Introduction and notes by Mary C. Austin. Honolulu: Univ. of Hawaii Press, 1989. 136pp. $15.95. ISBN: 0-8248-1252-2.

The illustrations are plain, black-and-white sketches, sometimes bordering on the grotesque, and add neither beauty nor information to these intriguing tales. The narrative has the ring of a translation, but this is not overly intrusive. Some of these stories we have heard before, such as "Tam and Cam," but we appreciate the new format. Others have a familiar ring and we wonder whether we heard the same story in another country. Many are completely new. In these stories we can see the influence of China on the culture of Vietnam, and also see how the several cultures within Vietnam are unique.

6–up.   Thich Nhat Hanh. *The Moon Bamboo.* Translated from the Vietnamese by Vo-Dinh Mai and Mobi Ho. Illus. by Vo-Dinh Mai. Introduction by Mobi Ho. Berkeley, Calif.: Parallax Press, 1989. 180pp. $12.00. ISBN: 0-938077-20-1.

The author of these original tales is both a poet and a religious man, actively working for world peace and a better understanding of the network of the universe. His experiences with the horrors of the war in Vietnam and the refugees from it inspired these stories. Readable and interesting, they offer insight into human relationships, war and peace, Vietnam, and the man himself.

4–up.   Timpanelli, Gioia. *Tales from the Roof of the World: Folktales of Tibet.* Illus. by Elizabeth Kelly Lockwood. New York: Viking, 1984. 53pp. $11.95. ISBN: 0-670-71249-3.

Symbolic Tibetan drawings grace the margins of these four intriguing and singular stories. An unusual introduction enjoins readers to make the interior journey of understanding that folktales offer. An appendix reveals the meanings of the Buddhist symbols used in the illustrations. This small book is a jewel.

4–7.   Uchida, Yoshiko, adapter. *The Sea of Gold, and Other Tales from Japan.* With a new introduction by Marcia Brown. Illus. by Marianne Yamaguchi. Boston: Gregg Press, 1965, 1980. o.p.

Here are retold a number of old, favorite Japanese tales. Some are so recognizable as to appear Western, such as one that reminds us of Rumpelstiltskin and several that are reminiscent of Aesop, but they merely remind us

of our common underlying humanity. The compelling black-and-white triptych drawings seem oddly discordant, yet work together to illustrate the story.

3–7.   Vuoung, Lynette Dyer. *The Brocaded Slipper.* Illus. by Vo-Dinh Mai. Reading, Mass.: Addison-Wesley, 1982. 111pp. $12.70. ISBN: 0-201-08088-5.

A brief introduction prepares us for these five Vietnamese versions of tales familiar to readers of Grimm, beginning with a lengthier version of Tam and Cam (Cinderella). The stories are well and simply told, and the large print helps younger readers. Author's notes at the end offer interesting tidbits of Vietnamese culture found in these satisfying read-alouds for any age.

HISTORICAL NOVELS

5–up.   Chetin, Helen. *Angel Island Prisoner, 1922.* Illus. by Jan Lee. Berkeley, Calif.: New Seed Press, 1982. English, 24pp.; Chinese, 31pp. pap. $7.00. ISBN: 0-938678-09-2.

In graphic detail, a young girl tells of the terror, uncertainty, and staunch determination in the face of hopelessness that accompanied her arrival in what she hoped would be a welcoming country, only to be thrown together with hundreds of other immigrants and corralled like cattle. A bit of humanity on the part of the "demons" finally does come through.

7–up.   Crew, Linda. *Children of the River.* New York: Delacorte, 1989. 213pp. $14.95. ISBN: 0-385-29690-8.

Set against the horror of the Cambodian bloodbath, this story far surpasses the trite boy-meets-girl teenage novel and surprises the reader with its depth of understanding of Cambodian culture and how the traditions of such a culture would clash with those of American life. The desire to remain true to Khmer values and old ways collides with the desire to become American.

American ways are represented by Jonathan, the popular, handsome football player who doesn't really like the glib, superficial social scene. His parents represent comfortably settled American idealism as Jonathan blurts out his indignation at the wrongs suffered by the Cambodians.

The conflict between the two very different ways of life is felt most deeply by Sukara, who is young and resiliant enough to be attracted to the delights of the new culture but old enough to feel the terror of war and of leaving home and family, and to want the safety of the known and the familiar.

6–up. Garrigue, Sheila. *The Eternal Spring of Mr. Ito.* New York: Bradbury Press, 1985. 163pp. $11.95. ISBN: 0-02-737300-2.

The mistreatment of the Japanese by both the United States and Canada after Pearl Harbor forms the backdrop for this story of a young Canadian girl who must struggle to understand and cope with the insanity of a nation terrified of indistinct dangers. Mr. Ito is the Japanese gardener for 12-year-old Sara's family in Vancouver, British Columbia. Through him and the suffering and indignities brought upon his family, Sara learns about grief and bitterness and about the hope that springs eternal.

6–up. Haugaard, Erik Christian. *The Samurai's Tale.* New York: Houghton Mifflin, 1984. 234pp. $12.95. ISBN: 0-395-34559-6.

This Danish author lived in Japan for a time to do research for this novel, which paints a graphic picture of the times of unrest between 1480 and 1603—the Japanese civil wars. A five-year-old boy is taken by his father's enemy when the rest of the family is killed. Working his way up from kitchen boy to stable boy to messenger, he eventually achieves his dream and becomes a samurai for a lord whom he admires and is proud to serve. Although there are no illustrations, the story will be appreciated by young people wanting a lively tale of heroic deeds, and also by those wanting a bit of insight into Japanese history, customs, and thought. The author has written several other books, some of them ALA Notable Books, and his latest title, *The Boy and the Samurai* (Houghton Mifflin, 1991), promises to be a good tale as well.

6–up. Irwin, Hadley. *Kim/Kimi.* New York: Macmillan, 1987. 200pp. $12.95. ISBN: 0-689-50428-4.

More universal than just the attempt of an adopted girl to find her real father, this tale takes us with a young Hapa girl (half Caucasian, half Japanese) on a quest to become acquainted with the half of herself that is Japanese. It is an identity-seeking journey that reaches beyond the racial and cultural into the personal, into the conflict between the inside and outside that don't quite match, into the struggle for self-expression. The story presents positive images and explanations of culture for first-, second-, third-, and fourth-generation Japanese Americans. The Japanese concentration camps in America during the Second World War are dealt with as well as some of the feelings of those who must try to live with one foot in each culture.

7–up. Kanazawa, Tooru. *Sushi and Sourdough.* Seattle: Univ. of Washington Press, 1989. 255pp. $19.95. ISBN: 0-2959-6713-7.

The driving force behind this well-integrated combination of newspaper reporting and human interest anecdotes is a Japanese man struggling to survive in a new culture. His adventures take him from California to Seattle to Alaska during the gold rush where he spends years battling the elements for his very life, the hordes of goldseekers for riches, and the culture for a new definition of self. Eventually, he brings his family from Japan, and the story becomes that of his son, triumphing over family and both cultures to become a new American.

3–4. Lim, Genny. *Wings for Lai Ho.* Illus. by Andrea Ja. San Francisco: East/West Publishing Co., 1982. 34pp. pap. $5.95. ISBN: 0-93401-4.

Poster-style black-and-white drawings illustrate this story of a young Chinese girl bound for the big new country where the streets are paved with gold, only to be detained for several months on arrival. Her story reveals the sadness of those Chinese, some detained on Angel Island for years, and their eternal hope that the new country, in spite of all, will be a better place. Told in Chinese as well as in English.

6–up. Paterson, Katherine. *Park's Quest.* New York: Dutton, 1988. 148pp. $12.95. ISBN: 0-525-67258-3.

The American involvement in Vietnam left behind many broken hearts, broken lives, and broken homes, and many children of American men and Vietnamese women. In this story, an American boy whose father died in Vietnam discovers he has a feisty little half-Vietnamese half-sister. The boy's reaction is as much an inward journey as a comment on the Vietnamese in America. The author is well known for her other books, which use Chinese and Japanese history as backdrops.

K–3. Say, Allen. *Tree of Cranes.* Illus. by the author. Boston: Houghton Mifflin, 1991. 32pp. $16.95. ISBN: 0-395-52024-X.

A young boy in Japan is puzzled when he notices that his mother seems oddly subdued. When she should have scolded him for playing in the pond, she simply sits quietly, folding a thousand paper cranes for a wish. She digs up the boy's special tree, brings it indoors in a pot, and decorates it with cranes and candles. This is a special day in the faraway place called California where she was born, a day of quiet and peace. This is a tender story of a boy's first glimpse of Christmas. Immaculate illustrations, vibrant with color, capture the quiet simplicity of a Japanese home. This book is a gem, both in artistry and in its portrayal of home life in Japan.

6–up. Watkins, Yoko Kawashima. *So Far from the Bamboo Grove.* New York: Lothrop, 1986. 183pp. $10.25. ISBN: 0-688-06110-9.

The evacuation and subsequent travels of a Japanese family living in North Korea in 1945 are seen through the eyes of a young girl. She and her older sister and mother are in danger because of the father's position in the war. The three of them leave a note for the brother and flee to the south—walking, hiding, starving, even being wounded. Here is the compelling inside story of homeless, penniless, and frightened but determined refugees. Several pages of historical notes are appended as an afterword.

7–up. Yep, Lawrence. *Mountain Light.* New York: Harper and Row, 1985. 281pp. $11.89. ISBN: 0-06-026758-5; PLB 0-06-026759-3.

The nineteenth-century uprising against the Manchu dynasty and its mistreatment of the Chinese, and the small-mindedness of family clans nursing old feuds form the backdrop for this story of 19-year-old Squeaky, who struggles with the dichotomy of how sane, loving human beings cope with the insanity of the self-righteous mob. Squeaky copes by clowning, which works sometimes. His friend Cassia copes by engaging in head-on fighting, which works sometimes. A combination of the two approaches helps a more mature Squeaky face the American mistreatment of the Chinese during the Gold Rush era as well as the continuing, self-feeding family feuds. A thought-provoking story.

NONFICTION

K–2. Behrens, June. *Gung Hay Fat Choy (Happy New Year).* Festivals and Holidays Series. Photographs compiled by Terry Behrens. Chicago: Children's Press, 1982. 31pp. $11.27. ISBN: 0-516-08842-4.

A few lines of large print accompany colorful photos of the Chinese New Year celebration, complete with dragons, lion dances, couplets written on red paper, oranges and special foods, and red envelopes with money for the children. Many of the pictures are of children or are taken from a child's point of view and so are good for introducing this aspect of the culture to younger children.

7–up. Blumberg, Rhoda. *Commodore Perry in the Land of the Shogun.* New York: Lothrop, 1985. 144pp. $13.00. ISBN: 0-688-03723-2.

This quite detailed history of the opening of Japan is complemented by many historical photographs and drawings, both Western and Japanese. The thought-provoking commentary attempts to be fair to both sides and provides much material for discussion. This book is worth delving into just for the drawings, but it is of rather limited and special use. Five appendixes, notes, a bibliography, and an index add to the book's usefulness.

7–up.   Bode, Janet. *New Kids on the Block: Oral Histories of Immigrant Teens.* New York: Watts, 1989. 126pp. $12.90. ISBN: 0-531-10794-9.

Each of the teenagers interviewed for this book recently immigrated to America, not always an entirely pleasant experience. Many came from the strife of war or poverty or from some other uncomfortable situation. Their families chose to come here for the same reason the very first immigrants came—for what they hoped would be a better life. Unfortunately for many, life in the United States proves to be a shock. Rather than being welcomed, they are met with distrust and sometimes open hostility. At best, they find such different cultural mores and expectations that daily life becomes quite difficult. The book was written partly to help them feel less alone and partly to encourage readers to realize that "our nation is richer because it is a rainbow of cultures and different points of view."

1–4.   Brown, Tricia. *Chinese New Year.* Photographs by Fran Ortiz. New York: Holt, 1987. 42pp. $12.95. ISBN: 0-8050-0497-1.

Personal family photos, unfortunately only in black and white, illustrate descriptions and explanations of the symbols that surround the Chinese celebration of the lunar New Year. Included are the Chinese zodiac, special foods, lion dances, parades, a dragon, and such traditional customs as visiting family and friends, spring cleaning, burning the kitchen god, and wearing new clothes.

2–5.   Elkin, Judith. *A Family in Japan.* Families the World Over Series. Photographs by Stuart Atkin. Minneapolis: Lerner, 1987. 31pp. $9.95. ISBN: 0-8225-1672-1.

Color photos concentrating on the daily life of children in Japan, with the text essentially describing the photos, make this a satisfactory introduction for small children. The book shows what children wear, what they eat, the games they play, and the houses they live in. A glossary and fact list add to the books usefulness. Other countries in the series are China, India, Singapore, and Sri Lanka.

7–up.   Fritz, Jean. *China's Long March: 6,000 Miles of Danger.* New York: Putnam's, 1988. 124pp. $14.95. ISBN: 0-399-21512-3.

The author interviewed many of the survivors of Mao's famed Long March for this very personal history that reads like a novel. The attitudes of each person, the struggles within individuals and within the group, the determination, the idealism, the new surge of life that Mao's brand of communism initially gave the peasants—all ring clear. A good catalyst for a discussion of Mao and his thought, of China and its recent history, and of the roots of Chinese communism, this book is also invaluable for the insight provided by those who were there. Notes, a bibliography, and an index enhance the text.

6–up.   _____. *Homesick: My Own Story.* Illus. with drawings by Margot Tomes and photographs. New York: Putnam's, 1982. 176pp. $9.95. ISBN: 0-399-20933-6.

A feisty young girl grows up in Shanghai, China, during the 1920s. Her introduction to Communism and her naive yet profound thoughts on the turns of Chinese civilization provide a measure of understanding for the Western reader as well. At that time in China foreigners were growing unpopular and eventually the family had to leave. The author's entry into American life with her adamant defense of things Chinese is both humorous and thought-provoking. Line drawings and photographs complement the text.

5–up.   Hamanaka, Sheila. *The Journey: Japanese Americans, Racism, and Renewal.* Paintings by the author. New York: Orchard, 1990. 40pp. $18.95. ISBN: 0-531-05849-2; LB $18.99. ISBN: 0-531-08449-3.

The paintings in this book are taken from five murals, each twenty-five feet long, which Hamanaka created to express her personal family history. Through her art, the author attempts to explain the concentration camps of World War II, the devastation at Hiroshima and Nagasaki, and the insidiousness of prejudice. The powerful paintings present a heavy political statement, but one that is understandable by older children.

7–up. Humphrey, Judy. *Genghis Khan*. World Leaders Past and Present Series. New York: Chelsea House, 1987. 111pp. $16.95. ISBN: 0-87754-527-8.

An intriguing personal history—from his wild boyhood on the Mongolian steppe to becoming the fiery leader of the Mongol horde—this biography reveals the underlying character of Genghis Khan. Unmerciful to enemies yet fiercely loyal to family and friends, the man described here lived a life of struggle and hardship and had to be strong and jaded in order to survive. Also a commentary on modern-day Mongol life and thought, this book gives the reader much to consider regarding morals and values. Photographs and historical drawings as well as a bibliography, a chronology, and an index add to the text. Other personalities in this series are Chiang Kai-shek, Ho Chi Minh, Sun Yat-sen, Zhou En-lai, Kim Il Sung, Kublai Khan, Mao Ze-dong, Jawaharlal Nehru, Sukarno, Pol Pot, and Deng Xiaoping.

4–7. Huynh, Quang Nhuong. *The Land I Lost*. Illus. by Vo-Dinh Mai. New York: Harper and Row, 1982. 115pp. $11.89. ISBN: 0-06-024592-1; 0-06-024593-X.

Poignant and amusing, these memoirs of a boyhood spent in the central highland jungle of Vietnam make the place and the people come alive as no National Geographic Special ever could. The misadventures of a boy and his pet water buffalo, "Tank," along with tales of his feisty grandmother and other characters in town draw us into a portrait of Vietnamese life as vivid and homey as that of Mark Twain's Tom Sawyer. Danger, death, and the endless war are dealt with matter-of-factly. Well-written and simply told, these stories are geared toward younger readers but will be appreciated by any age. Chinese ink washes illuminate the stories.

6–up. Ignacio, Melissa Macagba. *The Philippines: Roots of My Heritage (A Journey of Discovery by a Filipina American Teenager)*. San Jose, Calif.: Filipino Development Associates, 1977. $15.00

This book sounds like a teenager writing home, which is exactly what it is: A teenage girl journeys to the country of her roots, lives there for a year, and writes about what she finds both in the culture and within herself. It would be a fine step toward maturity for our culture as a whole if everyone were to do so, with much the same frame of mind as young Native Americans going on a vision quest.

5–up. Layton, Lesley. *Cultures of the World: Singapore*. New York: Marshall Cavendish, 1990. 128pp. $19.95. ISBN: 1-85435-295-4.

Wonderful color photographs, employing a variety of angles and close-ups, reveal the personal lives of the people of Singapore. The camera allows the reader to enter the world of the Chinese, the Muslims, and the Hindus, all of whom form an important facet of the city. Festivals, food, leisure activities, arts, language, religion, and social groups are explored. Several brief sections deal with history, politics, economy, and geography, and notes, a glossary, a bibliography, and an index add to the usefulness. Other books in this beautiful series cover India, Japan, Malaysia, Burma, and Indonesia.

7–up. Livo, Norma J., and Dia Cha. *Folk Stories of the Hmong: Peoples of Laos, Thailand, and Vietnam*. Englewood, Colo.: Libraries Unlimited, 1991. 135pp. ISBN: 0-87287-854-6.

Here is a collection of stories reminiscent of both Aesop and Grimm, but each very distinctively representing an aspect of Hmong culture. Along with the stories, the book details the history and culture of the Hmong, including beliefs and customs, festivals, marriage, jewelry, the story cloths which have become popular in the West, and a section on cultural conflicts. Thirty-six color plates of Hmong people in their native costumes add much to the text, and a bibliography is included. This well-done presentation of Hmong folklore and culture offers new light on a previously little-known group of recent immigrants.

7–up. Major, John S. *The Land and People of Mongolia.* Portraits of the Nations Series. New York: Lippincott, 1990. 200pp. $15.95. ISBN: 0-397-32386-7.

The fact that the photographs are all black and white detracts only slightly from this work, which is much more scholarly and detailed than the Cultures of the World[†] series. Here the fine points of history, geography, language, and social composition are complemented with maps, charts, and explanatory insets. A lengthy bibliography and an index are included. Also available in this series is *The Land and People of China* by the same author.

6–up. McLenighan, Valjean. *China: A History to 1949.* Enchantment of the World Series. Chicago: Children's Press, 1983. 127pp. $21.27. ISBN: 0-516-02754-9.

Comprehensive, clear, and sprinkled liberally with high-quality photos of temples, people, landscapes, arts, and artifacts, this book devotes a chapter to each dynasty in China's history. Beginning with the Great Wall, built to keep the barbarians (i.e., the rest of the world) out of China, the author reveals China's history, philosophy, and way of life in each era. Throughout, attention is drawn to special comments, notes, and explanations. A ten-page section of "facts at a glance" covers a variety of interesting items and is followed by a chronology, a list of important people, a list of dynasties, and an index. The book is also suitable for high school and adult collections.

6–up. _____. *People's Republic of China.* Enchantment of the World Series. Chicago: Children's Press, 1984. 143pp. $21.27. ISBN: 0-516-02781-6.

A continuation of the preceding volume, this book begins with the story of Pu-yi, the last emperor, and brings China into the twentieth century. Chapters are devoted to geography, city life, rural life, art and culture, and the people, including a section on women and the family. Three chapters cover modern history: the early days of the People's Republic, the notorious Cultural Revolution, and the subsequent changes in leadership, attitudes, and ways of life. Included in appendixes are a detailed map with gazetteer, short facts, important dates in China's history, and important people in the twentieth century. Other books in this series cover Hong Kong, Japan, Korea, the Philippines, and Thailand.

6–up. Meltzer, Milton. *The Chinese Americans.* Illus. with photographs. New York: Crowell, 1980. $8.95. ISBN: 0-690-04038-5; PLB 0-690-04039-3.

Meltzer has crafted an indignant history of the Chinese in America, emphasizing their hard work, their ingenuity, and their somewhat less than welcome reception in this country. The Chinese were left out of recognition for their major part in building the railroad, and suffered mistreatment in the gold fields, the farming fields, and the fields of the inner city. A few chapters on Chinese history and what life was like for the Chinese people in their own country before they came to America give some insights into their character. Meltzer has attempted to expose the stereotypes and mistreatment and give the Chinese credit for their role in America's history.

7–up. Moore, David L. *Dark Sky, Dark Land: Stories of the Hmong Boy Scouts of Troop 100.* Eden Prairie, Minn.: Tessera Publishing, 1988. 191pp. $14.95. ISBN: 0-9623029-0-2.

The personal stories of a troop of boy scouts, many of whom are Hmong and who have come to this country within the past few years, are here retold by their scoutmaster. The reader gains a closer, more personal understanding of what it means to leave home and belongings and possibly family, and to go out into an unfamiliar world on foot. The children graphically detail the fear of being struck down by enemy soldiers or by disease, the hunger and bewilderment, the terror of living moment to moment. Eventually, they make their way to the Big Country, America, where daily life presents a whole new set of struggles and problems. Each boy is portrayed in a delightful pencil sketch. Seven pages of Hmong chronology and a bibliography for further reading complement the text.

6–up. Neff, Fred. *Lessons from the Samurai: Ancient Self-Defense Strategies and Techniques.* Photographs by Bob Wolfe. Minneapolis: Lerner, 1987. 112pp. $9.95. ISBN: 0-8225-1161-4.

More than just an instruction manual on the ever-popular Asian martial arts, this book also offers a history of the ancient noble warriors of Japan—the samurai. Neff discusses their methods and philosophy, which includes "an understanding of the universe." Techniques for handling stress and human relations are followed by common questions and answers. The bulk of the book is devoted to body conditioning stretches, basic movements, stances, falls, dodges, punches, kicks, blocks, sweeps, throws, escapes, and, of course, meditation.

7–up. Perl, Lila. *Red Star and Green Dragon: Looking at New China.* Illus. with photographs. New York: William Morrow, 1983. 129pp. $11.95. ISBN: 0-688-01721-5.

Half of this book is history, half is a description of a modern nation struggling to find its place in the world of the twentieth century. Black-and-white photographs broaden the perspective, and a chronology, a bibliography, and an index add to the usefulness of the text.

7–up. Rau, Margaret. *Holding in the Sky: Young People in China.* New York: Dutton, 1983. 136pp. $12.50. ISBN: 0-525-66718-0.

Minute by minute, detail by detail, the daily lives of several young people living ordinary lives in the People's Republic of China are explored. Tidbits of historical and cultural explanation are sandwiched in to enhance understanding. Like the British television series "The Heart of the Dragon," this book offers insight into the country's ways of thinking, living, and behaving by closely following the personal lives of individuals. Black-and-white photos enhance the text, which includes Xin Jiang, Mongolia, and Tibet.

7–up. Ross, Frank, Jr. *Oracle Bones, Stars, and Wheelbarrows: Ancient Chinese Science and Technology.* Illus. by Michael Goodman. Boston: Houghton Mifflin, 1982. 177pp. $8.95. ISBN: 0-395-32083-6.

Everyone knows that the Chinese invented gunpowder, but here is revealed a myriad of other little-known inventions and ingenuities. This eye-opening book covers ancient astronomy, medicine, and technology as well as nearly every branch of the sciences, and shows that the Chinese contributions usually far preceded their European counterparts.

4–up. Schwaback, Karen. *Thailand: Land of Smiles.* Discovering Our Heritage Series. Minneapolis: Dillon Press, 1991. 127pp. ISBN: 0-87518-454-5.

Interesting tidbits of geography, history, folklore, and festivals, written in a flowing, nonpretentious style, make this book hard to put down. Included are well-selected color photos that enliven recipes (many are given in detail), a visit to school, and sports and games. A glossary, a bibliography, and an index add to the book's usefulness. Other countries in this series include Korea, Vietnam, and Indonesia.

4–7. Stanley, Fay. *The Last Princess: The Story of Princess Ka'iulani of Hawaii.* Illus. by Diane Stanley. New York: Four Winds, 1991. 40pp. $15.95. ISBN: 0-02-786785-4.

Both a beautifully retold tale and a well-researched though pointedly biased biography, this poignant story takes us from the glorious days of Ka'iulani's childhood—when Hawaii belonged to the Hawaiians and her uncle was king—to the transfer of political control to the United States. The infiltration of foreigners and the usurpation of control saddened and angered the Hawaiian people, who struggled against it to no avail. The revolutionaries were jailed, Hawaii was annexed, and the princess, almost willfully, became ill and died at the age of 23. All Hawaii mourned the beloved princess who had been next in line to be queen.

The full-page illustrations in rich earth tones complement Hawaii and are full of the detail of daily life: the elegant end-of-the-century dress, the interiors of gardens, the land, the formality of political meetings. The figures seem a bit wooden, but their personalities shine through. A note on the Hawaiian language and a bibliography make the book useful as well as beautiful.

7–up. Tames, Richard. *Japan in the Twentieth Century.* Twentieth Century World History Series. London: Batsford Academic and Educational Ltd., 1981. 96pp. $14.95. ISBN: 0-7134-3966-1.

Fine print and occasional black-and-white photographs do not detract from this well-written history of modern Japan. Questions for the "young historian" at the end of each chapter could be used as study guides. A date list, a bibliography, and an index complement the text.

7–up. _____. *Japan: The Land and Its People.* Silver Burdett Countries Series. Morristown, N.J.: Silver Burdett, 1975, 1986. 45pp. PLB $15.96. ISBN: 0-382-09256-2.

Almost qualifying as a traveler's guide with descriptions of shopping centers, theaters, vacation spots, and cuisine, this book also provides information about many other aspects of modern Japanese life, including industry, religion, history, language, and art. Although the color photographs are not always well selected and the fine print is sometimes distracting, the book is a good source of information on Japan.

7–up. _____. *The Japanese.* Today's World Series. London: Batsford Academic and Educational Ltd., 1982. 72pp. $14.95. ISBN: 0-7134-4453-3.

Not very inspired black-and-white photographs combined with a text of fine print would make this a rather dull book, except that the topics are beyond the usual for series books and provide some food for thought. The author delves into work (Is there a secret to Japan's postwar industrial success?), cars (including Japanese traffic and the export of small cars), family (Why are the causes of family strain different from those in Western families?), crime, religion, women, and that modern samurai—the company man. A chart comparing statistics between Japan and Britain is interesting, and a bibliography and an index add to the usefulness of the book.

4–7. Tang, Yungmei. *China, Here We Come!: Visiting the People's Republic of China.* New York: Putnam's, 1981. 64pp. $9.95. ISBN: 0-399-20826-7.

A group of American young people visiting China reveal their personal observations about the schools, the Forbidden City, the Great Wall, libraries, and a zoo. They also visit a Cultural Palace where children gather to learn the fine arts, handicrafts, and sports. Interesting black-and-white photographs complement the text.

6–up. Vander Els, Betty. *Leaving Point.* New York: Farrar, Straus and Giroux, 1987. 211pp. $12.95. ISBN: 374-34376-4.

The year is 1950, just after Liberation, when there was much mixed feeling in China about the new socialist lifestyle and the political fervor and idealism. It was an uncomfortable time to be an American missionary family in China, and eventually the author's family moves to Hong Kong, leaving behind most of their belongings and some good Chinese friends who tried to help them understand the Revolution.

This is the second of two books offering an autobiographical account of the experiences of a daughter of missionary parents in China, beginning with the 1942 Japanese invasion of China. The first book, *Bombers' Moon* (1985), rather amateurishly written, describes how the author and her younger brother are evacuated to India. With the second book, however, the author gains confidence and the saga of the family, now reunited in China, is much more flowing.

The focus is on the fourteen-year-old girl and her slightly older Chinese friend. This friendship is frowned upon by both the Chinese and the Americans, but it provides the two girls and the reader with an inside view of the reasons behind the Chinese Revolution, reasons that continue to be relevant today.

6–up. *We Live in China.* A Living Here Book. New York: Bookwright Press, 1984. 64pp. $11.90. ISBN: 0-531-04779-2.

Artisans, workers, officials, an opera teacher, a museum curator, and a storyteller are among the people who talk about their work, their families, their recreation, their daily lives, and their opinions on a variety of issues. A few photos accompany each of the twenty-eight interviews, which offer a unique perspective: China through Chinese eyes. A glossary and an index add to the usefulness of this book, one of a series that features about a dozen countries, including India and the Philippines.

6–up. Wolf, Bernard. *In the Year of the Tiger*. Photographs by the author. New York: Macmillan, 1988. 124pp. $14.95. ISBN: 0-02-793390-3.

A portrait of a people, this collection of fine black-and-white photographs, some of them true masterpieces, allows us a look at the inside life of the common citizen of China. The detailed and descriptive text gives the reader a view that no tourist would get. This is not a description of history or politics but rather a venture into the private lives of individuals and, through them, an understanding of the culture.

6–up. Yep, Laurence. *The Lost Garden*. Englewood Cliffs, N.J.: Julian Messner, 1991. 117pp. $12.95. ISBN: 0-671-74159-4.

Like the house and garden of his father, to which he returns in dreams, the author's childhood is now gone. But it lingers on in memories that he sets down vividly and poignantly in these musings on the past, ponderings of life's ways, and anecdotes. Growing up between two cultures in the America of the 1950s wasn't easy. Yep never wanted to acknowledge his Chinese side. Here he explores the strengths and weaknesses of his heritage, struggling to understand. This is also a book about writing, about where ideas come from, and about which characters from the author's past have inspired those who inhabit his books.

In a similar vein, *Star Fisher* (Morrow, 1991), also by Laurence Yep, recounts the move made by his grandmother when she was a girl from Ohio to West Virginia, and the difficulties the family encounters trying to hold together.

All ages. Zheng, Zhensun, and Alice Low. *A Young Painter: The Life and Paintings of Wang Yani—China's Extraordinary Young Artist*. Photographs by Zheng Zhensun. Introduction by Jan Stuart. New York: Scholastic, 1991. 80pp. $17.95. ISBN: 0-590-44906-0.

Yani began painting in her father's studio at the age of three. Now in her teens, she has exhibited her paintings in several Western countries, including the United States. This book tells of her early life in a small village in southern China, and includes color photos both of her paintings and of village life. Her development as a painter is presented in depth, and the art of Chinese painting is discussed in general. Both a beautiful art book and an inspiring biography, this book has an easy, flowing style that will appeal to children and young adults alike. A glossary of Chinese terms and a map of China are included.

PROGRAMMING IDEAS

Each culture has its own special festivals. Some occasions, such as New Year, are celebrated in many countries, but each country has its own particular way of celebrating. Tet in Vietnam, for example, is essentially the same holiday as the Chinese New Year. However, while the Chinese holiday is chiefly centered around family and friends, the Vietnamese celebration is much bigger and involves the whole community. In Korea, kite flying is a special event—all one's troubles fly away in the wind with the kites. In Guangzhou, we find Flower Street, in which several streets are lined with stalls selling cut flowers. The whole town turns out for three days, buying flowers to offer when visiting family and friends. And in Shang-hai, there are foods, such as *Ba Bao Fan*, that are found nowhere else.

The Moon Festival, which falls on the fifteenth day of the eighth lunar month, is a harvest festival celebrated in many Asian countries. In both China and Korea, it is a relatively quiet family affair, but in Hong Kong, families and friends gather for banquets and congregate in large, open parks to admire the moon. Children run around late into the night, carrying lanterns of all sizes and shapes. In Vietnam, the holiday is also called Children's Day and is celebrated with lanterns and a special white moon cake.

The key to understanding these celebrations is to use only materials as culturally authentic as possible. Reproductions from museums or even posters are more authentic than such crafts as making dragons from egg cartons. In China, no one makes dragons from egg cartons, partly because egg cartons are not widely used. Rather than scavenge household items and attempt to call them Chinese or Vietnamese, use the coloring books that have appeared recently in art stores. One such coloring book is *China*, published by Bellerophon Books*[3] (1988. 50 pp. $3.95. ISBN: 0-88388-077-6).

Many storytellers like to dress for their stories. If you are doing a Japanese story from an appropriate era, by all means dress in a Japanese kimono if you have an authentic one. Do not wear a bathrobe and call it Japanese. Rather, show the intricate detail of a real costume with a picture book, slides, or an authentic doll. Take the time to find out whether something is authentic. Do not use it just because it seems "Asian." For example, the little squares of paper that are folded into shapes to represent money to be burned for the dead may seem pretty, but they belong in a funeral and nowhere else. Similarly, it would be inappropriate to use paper in such colors as white (which is for funerals) or blue instead of the mandatory traditional red for writing New Year's couplets to hang on a doorway.

Following are brief descriptions of a few festivals from China, Japan, Korea, Singapore, Thailand, Burma, and the Philippines. Included are a story either about the origin of the festival or related in some way to it, and a song, dance, food item, or an appropriate craft.

FESTIVALS OF ASIA

There is an old fairy tale about a young man who desires to rescue a princess held in an impenetrable castle. A helpful and magical being offers him the golden key to the castle. "But what do I do once I am inside?" the young man asks. "Ridiculous boy!" exclaims the being. "If I have to tell you every step of the way what to do, then I deserve the princess, not you! I'm giving you the key that makes it possible. The rest is up to you. Go—and use your imagination!"

CHINA

New Year

The Chinese New Year falls during the first three days of the lunar year at the new moon, somewhat more than a month after the winter solstice. This usually puts it in late January or early February. It is the biggest celebration of the year in many Asian countries. The Vietnamese Tet is the same festival.

No one works during the festival. For some people, it is the only vacation they have all year long. All shops are closed, so everyone does all necessary shopping during the days preceding the festival, buying new clothes and ingredients for making special New Year's goodies. Houses are cleaned from top to bottom, and plum branches are put into vases to bloom at the proper moment. Narcissus bulbs are begun early in shallow planters so they too will bloom for New Year. Special New Year's couplets, written in large, black-ink characters on red paper, are hung vertically on either side of the front door. They offer luck for the coming year and welcome in the spring.

> In coming and going over this sill
> May all things go according to your will.

Kumquat trees, potted, are sold on the street and every family buys one or two for the living room. At midnight on the first day, the town explodes in a fury of firecrackers and fireworks, and the festival is on its way.

During the three days of celebration, everyone goes to pay respects to family and friends, bringing along gifts of oranges, New Year cake (made of sticky rice) (see figure 1), and other local specialties. By staying only a short time, long enough for a cup of tea, you can make the rounds of the homes of all your family and friends in one or two afternoons. Of course, someone must always remain at home to greet the people who come to your house to *bai nyan*. Sometimes it seems everyone is at someone else's house having tea, and certain bags of oranges come to look very familiar!

All married women give to the children of the family (by definition, all unmarried members of the household) small red envelopes decorated

---

[3] Complete addresses for all sources marked with an asterisk (*) can be found in the Distributors section at the end of this chapter.

with "gold" and containing money (usually bills). The amounts range from token to generous.

FOODS AND CUSTOMS

Ba Bao Fan
(Eight Treasure Rice)

2 cups red beans, cooked
1/2 cup margarine or lard
4 cups sticky rice, cooked
Dried fruit and Chinese sugar-pickled vegetables, as available
Brown sugar

1. Boil red beans and pound to paste with 1/4 cup lard or margarine and brown sugar.
2. Boil sticky rice, then mix with 1/4 cup lard or margarine.
3. Arrange pineapple bits, dried fruits, raisins, dates, coconut, sugar-pickled vegetables, lotus seeds, and so forth in an interesting pattern in a bowl. Press a layer of the sticky rice mixture around them, holding them in their pattern and covering the inside of the bowl but leaving a hollow in the center.
4. Fill that hollow with the red bean paste.
5. Steam to cook. Turn upside down on a plate and remove bowl to serve. Serve hot or cold.

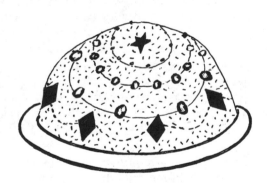

Figure 1. Ba Bao Fan

Gok Jai
(Chinese New Year Pastry)

1 cup shredded coconut
2 cups unsalted peanuts
1 cup sesame seeds
2 cups brown sugar
1 pound square wonton skins
Peanut oil

1. Brown sesame seeds over low heat until golden in color. No oil is necessary.
2. Brown peanuts over low heat until golden in color. No oil is necessary. After browning, remove peanuts and let cool. After cooling, chop the peanuts.
3. Mix together peanuts, sesame seeds, shredded coconut, and brown sugar.
4. Moisten the edge of one wonton skin.
5. Put a teaspoonful of the peanut mixture in the center of the skin.
6. Fold the skin in half. Squeeze the edges together. Flute the edges with your fingers. Repeat, using all wonton skins.
7. Fry in peanut oil (350°) until golden brown and crispy. Remove from oil and let cool.

Bai Nyan

Have small groups of students take fruits and candies to other classes to bai nyan and explain about visiting during Chinese New Year. Use a round, eight-compartment tray to represent wholeness. One child might pass the sweets while another explains to the class. Also pass out Lai See (red envelopes) if you can find any (or make your own—about 2 inches by 3 inches) stuffed with play money.

CALENDAR AND ZODIAC

When we speak of the lunar year, we mean that the months are defined by the movement of the moon. Thus, the first day of each month is, by definition, the first day of the new moon, and the fifteenth day is the full moon. This system leaves us somewhat short, so every once in a while, we need an extra month. This accommodation also occurs in the solar calendar, though the discrepancy is not as extreme. Every four years we need to add only one day—in leap year.

The Chinese system of naming the months is simply to call the first month (January) Month One, the second, Month Two, and so on. This system does not correspond exactly to January, February, and so on, but it is close. The days also are counted: Day One, Day Two, and so forth. Thus, a date such as January 5 would be Month One, Day Five. Some of the most popular festivals fall on dates in which the number of the day is the same as the number of the month. For example, Month 7, Day 7, also known as "Double Seven," is the Festival of the Spinning

Maid and the Herd Boy in July. These festivals are also known by their double date name. For example, Double Five is Dragon Boat Festival, and Double Nine is Hill Climbing Day.

The Chinese system of reckoning time is more complex than simply using the moon rather than the sun as a basis. About 4,690 years ago, Huang Ti, the semilegendary emperor of China, also called the Yellow Emperor, set up a system of ten heavenly stems and twelve earthly branches which, in combination, can be used to name the years in a sixty-year cycle. These cycles, begun in the sixty-first year of the reign of Huang Ti, have continued to the present. By this system of counting, A.D. 1992 is 4690 in the calendar of Huang Ti.

The twelve earthly branches are also associated with the twelve animals of the Chinese zodiac. Thus, each year in a twelve-year cycle is represented by a different animal. A person born in the year of a particular animal is said to have characteristics pertinent to that animal. See figure 2 and answer these questions.

1. What animal symbolizes this year?
2. List the symbolic animals.
3. What would the symbolic animal be for 1987, 1958, and the years that your parents were born?

The Chinese Zodiac

Present the zodiac animals, each with its own characteristics and years.

Make a dodecahedron (see figure 3).

Make a felt board or bulletin board of zodiac animals with appropriate years and characteristics. Find your own animal. Do the characteristics seem appropriate to you?

Chinese Fortune Zodiac Calendar

Year of the Rat
People born in the year of the rat have great personal charm. They strive for the better things in life. They are hardworking and thrifty and are able to save a great deal of money because they are penny-pinchers. Easily aroused to anger, they also can maintain self-control. They are honest and ambitious but are too fond of gossip.

Good mates: Dragon, Monkey, Ox
Disastrous mate: Horse

Rat	Rabbit	Horse	Rooster
1900	1903	1906	1909
1912	1915	1918	1921
1924	1927	1930	1933
1936	1939	1942	1945
1948	1951	1954	1957
1960	1963	1966	1969
1972	1975	1978	1981
1984	1987	1990	1993

Ox	Dragon	Sheep	Dog
1901	1904	1907	1910
1913	1916	1919	1922
1925	1928	1931	1934
1937	1940	1943	1946
1949	1952	1955	1958
1961	1964	1967	1970
1973	1976	1979	1982
1985	1988	1991	1994

Tiger	Snake	Monkey	Boar
1902	1905	1908	1911
1914	1917	1920	1923
1926	1929	1932	1935
1938	1941	1944	1947
1950	1953	1956	1959
1962	1965	1968	1971
1974	1977	1980	1983
1986	1989	1992	1995

Figure 2.   The Chinese zodiac calendar

Year of the Ox
People born in the year of the ox are serene and patient and make good listeners, yet they anger easily and display it openly. They speak little, yet can be most eloquent. They possess a great mental alertness and are clever with their hands and extremely dexterous. They are stubborn and hate to fail, and thus are likely to be very successful.

Good mates: Serpent, Rooster, Rat
Disastrous mate: Sheep

Year of the Tiger
People born in the year of the tiger are sensitive yet short-tempered. Friends surround them because of their compassion and sympathy. However, they can be a powerful and dangerous enemy, often entering into conflict with those who are older or in higher authority. Their greatest faults are narrow-mindedness and suspicion, yet they are deep thinkers and careful planners.

Good mates: Dragon, Horse, Dog
Disastrous mates: Snake, Monkey

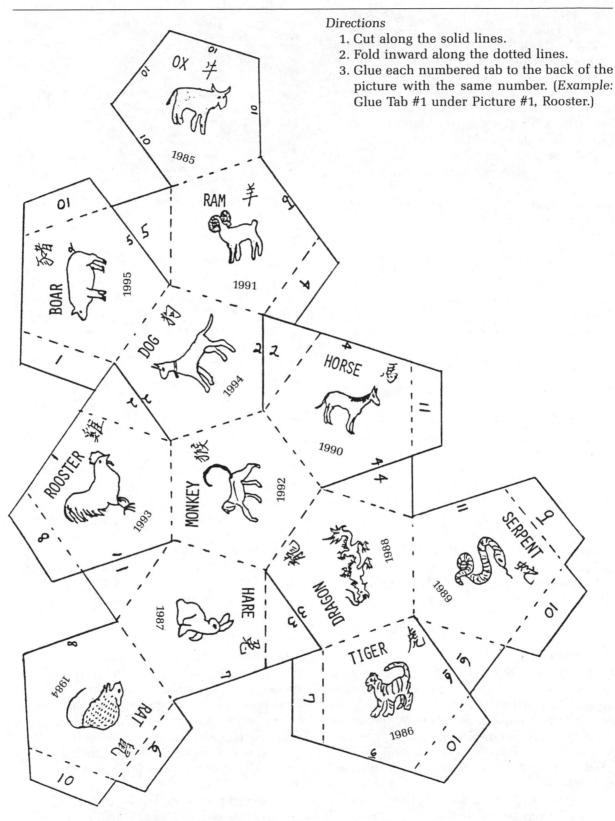

Directions
1. Cut along the solid lines.
2. Fold inward along the dotted lines.
3. Glue each numbered tab to the back of the picture with the same number. (*Example:* Glue Tab #1 under Picture #1, Rooster.)

Figure 3. Chinese animal signs dodecahedron

Year of the Rabbit

People born in the year of the rabbit are glib, talented, ambitious, and very slow to anger. They have fine tastes and are admired and trusted by their friends. Financially they are incredibly lucky and have an uncanny gift for picking a winner, which makes them good gamblers. They are conservative and do not plunge into anything without thinking it over carefully. However, if you sign a contract with a Rabbit person, you can never back out of it because they are very clever at business.

  Good mates: Sheep, Boar, Dog
  Disastrous mates: Rat, Rooster

Year of the Dragon

People born in the year of the dragon are healthy, energetic, excitable, short-tempered, and very stubborn. They do not like to borrow money or make flowery speeches. They are sincere and their opinions are valid. They are soft-hearted and can be taken in by any line, which gives other people a great advantage over them. They worry a good deal for no reason. They marry late or not at all, which may account for loneliness in old age, yet other people love them. The dragon represents great celestial power, symbolizing life and growth.

  Good mates: Rat, Snake, Monkey, Rooster
  Disastrous mate: Dog

Year of the Snake

People born in the year of the snake speak little and possess tremendous wisdom. They are fortunate in money matters, and money comes to them when they need it. They are vain and selfish, and stingy with their money, but always overdo their attempts to help their friends. They are calm but intense, passionate, and handsome, and sometimes have marital problems because they like to have deep affections outside the family.

  Good mates: Ox, Rooster
  Disastrous mates: Tiger, Boar

Year of the Horse

People born in the year of the horse are cheerful and garrulous, popular, and skillful in paying compliments. They are quick in everything and can guess a person's meaning even before the person is quite sure of it. They are decorative and showy in dress and manner. However,

inside they are weak and unsure. Often they fail at whatever project they attempt. They are not noted for patience. They are hot-blooded and will not listen to advice. They love theater and music, entertainment and large crowds. They can be so focused in their affections that they are blind to everything else.

  Good mates: Tiger, Dog, Sheep
  Disastrous mate: Rat

Year of the Sheep

People born in the year of the sheep are elegant, highly accomplished in the arts, passionate, and refined in their tastes. However, they are timid and shy and uncertain over which direction their life should go, and therefore never make great leaders. They are wise and gentle and easily stimulated to feel pity for the unfortunate.

  Good mates: Rabbit, Boar, Horse
  Disastrous mates: Ox, Dog

Year of the Monkey

People born in the year of the monkey are noted for their skills, talents, and flexibility. They can solve the most difficult problems with ease and are successful in nearly every field. They have a disconcerting habit of agreeing with others. If they cannot start a project at once, they become discouraged and give up before they begin. They have a strong drive to know everything and have good memories for fine points and details. They read a lot. They become famous if allowed to go their own way.

  Good mates: Dragon, Rat
  Disastrous mate: Tiger

Year of the Rooster

People born in the year of the rooster are deep thinkers and are devoted to their work. They try to do more than they are capable of and are disappointed when they fail. They do not trust other people and prefer to do things alone. They always think they are right and that they know what they are doing. It seems they are highly adventurous, but it is mostly talk. Not at all shy, they can be quite brave when need be.

  Good mates: Ox, Snake, Dragon
  Disastrous mate: Rabbit

Year of the Dog

People born in the year of the dog have a deep sense of duty and loyalty and are very honest. They inspire confidence and know how to keep secrets. They are admired by others yet are selfish, stubborn, and eccentric. They have very sharp tongues and an ability to find fault with everything. They champion just causes and their side nearly always wins. They are not good at social gatherings but are good at handling people in industry or business.

Good mates: Horse, Tiger, Rabbit
Disastrous mates: Dragon, Sheep

Year of the Boar

People born in the year of the boar have great fortitude and honesty. When they set out to do something they go straight for it with determination, drive, and great inner strength. They don't make many friends, but when they do, it is for life. They don't talk much, but when they do, it all comes out at once and there's no stopping them until they've finished. They have a thirst for knowledge, study much, and have a broad knowledge on the surface, though limited when probed. They are shy and do not seek outside help with problems.

Good mates: Rabbit, Sheep
Disastrous mate: Snake

RHYMES AND GAMES

New Year's Couplets

Make New Year's couplets to put on the door. Paint them in black ink on red paper so they read vertically. Make your own in English. Here is a sample:

All over town welcome spring;
For the New Year, praises ring.

In figure 4 are a few Chinese characters for you to trace and paint in black ink on red paper squares to put on your door. The characters, Gung Hay Fat Choy, are a New Year's wish: May you prosper.

Shuttlecock
(Janze)

In China, playing a shuttlecock is a sport. People kick it with one foot or both feet. There are many different ways to play with the shuttlecock. The most popular way is to use one foot to kick it up into the air and kick it again and again without letting it drop. You need to wear tennis shoes to play with it.

Materials

Yarn (6 yards)
One metal washer (slightly larger than a quarter)
Scissors
Cardboard or any thin book (8 inches wide)

Directions

1. Cut about 27 pieces of yarn, each eight inches long. An easy way to do it is to wrap the yarn completely around the cardboard or book, then cut through the yarn along both edges.
2. Fold one strip of yarn in two. Slip the loop through the hole of the metal washer. Holding the other ends, insert them through the loop and then pull to make a tight knot (also called a macrame basic knot or a Lark's head knot).
3. Repeat with the rest of the strips.

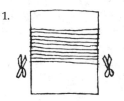

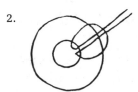

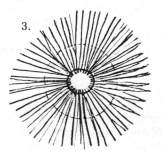

REFERENCE

Mann, Shiah. *Chinese New Year.* Illus. by Yeh Yung-ching. New York: A.R.T.S. Inc. 32pp. pap. $1.50.

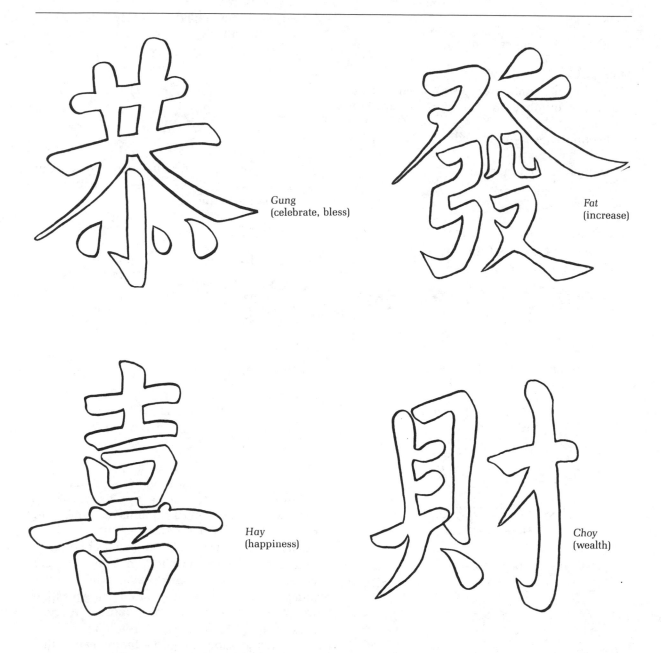

Gung
(celebrate, bless)

Fat
(increase)

Hay
(happiness)

Choy
(wealth)

Figure 4. Chinese characters form a New Year's wish: May you prosper

Lantern Festival

The full moon on the fifteenth day of the first month of the lunar year marks the official end of the New Year celebration. This day is celebrated with parades that include dragons, stilt-walkers in costumes and ornate masks, and lanterns ranging from simple to outrageous. Temples display a wealth of intricate lanterns and give prizes for the best. All manner of subjects are represented, including ships in full sail, elaborate buildings, and all kinds of animals, all made with great delicacy and finesse. Hordes of people throng to the parks to see the lanterns hung in trees and in the temples and to watch the dragons fight each other outside the Great Hall.

CRAFTS

Paper Lanterns

Materials

Matchstick bamboo or uninsulated number 16 or number 18 iron wire or drinking straws

Masking tape 1/4-inch wide

Paper napkins (use all colors except white, which is for funerals)

Glue

Scissors

Directions

1. Tape the ends of the bamboo, wire, or straws together.

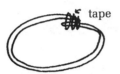

2. Assemble them into a globe with long verticals.

Vary the shapes and sizes.

Make two stars and attach them with small sticks (see Philippine Christmas lantern).

Five circles taped at each intersection make a butterfly.

3. Cover with paper. Glue along sticks. Cut paper off at sticks. Glue and paper one section at a time.

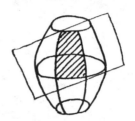 

REFERENCE

Mann, Shiah. *Paper Lanterns: Two Methods.* New York: A.R.T.S., Inc., 1974.

GAMES

Dragon Tag

This is a popular party game in China. Two children are chosen to be the heads of the dragons. One by one, as captains of teams, they choose the playmates they want for their "body." When all are chosen, each child holds onto the waist of the child in front. (Experienced dragons like to make belts of light rope to hang on to, as the ensuing battle can get rather rough and frail shirts fare poorly.) A good dragon might be fifteen children long.

The two dragons begin by facing each other with the "tail" out behind them. Each head tries to procure a handkerchief stuck into the back pocket of the last child in the opposing tail, at the same time protecting his or her own tail. Both head and tail must be expert players. Smaller children should go in the middle. The resulting maelstrom really resembles dragons fighting and writhing in the waves.

Stilt Walking

Make costumes of storybook characters and parade around the neighborhood or school on stilts. Costumes can be fairly simple or quite elaborate.

REFERENCE

The Candlewick Fairy. Adapted by Li Shufen. Illus. by Liu Shaohui. Beijing: Foreign Language Press, 1985. Order through Guoji Shudian.*

Ice Festival in Harbin

It is midwinter in Harbin in the heart of what used to be called Manchuria. From all over China, indeed from all over the world, come ice sculptors with their entries for this year's contest. A local park contains the life-sized figures, many of them masterpieces. Represented are animals, storybook characters, boats and other vehicles, groups of people (dancers, children, parents), and personalities from history and legend.

Some of the sculptures have colored neon lights inside, but all catch the late afternoon winter sun and glow in the cold like the cheeks of their admirers. From all over China people flock to view this marvel.

CRAFT

Ice Sculpture

Freeze blocks of ice in your freezer or outside, if you are lucky enough to live in a climate that has a decent winter. Try your hand at ice sculpture. Even the simplest ones can be impressive. Look at some Eskimo carvings for inspiration. They are usually simple in form but alluring and wonderful. Use chisels and hammers and planes as you would on wood.

Younger children can have a sculpture contest using snow rather than ice. Display with lights around your school and watch your community glow. It's as good as Christmas!

FOOD

Hot Pot

If you have access to electricity, you may use a hot plate and a soup pot. But the authentic way is to light a charcoal fire inside a chimney pot. In any case, a bowl is filled with water that is kept nearly boiling. The guests sit around the bowl and dip into it bits of meat, vegetables, and noodles. As each item is done, it is removed, dipped in one of a variety of sauces, and eaten immediately. The fare may range from paper-thin slices of pork or beef and a few vegetables to lamb, fish, octopus, squid, scallops, oysters, watercress, and a variety of noodles (often the very thin transparent rice noodles). When dinner is over, you have a wonderful soup to end your meal.

To really enjoy the hot pot, have it in a cold storage shed or garage as they do in Harbin. Everyone huddles around the fire to keep warm, boiling the meat together.

Ching Ming

Usually falling on April 5 or 6, this festival, sometimes called the grave sweeping festival, is the time when families get together and go to their ancestors' graves. Families clean up the graves, sometimes repainting the inscriptions, and offer flowers, fruits, incense, a picnic lunch, and firecrackers. Then the people eat the picnic lunch and enjoy the "clear and bright" (*Ching Ming*) afternoon.

CEMETERY VISIT

Take a group on an outing to a local graveyard on a bright spring day. Take along incense and candles (if not firecrackers), flowers, and a nice picnic. If no one has ancestors there, simply choose a grave on which to place the flowers. Wandering in cemeteries, especially old ones, can be quite interesting, reading inscriptions and pondering the lives of those left behind. Try to maintain a certain decorum for the sake of other visitors and to show respect for those whose ancestors you are adopting.

Dragon Boat Races   Moon 5, Day 5

A month before this event, long, slim boats filled with fifteen to fifty-five able-bodied young men practice for speed on local rivers and canals. Children gather to watch and cheer. The date "Double Five" is set for the real race, when many boats crowd the river to vie for trophies.

This tradition comes from the story of Chu Yuan (3rd c. B.C.), who was an adviser to the king of one of many small, warring states. Because of unscrupulous political adversaries, Chu Yuan's ardent, heartfelt, and wise advice was rejected, along with the man himself. Chu Yuan then became one of China's most famous poets and wandered in exile for several years writing poetry describing his disappointment, including his masterpiece, "Song of Encountering Sorrow." Then, disheartened with his king, with politics, and with the world in general, he threw himself into the Milo River and drowned.

At his death, legend has it, the people realized how wronged he had been and set out in boats to rescue him but were too late. They threw rice into the river, some say to offer to the fish so the fish wouldn't touch his body, others say wrapped in leaves as an offering to the soul of Chu Yuan. In either case, sticky rice dumplings, sometimes with a meat filling, wrapped in banana leaves and steamed, are eaten on this day.

Other Southeast Asian countries also celebrate spring festivals in which there are water parades and boat races. One type of dragon in ancient lore is said to live in water or clouds and be responsible for bringing needed rains.

These dragons also decorate the boats of other Southeast Asian festivals.

GAME

If you have access to boats and water, have races. If not, make dragon heads and tails, attach them to lines of wagons, roller skaters, or runners, and stage your own dragon races. As many children as are comfortable can be in one line. Each child holds onto a ribbon strung from the head runner to the tail, so that, for safety's sake, any child can leap out of line if need be.

Dragon Races

Enlarge the dragon's head shown in figure 5. Attach it to cardboard and cut out. Using a hole punch, make holes in strategic places and tie on red, orange, and yellow yarn. Paint the dragon's head and attach it to a small, sturdy dowel. The first runner will hold the head aloft.

Figure 5. Dragon's head used for dragon races

Where the dowel adjoins the head, attach a long, green ribbon decorated with paper or cloth scales (circles will do) to represent the body of the dragon and ripple in the wind. For a more elaborate effect, use a long swath of green cloth draped over a string running from head to tail. Each runner will hold onto the string and cloth and thus support the body. As an alternative, attach foot-long green crepe paper streamers to the body ribbon. The only really necessary item is the body ribbon, which runs from head to tail and keeps the runners together in one dragon.

A tail can be added to the end of the line. If you are using a green cloth, leave a couple of feet extra at the end. Attach a tail-shaped piece of cardboard to make the cloth stick out and let it flutter behind the last runner. Be sure to allow enough space between runners.

FOOD

Jung Zi

Jung Zi are sticky rice dumplings wrapped in banana, bamboo, or other large grass leaves. They can be plain sticky rice (*nuo mi*) or have a filling of red beans, peanuts, pork, or so forth. Put the ingredients together uncooked, wrap tightly with the long leaves, then steam for several hours.

POETRY

Encountering Sorrow

Study Chu Yuan's poem "Li Sao" and consider the story of Chu Yuan. Why did he feel so disappointed with his government? With his life? What could he have done instead of drowning himself? What would you do if someone important to you (your teachers, parents, or boss) rejected your ideas, which you felt were wonderful? This dicussion will be most meaningful to older children. The following excerpts from "Li Sao" can guide the discussion. The complete poem can be found in *Ch'u Tz'u: The Songs of the South* by David Hawkes (see References).

The fools enjoy their careless pleasure,
But their way is dark and leads to danger.
I have no fear for the peril of my own person,
But only lest the chariot of my lord should be
  dashed.
I hurried about your chariot in attendance,
Leading you in the tracks of the kings of old.

But the Fragrant One refused to examine my
  true feelings:
He lent ear, instead, to slander, and raged
  against me.

lines 17–20

There was a time when he spoke to me in
  frankness;
But then he repented and was of another mind.
I do not care, on my own count, about the
  divorcement,
But it grieves me to find the Fair One so
  inconstant.

lines 24–25

What I do resent is the Fair One's
  waywardness:
Because he will never look to see what is in
  men's hearts.

line 44

Truly, this generation are cunning artificers!
From square and compass they turn their
  eyes and change the true measurement.
They disregard the ruled line to follow their
  crooked fancies:
To emulate in flattery is their only rule.
But I am sick and sad at heart and stand
  irresolute:
I alone am at a loss in this generation.
But I would rather quickly die and meet
  dissolution
Before I ever would consent to ape their
  behavior.

lines 46–49

I have looked back into the past and forward
  to later ages,
Examining the outcome of men's different
  designs.
Where is the unrighteous man who could be
  trusted?
Where is the wicked man whose service
  could be used?
Though I stand at the pit's mouth and death
  yawns before me,
I still feel no regret at the course I have
  chosen.
Straightening the handle, regardless of the
  socket's shape:
For that crime the good men of old were
  hacked in pieces.

lines 86–89

Deep in the palace, unapproachable,
The wise king slumbers and will not be
    awakened;
And the thoughts in my breast must all go
    unuttered.
How can I bear to endure this for ever?

                              lines 128–129

Enough! There are no true men in the state:
    no one to understand me.
Why should I cleave to the city of my birth?
Since none is worthy to work with in making
    good government,
I will go and join P'eng Hsien in the place
    where he abides.

                              lines 186–187

                              —Chu Yuan

Note: P'eng Hsien was a shaman ancestor.
Some take this last line to mean an intent to
commit suicide. Others believe that Chu Yuan
simply intends to retire into mysticism.

REFERENCES

Ch'en Shou-yi. *Chinese Literature: A Historical Introduction.* New York: Ronald Press, 1961. 665pp.

Hawkes, David. *Ch'u Tz'u: The Songs of the South; An Ancient Chinese Anthology.* Boston: Beacon Press, 1959. 229pp.

Cowherd and Spinning Maid
Moon 7, Day 7

This festival is celebrated at home "with offerings to the lovers and a look into the future to see who will marry whom."

Retold many times, the popular story behind this festival has a number of versions. One version has it that there were seven sisters who were immortal. Their job was to weave clothing for the Queen of Heaven. Every day they went to bathe in the river on earth. One day a cowherd saw them and mischievously stole the gown of one of them. She had to ask him for her clothes. Once he saw her naked, she had to marry him. So they lived happily on earth for several years. But then the Queen saw that the maiden was not attending to her weaving duties and ordered her back to heaven. When the cowherd died, he too became a star and hurried to meet his be-loved. But the Queen was jealous and with one stroke of her hairpin formed a river (the Milky Way) between them. Only once a year (on Double Seven) are they allowed to meet, crossing a bridge formed by all the magpies of the world.

A PLAY

Read or tell the story of the seven sisters, then have the children reenact the story. Choose a cowherd, a Queen of Heaven, and seven sisters, one of whom will be the spinning maid. All the others can be the magpies, forming the bridge. Let the cowherd choose which sister will be the spinning maid by which "robe" he steals. He may or may not know which robe belongs to which girl. The story is short so it is possible to do it several times, with changes of hero, heroine, and Queen. Let the children decide for themselves what they will say. Each performance will thus be unique.

Birthday of Confucius (September 28)

This is celebrated as National Teacher's Day in Taiwan, and possibly is also noted on the mainland, depending on the current status of things ancient.

Confucius is revered as one of China's great sages but, though there are temples in his honor, he is not worshiped as a god. Teachers have always held great respect in China. The students and disciples of Confucius wrote down what he said. These discourses and those of one of his most famous followers, Mencius, are collected in four books called *The Analects, The Doctrine of the Mean, The Great Learning,* and *The Book of Mencius.* These are the Confucian classics, from which are taken the many sayings people even today are fond of repeating.

Confucius spent his career wandering from one political post to another as an adviser. In his day, many people made their living in this way. When a king would listen to him, Confucius was in favor. If not, he would wander. Finally, near the end of his life, he gave up trying to curry favor with royalty and began gathering disciples about him.

CONFUCIUS SAYS

The following are some things Confucius really did say. Have a group of older children examine them and decide whether they are good ideas. Do any of them apply to us today? Do you think we might be wise enough to say something that could apply to people 2,500 years from now living on the other side of the earth? What do you think accounts for this kind of wisdom?

Confucian sayings always begin with *Zi Yue*, which means "The Master says."

The Master says: I will not be bothered if men do not know me [if I am not famous]; I will be bothered if I do not know men [understand them].

The Master says: See what a man does, notice his motives, examine in what things he takes his leisure. How can a man conceal his character?

The Master says: Learning without thought is labor lost. Thought without learning is perilous.

The Master says: Shall I tell you what knowledge is? When you know a thing, to hold that you know it. When you do not know a thing, to allow that you do not know it. That is knowledge.

The Master says: In festive ceremonies, it is better to be sparing than extravagant. In ceremonies of mourning, it is better that there be deep sorrow than a minute attention to observances.

The Master says: It is virtuous manners which constitute the excellence of a neighborhood. If a man, in selecting a residence, does not fix on one where such manners prevail, how can he be wise?

The Master says: A scholar whose mind is set upon truth but who is ashamed of bad clothes and bad food is not fit to be discoursed with.

The Master says: He who acts with a constant view to his own advantage will be much murmured against.

The Master says: When we see men of worth, we should think of equaling them; when we see men of a contrary character, we should turn inwards and examine ourselves.

The Master says: Fine words, an insinuating appearance, and excessive respect. I am ashamed of that. To conceal resentment against a person and yet appear friendly with him. I am also ashamed of that.

The Master says: I have not yet seen one who could perceive his own faults and inwardly accuse himself.

The Master says: When I have presented one corner of a subject to anyone, and he cannot from it learn the other three, I do not repeat my lesson.

The Master says: Virtue! Is it a thing far away? If I desire virtue, Lo! Virtue is at hand!

The Master says: Study as though you were chasing something you could not catch up with, and were afraid of losing it.

The Master says: Wherever there are three men walking, one of them is my teacher. I will select his good qualities and follow them. I will pick out his bad qualities and avoid them.

Mid-Autumn Festival (Moon Festival) Moon 8, Day 15

Typical of harvest festivals, this one is celebrated with a feast, usually with a gathering of the clan. The full moon, traditionally the biggest and brightest of the year, is honored. Families gather in parks in the evenings to drink tea and eat moon cake and gaze at the full moon. Because the moon is round, all things round are offered in tribute. Oranges and apples are presented in round dishes. Moon cakes are made by enclosing sweet red bean paste or lotus seed paste in a round, scalloped pastry shell. Sometimes a hardboiled egg yolk, round and yellow like the moon, is added to the filling.

The moon goddess, Chang O, is remembered on this day. Her husband, the archer Yi, shot down nine of the ten suns blazing in the sky to save the earth from being scorched and was rewarded with the peach of immortality. Only one person could eat it and become immortal, so Chang O stole it and ran away to the moon to escape her husband's wrath. Many poems are written about her in her lonely abode.

Is Chang O sorry she stole the magic herb,
Between the blue sky and the emerald sea,
  thinking night after night?

—Li Shang Yin

ACTIVITIES

1. Find as many round delicacies as you can. Find pictures to put on a bulletin board or provide the real items. Have tea and eat them. Include moon cake if possible. (You will have to buy it at a Chinese products store or send for it.) Make a full moon to gaze at or have the gathering in a park under the full moon in the evening.

2. Have older children use books and reference tools to find out all they can about harvest festivals around the world. How are they celebrated? Note the similarities and differences in various parts of the world. Have clues ready for the treasure hunters.

Hill Climbing Day   Moon 9, Day 9

On the ninth day of the ninth month, everyone goes up into the hills with a picnic and a jug of chrysanthemum wine in commemoration of a Han dynasty scholar who was warned of a disaster about to befall his town. He took his family and went up into the hills for the day, well supplied with food and wine, and returned home in the evening to find all his cattle dead. Every year on that day, in thanks for being allowed to escape such a fate themselves, people climb hills just on the chance that it might once again prove fatal to stay home.

ACTIVITY

Autumn in China is the best season, with clear, crisp days and bright, blue skies just before winter sets in. Take a picnic and go early up into the hills.

Winter Solstice

On December 21 or 22, at the winter solstice, families get together and have a simple dinner. Although this is a minor festival, with the lunar New Year still about a month away and in the midst of gray skies and cold, it provides an opportunity for families to gather at home.

JAPAN

Japan's two most important festivals, or *Matsuri*, are the New Year, or Oshogatsu, and a midsummer commemoration of the dead known as O-Bon. The Japanese celebrate the religious festivals and ceremonies of both Shinto and Buddhism. Every major shrine and temple has an annual festival. Eight of the largest and most important of these festivals are national holidays.

The five festivals most familiar to Japanese Americans are Oshogatsu, Hinamatsuri (Girl's Day), Tango No Sekku (Boy's Day), Tanabata (Star Festival), and Bon Odori (Bon dance). Here we will describe only two festivals, the New Year and Children's Day.

New Year

New Year lasts from January 1 to 3. Business and government offices begin closing down around December 29. Homes are thoroughly cleaned, pine branches and decorated bamboo are placed on both sides of the entryway, sacred straw festoons are hung, and traditional foods are prepared. On New Year's Eve, *koshi soba* (end-of-the-year buckwheat noodles) is eaten for longevity, and the end-of-the-year bell tolls 108 times from Buddhist temples to symbolize the elimination of 108 bad things during the past year.

Many people visit the temples on the following days to pray for a good year. Wearing new clothing, families join in a toast with *otoso* (sweet sake) and *sake* (rice wine). *Ozoni* (soup with *mochi*) is eaten. Children receive gifts of money called *otshi-dama* in envelopes from family and relatives. Such games as battledore and shuttlecock (similar to badminton) and *karuta*, a card game with one hundred cards, are very popular.

CRAFT

The Tsuru, the crane, is one of the symbols for the New Year. String several paper cranes and hang them from the ceiling. Most origami books will have instructions for folding them.

Children's Day

May 5 is Children's Day, or Kodomo No Hi. It is a time to honor the children of Japan. It shares the same day with Tango No Sekku (Boy's Day). The festival symbolizes the hopes of parents that their sons will grow to be strong, healthy young men. Warrior dolls are displayed, and large banners shaped like carp are flown on poles over the boys' homes. The *koi*, or carp, symbolizes perseverance because of its attempt to swim upstream against all odds.

Although girls do participate in this festival and can also fly paper carp and display warrior dolls, the dominant theme here is for the boys. There are no special activities just for the girls on this day. However, there is another day, "Doll Festival," which is especially for girls and falls on March 3. Traditional dolls are displayed on a background of red cloth to symbolize the energy of the sun and good luck. On this day, girls dress in their best kimono and serve tea and cakes to family and friends who come to admire the doll display.

CRAFT

Look for carp streamers in any Japanese gift-shop. The streamers are very colorful and come in different sizes.

Carp Streamer
(Koi Nobori)

Use white cloth, such as an old sheet. Fold the sheet in half and cut out a fish shape. Pencil in a fish design and color with fabric markers (so the color will not run). Many designs are used. Sew up the belly but leave the mouth and tail open for the wind. Using thin wire, make a circle to match the mouth. Fold the mouth around the wire circle and hem. Using heavy thread, tie four lines from the fish's mouth. Join together and attach to a pole. Now you are ready to fly your carp in a parade or from a window.

REFERENCES

Araki, Nancy K. and Jane M. Horii. *Matsuri = Festival.* Union City, Calif.: Heian International, 1984. 150pp. pap. $9.95. ISBN: 0-89346-019-2.

DeMente, Boye. *Passport's Japan Almanac.* Passport Books, 1987. ISBN: 0-8442-8508-0.

Gakken Company. *Pictorial Encyclopedia of Japanese Culture: The Soul and Heritage of Japan.* New York: Kodansha International, 1987. 130pp. $29.95. ISBN: 0-87040-752-X.

KOREA

There are two important holidays for Koreans. The biggest one of the year is called Sol Day, or New Year's Day. It is celebrated on the first day of the first lunar month, which falls sometime in January or February. The other holiday is the Ch'usok, or Harvest Moon, which is on the fifteenth day of the eighth month—that is, sometime in September or October.

New Year's Day

Koreans dress in their best clothes or in traditional costumes and gather together to visit the gravesites of their ancestors to pay respect. After the ceremony, the formal New Year's greeting, *Sebae,* is said with deep bows to the elders. The children receive special words of advice and gifts. Everyone enjoys a special rice cake soup called *duk-kuk,* which symbolizes being one year older.

A popular New Year's game is *yut.* It is similar to a dice game, but uses four sticks instead. The sticks are thrown up into the air by twisting the wrist.

Flying kites, or *yeon,* is another favorite activity for New Year's day. For the Koreans, flying a kite on this day symbolizes escaping disaster or letting bad luck fly away. Kites thus are inscribed with the symbol of bad luck, *aik.* Many kites are made in the shape of auspicious divinities, such as turtles, dragons, or tigers. Sometimes a kite-fighting contest is held in which the better-maneuvered kite cuts the strings of the weaker.

Girls play on the seesaw with great skill and good balance. One girl stands on the end of a long plank that is balanced on a sack of rice straw, and is tossed high into the air as her companion jumps onto the opposite end. According to custom, this game originated long ago when women, confined to their homes, found the seesaw not only a source of enjoyment but also a means by which they could see the outside world over the courtyard walls.

GAME
Yut

The *yut* game originated in the ninth century during the Paekche dynasty. It is played by two to four players, or by two to four teams.

Materials
- 4 pieces of flat wood or popsicle sticks, one side marked "back" and the other side marked "face."
- 4 red and 4 green pawns. Use buttons or checkers.
- Cardboard or heavy paper for board (see figure 6).

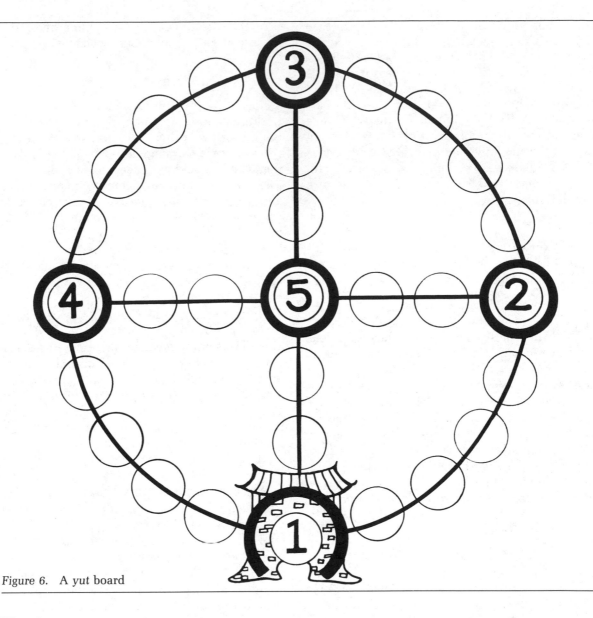

Figure 6.   A yut board

Directions

1. The players alternate tossing the four wooden sticks in the air. Each player moves a pawn according to the fall of the sticks:

    *mah:** All four pieces show their backs. (Move five spaces.)

    *yut:** All four pieces show their faces. (Move four spaces.)

    gul: Three pieces show their faces. (Move three spaces.)

    kae: Two pieces show their faces. (Move two spaces.)

    toh: One piece shows its face. (Move one space.)

    *Take an extra turn.

2. If the player's pawn lands on the same spot as the pawn of an opponent, the opponent's pawn must return to the beginning (circle 1).

3. A player can take a short-cut if the pawn lands on a short-cut junction. These are marked by double circles, which allow a player to turn to the left and follow the shorter route on the next turn.

4. If two pawns belonging to one player land on the same spot, they may be moved together as one.

5. The first player who moves all four pawns to the final goal wins.

Harvest Moon

Ch'usok is the day of thanksgiving. All families visit their ancestors' graves to offer thanks. Each family makes rice cakes and wine from the harvest. Special foods include bluebell, water lily root, candied walnuts, persimmons, honey cakes, rice balls, and nut-flavored drinks. Sometimes this is called Children's Day, for there are many entertaining activities, such as cow and tortoise games, tug-of-war, and traditional round dances.

SINGAPORE

The official emblem of Singapore is the Merlin—half lion, half fish. At the mouth of the Singapore River, the Merlin Statue stands over twenty-six feet high, spewing a fountain of water from its mouth.

In Singapore and Malaysia, the Chinese, Hindus, and Muslims celebrate many religious festivals and processions. They also have many local market feasts.

Chinese

The Chinese in Singapore, like their counterparts in China, Hong Kong, and Taiwan, celebrate their most important holiday, the lunar New Year, in January or February with a dragon dance and parade. The other festivals are similar to those held in other countries and include the Dragon Boat Festival, the Festival of the Hungry Ghosts, and the Mid-Autumn Moon Festival. There is one uniquely Singaporean celebration, however—the Birthday of the Monkey God.

Hindus

The Hindus celebrate a harvest festival called Thai Pongal in January, which is considered the luckiest month of the year. One of the most dramatic of the Hindu festivals is the Thaipusam, also held in January. Male devotees of Thaipusam march in a procession to the temples. Each participant carries a *Kavadi,* an oversized, metal frame weighing some seventy pounds and decorated with peacock feathers, fruits, and flowers, which represent aspects of God. The frame is anchored onto each man's body with sharp hooks that pierce the flesh. Other barbs are also stuck through cheeks and tongue. This is a ritual of atonement or of thanks for a prayer granted. Very few participants show pain or even blood on their bare chests or their cheeks. Women carry a smaller kavadi on their shoulders, and pierce their cheeks and tongues. Other rituals offer similar ordeals during which the participants' faith protects them from pain and blood.

Muslims

Muslims celebrate their New Year, Hari Raya Ruasa, during July. This festival marks the end of Ramadan—a 30-day period of fasting. Dressed in new clothing, devout Muslims pray at the gold-domed mosques and visit friends and relatives. In the marketplaces, dozens of stalls sell many kinds of Malay cakes and Indian food. Houses are cleaned and sweet pastries are made. Families visit cemeteries to tidy gravesites and to recite verses from the holy book, the Quran. Children receive money in green pockets similar to the red envelopes Chinese children receive.

Crafts

Make a Merlin face mask. Enlarge the mask shown in figure 7. Paste the enlargement onto cardboard or tag board. Add color. Mount your mask onto long dowels to hold in a parade, use many to decorate a room, or cut eye holes and use as a face mask.

THAILAND

Loy Krathong

One of the most colorful celebrations in Thailand is the Loy Krathong Festival, which takes place on the night of the full moon of the twelfth lunar month (November).

A *krathong* is a small, lotus-shaped boat often made of banana leaves and containing a candle, incense sticks, clay figures, offerings of food and flowers, and often a coin. It is placed in the rivers and canals by children and adults to honor the water spirit. People gather around to watch thousands of twinkling lights as the candle boats float down streams and canals to

Figure 7. Merlin mask

the sea. There are many elaborate and huge royal krathongs to view, and the night ends with fireworks.

The artistic Thai people show great skill in making over a thousand styles of garlands and floral offerings. Some of the elaborate boats are woven from green banana-leaf baskets shaped like lotus flowers with pink, red, or golden lotus petals. Traditionally, the boats have been thought to be offerings for the Lord Buddha. Most people, however, float away their worries and sufferings in the krathong.

The Thai start the morning with a colorful, traditional costume parade with music. Schoolchildren make lanterns and carry them in the parade. There are krathong-making contests and competitions that result in floating floral barges, palaces, and houses. A beauty contest called the Noppamas Queen Contest commemorates the legendary royal consort of the Kukhothai king who made the first elaborately decorated krathong to be floated down the river.

We hesitate to advocate a simple paper boat project or even an origami boat after our admonition to stick with real things (i.e., to make real dragons and not egg carton dragons; to wear a real kimono or show a picture of one, and not wear a bathrobe). The Thai children use banana leaves to make their tiny boats. We don't have many banana leaves available in the United States. The Thai children have plenty of canals, which carry these boats with their offerings to the sea. If we were to advocate setting paper boats adrift on local rivers, we would be counseled for littering. Origami is Japanese, not Thai.

CRAFT

Weave paper boats, using shades of green construction paper to represent banana leaves, in the same style as Valentine Heart Baskets or May Day Baskets. Any small basket design will do, as it will not be exactly authentic in any case. Put inside a coin, a flower, little clay figures, some candy. Hang them from the ceiling or from light fixtures in the classroom, or attach them to a bulletin board with a meandering blue paper river. Add Thai houses on stilts at river banks. If you have in your library a book on Thailand, you could add paper dolls of children sending off the boats, dressing the children according to the pictures in the book. After the festival, the children can take their boats home and eat the candy.

CRAFT

A spirit house is a miniature structure elevated on a pole and found in front of a Thai house or building. It houses the spiritual guardian Phi and often is a simple wooden replica of a traditional Thai dwelling. Some spirit houses are elaborate, colorful models of religious temples. The spirit house is supplied with regular offerings of incense, flowers, and food, and inside are doll-like figures that represent spiritual attendants.

Make a spirit house from cardboard or wood. The most popular colors used in Thailand for the houses are yellow, lilac, and yellow-green. The roof is usually orange.

Some spirit houses are elaborate and ornate. Others are very plain and resemble our birdhouses. For your own spirit house, buy or make a simple house, then decorate it as elaborately as you can. Place it either in a special place on a porch or in your room. The best idea would be to mount the spirit house on a pole and place it in the front yard of the school. Furnish it with oranges, incense, flowers, and a few small dolls.

REFERENCE

Schwabach, Karen. *Thailand: Land of Smiles.*[†]

BURMA

Most of the festivals in Burma are connected with the full moon and are concerned either with some aspect of Buddhism or with natural phenomena often related to the seasons. Every month there is an all-night celebration of solemnity or joy or rambunctiousness. Many festivals take on the qualities of a country fair, with stalls selling delectable tidbits and offering games of skill and chance, and sometimes go on for days or even weeks. Other minor festivals take place just before or just after the full moon. The Burmese also celebrate modern political holidays, such as Independence Day (January 4), Peasants' Day (March 2), and Workers' Day (May 1).

Islam and the Christian religions are also represented in the holiday scene, as are vestiges of past invasions and indications of an awareness of the modern world, although the Burmese tend to discourage much outside contact.

The figures most dominant in the festivals of Burma, however, are the saffron-robed Buddhist monks. Usually around the age of nine or ten, every boy dons the saffron robe, has his head shaved, and becomes a monk for several weeks or several months or even longer. Some remain monks for their entire lives. This period is regarded as the boy's growing up and is celebrated with much feasting, music, drama, and pride.

Thingyan

Thingyan is the Burmese version of the water festival popular all over Southeast Asia in April. In Burma, as elsewhere, it is considered the New Year. It is a Buddhist festival, and accordingly there are a few religious observations, such as the washing of the Buddhas and perhaps the washing of the hair of the elders, but for three days the emphasis of the populace lies in drenching each other with buckets upon buckets of water. In other countries a few sprinkles suffice, or perhaps a touch of perfume, but in Burma everyone must be waterlogged. A spirit of fun prevails.

ACTIVITY

The only activity that presents itself is to entice friends, foes, students, teachers, and colleagues out into an open space, arm everyone with buckets and hoses, and ensure that no one stays dry. (Do you dare keep this up for the prescribed three days?)

In May, for the full moon festival of Kason, participants may more sedately carry jugs of water to pour ceremoniously over the roots of any local banyan trees to celebrate the thrice-honored day of the Buddha's birth, his enlightenment, and his entrance into Nirvana.

Thadingyut

Thadingyut falls around October and represents the end of the Buddhist Lent, which lasts for three months. During that period no one may marry, so Thadingyut is welcomed and celebrated with many marriages. The rains show signs of stopping, the weather turns cooler, and the sky becomes gloriously bright. This is also the time when Buddha returned to earth, radiating his own brilliance along a pathway of candles. For the three days of the festival, all of Burma is alight with candles, lanterns, lamps, and lights of all kinds, ancient and modern. People celebrate all night. Fire balloons are filled with smoke and sent skyward. After the solemnity of the three months of Lent, this is a welcome time of lightheartedness and joy.

The festival for the previous month, Tawthalin, takes advantage of the rivers that are swollen with the rains and offers boat races. In the month following, Tazaungmone, there is a weaving festival in which all the young girls compete, staying up all night to weave robes for the monks. This festival is also celebrated with many lights and balloons.

ACTIVITY

Make paper lanterns, light candles and oil lamps, and adorn the inside and outside of the house with light.

REFERENCES

Burma. Directed and designed by Hans Johannes Hoefer. Written by Wilhelm Klein. Photographed by Gunter Pfannmuller. Edited by Jogn Gottberg Anderson. Insight Guides Series. Singapore: APA Productions; New York: Prentice-Hall, 1986. 332pp. pap. $16.95. ISBN: 013-090902-5.

Trager, Helen G. *We the Burmese: Voices from Burma.* New York: Praeger, 1969. 297pp. o.p.

Wheeler, Tony. *Burma: A Travel Survival Kit.* Victoria, Australia and Berkeley, Calif.: Lonely Planet Publications, 1988. 180pp. pap. $8.95. ISBN: 0-86442-017-X.

PHILIPPINES

Christmas

In the Philippines, Christmas begins on December 16 and ends on January 6, the Day of Epiphany. Church bells chime at dawn to herald the first Mass. The smell of sweet rice cakes fills the streets and hundreds of lanterns and multi-colored lights appear over windows and doorways. Better known as *Parol*, the Philippine Christmas star is constructed from bamboo frames or cardboard and covered with colored cellophane. In a town near Manila, the lantern tradition is climaxed on Christmas Eve by a colorful parade of lanterns as big as houses. Each lantern is carried in a truck and has its own brass band, dancers, and singers.

At the midnight supper, Noche Buena, family members gather to enjoy special foods: *rellenos* (boned, stuffed chicken), *pastel* (chicken pastry), *lechon* (roast suckling pig), and desserts of *leche flan* (egg yolk custard), *jalea de ube* (pudding made from violet tubers), and coconut *makapuno* in syrup.

On Christmas morning, the children visit their *ninangs* and *ninongs* (godparents). After the handkissing ritual, the children receive gifts and new coins. All the homes are open for visitors and many delicacies are set out for them.

Christmas festivities flow into the celebration of New Year with firecrackers and carolers, and culminate with the coming of the Three Kings on January 6. The Three Magi on horseback pass through the main street dressed in their finest royal costumes and distribute gifts to the children and alms to the poor.

CRAFT
Christmas Star Lantern

During Christmastime, Filipinos make and display a star-shaped lantern called *Parol* (pah-roh), like the one in figure 8.

Materials

> 10 kite ribs or bamboo strips, each two feet long. You will use 5 for the front and 5 for the back.
> 5 smaller ribs, each 3–5 inches long
> Tape
> String
> Tissue paper or foil

Directions

Form the front of the star by crossing 5 large ribs and taping or tying them together. Repeat for the back. Tie the two completed frames together at the five points of the star. Tape or tie the 5 smaller ribs as spacers between the front and back frames where the center ribs cross each other. This should form a three-dimensional star. The faces or surfaces of the star can be decorated with tissue or crepe paper. Use several colors. Some stars are plain white with the outer rims trimmed with shiny garlands and the center surfaces decorated with designs. Tassels made of strips of tissue paper or foil can be tied to the points of the star.

RESOURCES

Araki, Nancy K., and Jane M. Horii. *Matsuri = Festival. Japanese American Celebrations and Activities.* Illus. by the authors. South San Francisco: Heian International Publishing Co., 1978. 140pp. $9.95. ISBN: 0-89346-019-2.

Behrens, June. *Gung Hay Fat Choy: Happy New Year.* Festivals and Holidays Series. Photographs compiled by Terry Behrens. Chicago: Children's Press, 1982. 31pp. $14.60. ISBN: 0-516-08842-4.

Borja, Robert. *Making Chinese Paper Cuts.* Niles, Ill.: Whitman, 1980. $12.95. ISBN: 0-8075-4948-7.

Brown, Tricia. *Chinese New Year.* Photographs by Fran Ortiz. New York: Holt, 1987. 42pp. $13.95. ISBN: 0-8050-0497-1.

Carter, Michael. *Crafts of China.* Crafts of the World Series. New York: Doubleday, 1977. 144pp. o.p.

The Celebration of Children in Japan. Office of Bilingual Crosscultural Education. San Jose, Calif.: Franklin-McKinley School District, 27pp.

Cheng, Hou-Tien. *The Chinese New Year.* Scissor cuts by the author. New York: Holt, 1976. 32pp. o.p.

Chhim, Sun-him. *Introduction to Cambodian Culture.* San Diego: Multifunctional Resource Center, San Diego State University, 1987. 60pp.

Chinatown: San Francisco. Photographs by Peter Perkins. Text by Richard Reinhardt. Berkeley, Calif.: Lancaster-Miller, 1981. 86pp.

Chinese American Culture Curriculum Material Packet. Oakland (Calif.) Unified School District* and the Department of State and Federal Programs, Office of Bilingual Bicultural Education, Chinese Component, 1980. 130pp.

Christie, Anthony. *Chinese Mythology.* New York: Hamlyn, 1968. 141pp. $22.50. ISBN: 0-87226-015-1.

Cole, Ann, et al. *Children Are Children Are Children.* Boston: Little, Brown, 1978.

Fawdry, Marguerite. *Chinese Childhood.* New York: Barron's, 1977. 192pp. $17.95. ISBN: 0-9505588-0-X.

Huynh Dinh Te. *Introduction to Vietnamese Culture.* San Diego: Multifunctional Resource Center, San Diego State University, 1987. 80pp.

Indochinese Cultures. Cambodian, Laotian, Vietnamese. Curriculum Packet. Oakland Unified School District and the Office of Bilingual Education, Asian Bilingual Component, 1983. 93pp.

Indochinese New Year's Festivals: Tet, the Vietnamese New Year's Day. Cambodian New Year Begins. New Year in Laos. Sacramento: Office of Bilingual Bicultural Education, California State Department of Education, 1979. 37pp.

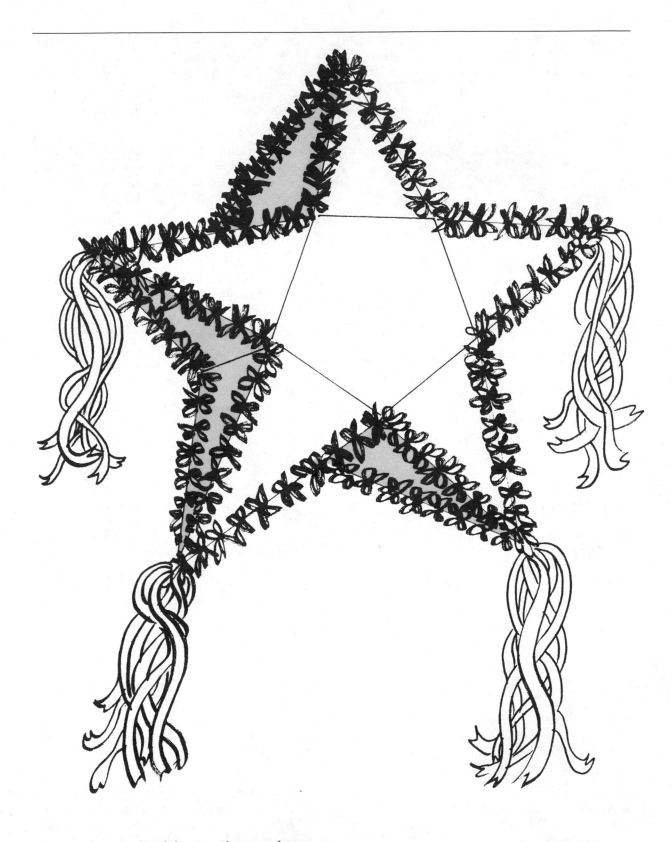

Figure 8.   Parol: The Philippine Christmas lantern

Jing Ho Hauk Ho #1 and #2. A Make It, Do It, Learn It Book of Chinese Activities for Children. Written and illustrated by C. K. Rekdal and Bettie Sing Luke Kan. Seattle: Fortune Cookie Press, 1976. 26pp.

Law, Joan, and Barbara E. Ward. *Chinese Festivals in Hong Kong.* Hong Kong: A South China Morning Post Publication, 1982. 95pp. ISBN: 9621000025.

Luangpraseut, Khamchong. *Laos Culturally Speaking: Introduction to the Lao Culture.* San Diego: Multifunctional Resource Center, San Diego State University, 1987. 48pp.

Mann, Shiah. *Chinese New Year.* Illus. by Yeh Yung-Ching. New York: A.R.T.S., Inc., 1976. 32pp. pap. $1.50.

Miller-Lachmann, Lyn. *Our Family, Our Friends, Our World: An Annotated Guide to Significant Multicultural Books for Children and Teenagers.* New Providence, N.J.: R. R. Bowker, 1992. 710pp. ISBN: 0-8352-3025-2.

Negron-Tokumoto, Lillie. *Chinese Creative Cultural Activities for Elementary School Children, K–5.* San Jose (Calif.) Unified School District,* 1986. 136pp.

St. Tamara. *Asian Crafts.* Illus. by the author. New York: Lion Press, 1970. 63pp. $12.95. ISBN: 0-87460-148-7.

Schubert, Barbara, and Marlene Bird. *Chinese: A Book of Culturally Based Activities for K–6 Children.* San Jose, Calif.: Reflections and Images,* 1976.

Yeh, Yung-Ching. *Chinese Folk Songs.* New York: A.R.T.S., Inc., 1979. 40pp.

Yip Wang Law. *Things Chinese.* Illus. by Roger Moses. Honolulu: Ethnic Resource Center for the Pacific, Educational Foundations, College of Education, Univ. of Hawaii. 23pp.

DISTRIBUTORS

Bellerophon Books
36 Anacapa Street
Santa Barbara, CA 93101

Charles E. Tuttle, Inc.
28 S. Main Street
P.O. Box 410
Rutland, VT 05701-0410

China Publications Centre (Guoji Shudian)
P.O. Box 399
Beijing, China

Chinese Cultural Center
750 Kearny Street
San Francisco, CA 94108
(415) 986-1822

Filipino Development Associates
5089 Yucatan Way
San José, CA 95118

Follett Library Book Co.
4506 Northwest Highway (Routes 14 & 31)
Crystal Lake, IL 60014
1-800-435-6170

Fortune Cookie Press
7558 Ravenna Avenue N.E.
Seattle, WA 98115

Greenshower Corp.
Bilingual Quality Children's Books
10937 Klingerman St.
S. El Monte, CA 91733
(818) 575-1000
Collect Calls: (848) 575-0294

Harcourt Brace Jovanovich Publishers
1250 Sixth Ave.
San Diego, CA 92101

Heian International, Inc.
1260 Pacific Street, P.O. Box 1013
Union City, CA 94587
(415) 471-8440

Holt, Rinehart and Winston
383 Madison Ave.
New York, NY 10019

Japanese American Curriculum Project, Inc.
414 East Third Ave.
San Mateo, CA 94401

Kane/Miller Book Publishers
P.O. Box 8515
La Jolla, CA 92038-8515
(619) 456-0540
P.O. Box 529
Brooklyn, NY 11231-0005
(718) 624-5120
   Specializing in Foreign Children's Books

Lothrop, Lee and Shepard Books
105 Madison Ave.
New York, NY 10016

Oakland Unified School District
1025 Second Avenue
Oakland, CA 94606

Philippine Expressions
8565 Wilshire Blvd., #11
Beverly Hills, CA 90211

Reflections and Images
6607 Northridge Drive
San Jose, CA 95120

San Jose Unified School District
1605 Park Avenue
San Jose, CA 95126

Viking Kestrel
Viking Penguin Inc.
40 West Second Street
New York, NY 10010

CHAPTER 4

Hispanic Materials and Programs

by Oralia Garza de Cortes and Louise Yarian Zwick

Hispanics are the fastest growing minority population in the United States. Between 1980 and 1987, the total number of Hispanics in the United States increased 30 percent, an increase five times greater than that of any non-Hispanic group. The term *Hispanic* encompasses the members of subgroups of Mexican, Puerto Rican, Cuban, and Central and South American origin, as well as other people of Spanish origin. Among these subgroups, that of Mexican origin is the largest, constituting 62.8 percent of the total Hispanic population, followed by Puerto Ricans at 12.2 percent, and Central and South Americans at 11.2 percent. Cuban Americans constitute 5.3 percent. The category "Other Hispanics" consists primarily of people of Spanish origin, who constitute 8.5 percent of the Hispanic population. A total of 18.8 million people of Hispanic descent currently live in the United States. The implications of these recent U.S. census figures in terms of library and social services for Hispanic people are far reaching, especially because more than one-third of the total Hispanic population in the United States is under eighteen years of age (see Refugio I. Rochin, *Economic Perspectives of the Hispanic Community* [Davis: Dept. of Agricultural Economics, Univ. of California, 1988]).

This bibliography was compiled to provide librarians, educators, and parents with a selection of literature for children that focuses on various aspects of Hispanic culture. The primary criterion for selection was the relevancy of culture. In addition, a work must accurately depict the cultural life of the subgroups mentioned. Cultural aspects of life were evaluated in relation to the portrayal of positive and nonstereotypical images.

Although other writers have criticized the assimilative, patronizing, and pastoral images of Hispanic characters cast by well-meaning authors and illustrators, those distorted images continue to be portrayed. The challenge of bridging the gap between how we see ourselves and how others see us is one that we hope will one day be met as people learn more about each other and come to value and respect each other's cultures. Librarians play a vital role in such a challenge and have become increasingly sensitive to the effects that stereotypes or a negative self-image can have on the character of a young child. It is for these reasons that quality materials must be provided.

This section is divided into two primary areas—works in English and works in Spanish. Bilingual works are included in the English section, while works in Spanish printed in the United States are listed in the Spanish section. Mixed-media items (i.e., recordings, film) are also listed separately in their respective Spanish or English categories. In addition, a special Resource section includes materials that are primarily curriculum related but which we found quite useful, especially in planning story hour programs. The Resources for Adults section lists articles and books that contain useful information about Hispanic materials and about issues affecting library services.

The Spanish section is not just a listing of books in Spanish but is a compilation of what we consider to be the best of the literature in Spanish for children that also reflects the cultural attributes of Hispanic populations. Consistent with our training as librarians and educators, we recognize the need to provide materials for the development of language in the first language of the child. The Spanish story hour program is an excellent means toward that end.

In light of the alarming dropout rates among Hispanic youth, can we do less than insist that Hispanic children's literature find its rightful place on the shelves of public and school libraries? Although interlibrary loan serves an important role in providing many materials not locally available, it cannot replace the need to develop special collections of books in Spanish as well as in English that realistically and accurately affirm the rich traditions and heritage of Hispanic culture.

Finally, the role of the distributor is vital if such a collection is to be developed. The distributors listed here have a proven track record of identifying, locating, and providing needed titles. Their commitment to locating often-hard-to-find materials is noteworthy, and the impor-

tance of their role in the selection-acquisition process cannot be overemphasized.

As we approach the twenty-first century, we must recall the legacy of many dedicated librarians who demonstrated their commitment to the youth of America. The identification of Hispanic materials through this list and the subsequent programs that we hope will take place in public and school libraries are further steps toward a century-old goal of bringing together children and books. In the process, we hope to instill in children a love of reading as well as a deeper understanding of and appreciation for their own and others' cultures. We believe that introducing good books and presenting quality programs in library settings will initiate the transformation process that must take place if we are to educate and empower the next generation of America's children.

BIBLIOGRAPHY

FICTION

English

K–6. Anaya, Rudolfo A. *The Farolitos of Christmas: A New Mexican Christmas Story.* Illus. by Richard C. Sandoval. Sante Fe: *New Mexico* Magazine, 1987. 32pp. pap. $6.95. ISBN: 0-937206-06-7.

Every year during the Christmas season, Luz's *abuelito* (grandfather) lights the largest bonfire in the area, which the traveling shepherds then select as the place to perform their traditional play. But this year Grandpa has caught a cold and cannot light the fire. Luz's ingenuity leads her to find a creative solution to this dilemma. The author offers a plausible explanation for the popular New Mexican tradition of *luminarias.* This modern story by a distinguished Chicano writer is enhanced with rich color illustrations.

K–5. Argueta, Manlio. *Magic Dogs of the Volcanos/Los Perros Mágicos de los Volcanes.*

Illus. by Elly Simmons. San Francisco: Children's Book Press, 1990. 32pp. $12.95. ISBN: 0-89239-064-6.

This beautiful, bilingual story from El Salvador features the *cadejos,* magic dogs prominent in the country's folklore tradition. Although the magic dogs befriend and protect the people who live on the slopes of the volcano, Don Toñio and his thirteen brothers send soldiers to hunt the dogs. With the help of their great-great-grandparents, the volcanos, the magic dogs vanquish the soldiers and restore peace in the land. Folk-primitive illustrations in deep colors complement this allegorical story of El Salvador.

P–3. Atkinson, Mary. *María Teresa.* Illus. by Christina Engla Eber. Chapel Hill, N.C.: Lollipop Power, 1979. 39pp. $5.95. ISBN: 0-914996-21-5. (Dist. by Carolina Wren Press.*[1])

The new girl in school with a funny-sounding name is the focus of this heart-

---

[1] Complete addresses for all sources marked with an asterisk (*) can be found in the Distributors section at the end of this chapter.

warming story about Maritere (short for María Teresa), who finds her new classroom both alienating and very different from her New Mexican origins. She finds solace, however, in her pet, a lamb puppet who converses with her in Spanish, reassuring her in the sentiments that only her language can offer. She takes her pet to school for show-and-tell and amazes her classmates with the puppet's unique ability to speak only Spanish. The other children must also learn Spanish if they want to converse with the puppet. This title is on the state of California's recommended list of books for Spanish readers.

P–3. Belpré, Pura. *Once in Puerto Rico.* Illus. by Christine Price. New York and London: Frederick Warne, 1973. o.p.

Puerto Rico's past comes alive in these legends collected from research centers and from the oral tradition by a renowned children's storyteller. Simple black-and-white line drawings complement the text.

2–5. _____. *The Rainbow-Colored Horse.* Illus. by Antonio Martorell. New York: Frederick Warne, 1978. 44pp. ISBN: 0-723-261512. o.p.

One of many variants of the well-known story about a magical horse of many colors, this version tells of a Taino farmer's son and his endurance during the many trials he must undergo to win the hand of the young princess he loves. A male variant of the Cinderella story, this is rich in the many ingredients characteristic of classic folktales.

5–8. Betancourt, T. Ernesto. *The Me Inside of Me.* Minneapolis: Lerner, 1985. 155pp. $10.95. ISBN: 0-8225-0728-5.

Alfredo Flores is orphaned at the age of seventeen by the death of his entire family in a plane crash while en route to Mexico City. He becomes heir to the travel insurance they purchased shortly before the crash. Flores experiences much guilt and grief over the death of his family, but his Southern California barrio lifestyle changes drastically overnight—he now has access to many things once denied him, including a new car and life as a student in an exclusive prep school. His

inner struggles to figure out who he is in this new environment form the focus of this book, written by a well-known children's author of Puerto Rican heritage who also uses the pseudonym Tom Paisley.

P–2. Bierhorst, John, translator. *Spirit Child: A Story of the Nativity.* Illus. by Barbara Cooney. New York: Greenwillow, 1990. pap. $4.95. ISBN: 0-688-09926-2.

Stunning, full-color, primarily earth-tone illustrations portray the birth of Christ as imagined by the Aztec Indians, based on the story as told to them by the Spanish missionary Fray Bernardino de Sahagún, who converted the Indians to Christianity. The text is not free flowing, and Bierhorst would have done well to adapt it for children, yet the exactness to the original telling adds authenticity to the folkloric approach.

K–3. Blackmore, Vivien, reteller. *Why Corn Is Golden: Stories about Plants.* Illus. by Susana Martínez-Ostos. Boston and Toronto: Little, Brown, 1984. 47pp. $12.95. ISBN: 0-316-54820-0.

These short, etiological legends relate the origins of such pre-Columbian plants and foods as corn and cacao beans. Soft, pastel watercolors augment this edition of simple yet informative tales suitable for beginning storytelling.

1–5. Brenner, Anita, reteller. *The Boy Who Could Do Anything and Other Mexican Folk Tales.* Illus. by Jean Charlot. Hamden, Conn.: Linnet, 1992.

Popular tales told about Tepoztón, the boy wanderer, combine pre-Columbian beliefs and biblical motifs in this collection of stories from the oral tradition. The author, a noted historian and author of the important work *The Wind That Swept Mexico,* lived in Mexico during the Mexican Revolution. Jean Charlot, a renowned French artist and illustrator of children's books, was involved in the muralist movement in Mexico during this period.

2–5. Bruni, Mary Ann Smothers. *Rosita's Christmas Wish.* Illus. by Thom Ricks. San

Antonio: TexArt Services, 1981. 48pp. $14.95. ISBN: 0-935857-00-1. (Dist. by Texas Monthly Press.*)

Rosita is a young Mexican-American child from the *barrios* of San Antonio whose foremost wish is to play the part of Gila, the Shepherdess in the age-old Christmas shepherd's play "Los Pastores." The excitement surrounding the presentation of the drama and Rosita's eventual role are part of a well-told, realistic story drawn from the rich cultural experiences of present-day U.S. Mexican Americans. Mixed media consisting of watercolor wash, painting, and pen and ink beautifully illustrate the vivid costumes used by the cast. A vocabulary list includes characters, places, and names used in the text.

P–3. Cruz, Manuel and Ruth. *A Chicano Christmas Story/Un Cuento Navideño Chicano.* Illus. by Manuel Cruz. South Pasadena, Calif.: Bilingual Educational Services, 1981. 48pp. pap. $3.95. ISBN: 0-86624-000-4, RM7.

On a ranch somewhere in the Southwest, a Chicano family is caught in an economic crunch at the peak of the Christmas season. Their giving spirit and generosity, however, restore the spirit of Christmas, symbolized by a Chicano Santa Claus who brings Diego and Elenita their first gifts from Santa. This hopeful story, illustrated with simple line drawings in two-tone pen and ink, is also available in sound filmstrip format.

3–6. De Gerez, Toni, adapter. *My Song Is a Piece of Jade: Poems of Ancient Mexico in English and Spanish/Mi Canción es un pedazo de Jade: Poemas del México Antiguo en Inglés y Español.* Illus. by William Stark. Boston and Toronto: Little, Brown, 1984. 45pp. o.p.

In this bilingual collection of ancient poems of the Toltecs of pre-Columbian Mexico, the English translations are as smooth flowing as those in Spanish. Both translations are derived from the Nahuatl language. The lovely watercolor illustrations enhance the design of the book, which places both translations of a poem on the same page. An illustrated glossary of items used by the Toltecs is included.

P–3. Delacre, Lulu, selector. *Arroz con Leche: Popular Songs and Rhymes from Latin America.* Illus. by Lulu Delacre. New York: Scholastic, 1989. 32pp. pap. $12.95. ISBN: 0-590-41887-4.

This dual nursery rhyme and music book includes the musical accompaniments to the most popular nursery rhymes from Mexico, Puerto Rico, and Argentina. Beautiful, soft pastel illustrations capture the sheer joy and kindred spirit of children at play in their natural surroundings. The translations, though not literal, capture the essence of play.

3–6. De Paola, Tomie, reteller. *The Lady of Guadalupe.* Illus. by the author. New York: Holiday House, 1980. 48pp. $14.95. ISBN: 0-8234-0373-4; pap. $5.95. ISBN: 0-8234-0403-X.

Our Lady of Guadalupe is known as the patron saint of Mexico and of the Américas. The popular religious story about this well-known icon is based on an eye-witness account of her appearance to Juan Diego, an Aztec Indian who delivered her message—to build a shrine at the site of a former Aztec temple—to the newly established Catholic bishop. The bishop finally became convinced of the authenticity of the miracle of roses and ordered a shrine built. Colorful, naive-style illustrations, typical of de Paola, augment an accurate rendition of the story.

3–6. García, María. *The Adventures of Connie and Diego/Las Aventuras de Connie y Diego.* Illus. by Malaquías Montoya. San Francisco: Children's Book Press/Imprenta de Libros Infantiles, 1986. 24pp. $12.95. ISBN: 0-89239-028-X.

Connie and Diego, two children of multi-ethnic origins, suffer the anxieties associated with feeling that they don't belong. In their desperation, they leave their home and travel to the land of the animals. They ask each animal they meet if they may join it, and each one refuses them shelter. The children finally realize that they must accept themselves for who they are. Bold, color illustrations by a well-known Chicano muralist enhance the story line.

3–6.   García, Richard. *My Aunt Otilia's Spirits/ Los Espiritos de Mi Tía Otilia.* Rev. ed. Illus. by Robin Cherin and Roger I. Reyes. San Francisco: Children's Book Press, 1987. 24pp. $12.95. ISBN: 0-89239-029-8.

This is a delightful, scary story about Aunt Otilia, the weird aunt from Puerto Rico who visits her kinfolk in San Francisco each year. Aunt Otilia delves into "spirits" in the evening when all is quiet. The result is a hilarious series of events that make Aunt Otilia "split," never to return, which pleases her nephew even though he receives a spanking for chasing his aunt's spirits away. The bilingual format adds to the usefulness of the text.

P–2.   Griego, Margot C. et al. *Tortillitas Para Mama and Other Nursery Rhymes.* Illus. by Barbara Cooney. New York: Holt, 1981. unp. ISBN: 0-03056-704-1.

Beloved nursery rhymes from the Spanish oral tradition are beautifully illustrated in deep colors by a noted children's illustrator. Unfortunately, most of the Mexican women in the illustrations are overweight. Also, children should understand that many of the illustrations portray rural rather than modern urban settings. The nursery rhymes are in both English and Spanish, though the English translations are more literal than rhyming.

5–8.   Guifford, Douglas. *Warriors, Gods, and Spirits from Central and South American Mythology.* Illus. by John Sibbick. World Mythologies Series. New York: Schocken Books, 1983. 132pp. o.p.

Alternating black-and-white pen-and-ink sketches and surreal, full-page color illustrations bring very much to life the monsters, giants, dwarfs, and ancient peoples of the many myths in this excellent collection. Information on the meaning and significance of the symbols of the animals and plants, a bibliography of reference sources, and an analytical index enhance the usefulness of this fine work.

K–3.   Janda, J. *The Legend of the Holy Child of Atocha.* Illus. by William Hart McNichols. New York and Mahwah, N.J.: Paulist Press, 1986. 45pp. pap. $2.95. ISBN: 0-8091-6559-7.

Here is the legend behind the statue of the Christ Child found in many home altars in the Southwest. The story is said to have originated in the old town of Atocha in Spain. It is said that the Christ Child wore out his sandals as he journeyed through the prisons, feeding the fathers from the town who were being held captive by the Moors during the days of the invasion. Tender line drawings in brown tones augment the simple story of a miracle.

P–3.   Kouzel, Daisy, adapter. *The Cuckoo's Reward: A Folktale from Mexico in Spanish and English/El Premio del Cuco: Cuento Popular de México en Español y Inglés.* Trans. by the author. Illus. by Earl Thollander. Garden City, N.Y.: Doubleday, 1977. unp. o.p.

One day Chac, the god of rain and harvest, gathers many birds—the owl, the crow, the cuckoo, the nightingale, and the sparrow—and warns them that they must all help save the crops from destruction at the hands of the god of fire. But the god of fire plays a trick on the birds and begins the destruction much sooner than anticipated. The cuckoo risks her life trying to save the crops and, in the process, loses her splendid feathers. In return for her bravery, the birds agree to care for her offspring forever. That is why today the cuckoo bird lays her eggs in other birds' nests. Here is an excellent recounting of this beloved etiological legend from ancient Mexico.

3–5.   Kurtycz, Marcos, and Ana García Kobeth, adapters. *Tigers and Opossums: Animal Legends.* Trans. by Felicia M. Hall. Illus. by the adapters. Boston and Toronto: Little, Brown, 1984. 46pp. $12.95. ISBN: 0-316-50718-0.

Why the hummingbird's cries are so beautiful, why the oppossum's tail is hairless, and why the bat flies through the night are some of the etiological tales that eloquently capture the spirit of wonder emanating from this collection. Finely sketched pen-and-ink drawings by well-established contemporary Mexican painters enhance the text.

3–6.   Kurusa. *The Streets Are Free.* Illus. by Monika Doppert. Trans. by Karen Englander.

Toronto: Annick Press, 1985. unp. pap. $6.95. ISBN: 0-920303-07-2; $12.95. ISBN: 0-920303-09-9.

See Kurusa's *La Calle es Libre* in the Spanish Fiction section of this Bibliography.

K–3. Martel, Cruz. *Yagua Days.* Illus. by Jerry Pinkney. New York: Dial, 1987. 34pp. pap. $3.95. ISBN: 0-80370-457-7.

Adán, a young Puerto Rican New Yorker, has long heard about "yagua days" in Puerto Rico but has never understood the significance. When he finally gets the opportunity to visit his relatives on the island, he discovers the joy and fun in the phrase. Black-and-white drawings capture Adan's joyful spirit and convey the fun and laughter of "yagua days."

3–6. Mohr, Nicholasa. *Felita.* Illus. by Ray Cruz. New York: Dial, 1979. 112pp. $12.89. ISBN: 0-8037-3144-2.

Felita, an eight-year-old Puerto Rican child growing up in New York City, experiences at an early age the pain and humiliation caused by prejudice and racism. She relates her indignation at being evicted from a new neighborhood and at not being accepted at the new school because of her nationality and her language. Felita's resilient spirit, however, as well as her tender relationship with her grandmother sustain her throughout her hardships.

4–6. _____. *Going Home.* New York: Dial, 1986. 176pp. $13.95. ISBN: 0-8037-0269-8.

In this sequel to *Felita*, the protagonist is now a growing adolescent who travels with her uncle to Puerto Rico, her parents' native home, for the first time. Felita discovers to her chagrin how much she feels out of place on this island that she had always heard called "home." She is humiliated by the island children who tease her for her lack of proficient Spanish and her "different" cultural upbringing. Another cultural shock takes place as Felita discovers the restrictive island upbringing, especially for girls. Her anxiety and frustration take their toll on her uncle, who had looked forward to sharing the beauty of

the island with her and who is disappointed with the turn of events. Another important young adult book by Mohr is *Nilda*.

K–6. Peña, Sylvia Cavazos, ed. *KiKiRiKi: Stories and Poems in English and Spanish for Children.* 2d ed. Illus. by Narciso Pena. Houston: Arte Publico, 1989. 116pp. pap. $7.50. ISBN: 0-685-34571-8.

Thirteen Spanish and fifteen English poems and short stories make up this anthology. Contributors include some well-known writers of Hispanic literature from throughout the United States, such as Nicholasa Mohr and Sandra Cisneros. Not all entries appear in both languages.

4–6. _____. *Tun-Ta-Ca-Tun: More Stories and Poems in English and Spanish for Children.* Houston: Arte Publico, 1985. 80pp. pap. $8.50. ISBN: 0-934770-43-3.

This unique anthology of short stories and poems emphasizes the cultural life of Hispanics. Stories range from a modern rendition of the legend of the poinsettia to Nicholasa Mohr's "The Conch Shell," a story of a little boy who finds himself holding on to an object that reminds him of home until he is able to accept the reality of his new environment. All entries appear in both languages.

P–3. Pomerantz, Charlotte. *The Tamarindo Puppy and Other Poems.* Illus. by Byron Barton. New York: Greenwillow, 1980. 31pp. o.p.

Poems ranging from sweet and tender to more interactive combine both Spanish and English to produce unique rhymes. Primitive illustrations in predominantly orange and yellow tones portray Puerto Rican children and animals in their island environment.

P–2. Prieto, Mariana. *The Wise Rooster/El Gallo Sábio.* Illus. by Lee Smith. New York: John Day, 1962. o.p.

As all the barnyard animals gather around the manger on Christmas Eve, they discover that they can talk. That evening they all agree that they should use their newfound voices to speak only of the special things that they will do for the newborn king. But when the time comes for the vain donkey Palladín to have his say, he begins to speak only of himself. The barnyard animals are stunned as they realize that Palladín can only stutter. Even more tragically, they too are no longer able to speak. Because of that, every year on Christmas Eve (La Noche Buena—the Good Night), you can hear the rooster crowing *Qué verguenza* (What a shame), a reminder of that brief time when the animals could speak the same language as humans. This Spanish legend is lovingly retold.

2–6. Rohmer, Harriet, adapter. *The Legend of Food Mountain/La Leyenda de la Montana de Alimento.* Illus. by Graciela Carrillo. Trans. by Alma Flor Ada and Rosalma Zubizarreta. San Francisco: Children's Book Press, 1982. 23pp. $12.95. ISBN: 0-89239-022-0.

When the great god Quetzalcoatl, the creator, first made the people of the earth, he forgot to provide them with needed nourishment. A red ant discovered food in the mountain, and Quetzalcoatl wanted the mountain moved so that the people could be nourished forever. The mountain was struck open by the rain god and the rain dwarfs stole all the food, which is why people pray to the rain god for food. Rohmer adapted this legend from one of the first picture-writing manuscripts of the Americas, and the color sketches incorporate many of the symbols used by the Aztecs. The bright, bold colors enhance the text.

2–6. _____, and Dorminster Wilson. *Mother Scorpion Country: A Legend from the Miskito Indians of Nicaragua/La Tierra del la Madre Escorpion: Una Leyenda de los Indios Miskitos de Nicaragua.* Illus. by Virginia Stearns. Trans. by Rosalma Zubizaretta and Alma Flor Ada. Stories from Central America. San Francisco: Children's Book Press, 1988. 31pp. $12.95. ISBN: 0-89239-032-8.

Kati and Naklili are a happily married couple from the Land of the Miskitos. When Kati dies, Naklili refuses to be separated from her and travels with her to Mother Scorpion Country, the land of the dead. While there, he realizes his happiness is short-lived because the living cannot share the beauty of the land. Illustrations in deep, bold colors greatly enhance this love story. The book has a bilingual format.

2–6. _____, and Mary Anchondo, adapters. *How We Came to the Fifth World/Como Vinimos al Quinto Mundo.* Rev. ed. Illus. by Graciela Carrillo. San Francisco: Children's Book Press, 1988. 24pp. $12.95. ISBN: 0-89239-024-7.

According to the Aztecs, the world was created in five epochs, each ruled by a god representing one of the four elements of nature—earth, air, fire, and water. How each world was created and how each was ultimately destroyed are the essence of this story. Dramatic, bold, color illustrations eloquently recount this popular myth.

2–6. _____, Octavio Chow, and Morris Vidaure. *The Invisible Hunters: A Legend from the Miskito Indians of Nicarágua/Los Cazadores Invisibles: Una Leyenda de los Indios Miskitos de Nicarágua.* Illus. by Joe Sam. Trans. by Rosalma Zubizarreta and Alma Flor Ada. San Francisco: Children's Book Press, 1987. 32pp. $12.95. ISBN: 0-89239-031-X.

Three hunters come into contact with another culture and begin to compromise their values and promises, violating the tribal laws set out by the Wari. The voices that people hear coming from the bushes near the village of Ulruas on the Coco River of Nicaragua are said to be the voices of these three hunters. The unique illustrations—mixed-media collages using marbleized paper—and the bilingual format complement the text.

2–4. Stanek, Muriel. *I Speak English for My Mom.* Illus. by Judith Friedman. New York: Albert Whitman, 1989. 32pp. $10.95. ISBN: 0-8075-3659-8.

Lupe, a young immigrant, serves as her family's translator. Her mom, a widow, does not know English and so is unable to communicate. Lupe finds herself translating at the dentist's office and even at her own parent-teacher conferences. Sometimes the task is overwhelming, especially when it interferes with playtime. But Lupe and her mom are brought closer together in that special relationship, and Lupe helps her mom with the decision to learn English. Tender black-and-white illustrations with Aztec border motifs complement the text.

1–3. Taha, Karen T. *A Gift for Tía Rosa.* Illus. by Dee de Rosa. Minneapolis: Dillon, 1986. 36pp. $10.95. ISBN: 0-87518-306-9.

Ten-year-old Carmela is saddened by the death of Tía Rosa, the elderly neighbor who taught her to knit. Tía Rosa died before being able to finish a blanket for her first-born granddaughter, whom she did not get to meet. Carmela realizes that the best gift she can give the baby is to finish the blanket Tía Rosa had begun. Full-color illustrations of modern-day Hispanics in urban settings add credence to a touching story.

Spanish

4–6. Armellada, Fray Cesareo de, reteller. *El Cocuyo y la Mora: Cuento de la Tribu Pemón* (The firefly and the raspberry: Legend of the Pemón Tribe). Adapted by Kurusa and Veronica Uriba. Illus. by Amelie Areco. Colección Cascada. Mexico, D.F.: Secretaria de Educación Pública, 1986. unp. $7.95. ISBN: 968-29-1176-1.

A raspberry falls in love with a firefly but is rejected because she is not as attractive. Intricate, colorful pen-and-ink drawings highlight this poignant, eloquently told love story. This is a traditional story of the Pemon Indians of Venezuela.

3–6. Arredondo, Inés. *História Verdadera de una Princesa.* Illus. by Enrique Rosquillas. Reloj de Cuentos Series. Mexico: Centro de Información y Desarrollo de la comunicación y la Literatura Infantiles (CIDCLI) and CONAFE, 1984. 37pp. $6.95. ISBN: 968-494-016-5.

Several biblical motifs are incorporated into the story of the young Mayan slave girl known in Mexican history as "La Malinche." Her linguistic abilities enabled her to communicate directly with the many tribes who joined with Hernando Cortés in the infamous defeat of the Aztecs by the Spanish conquerors. Excellent illustrations enrich the beauty of the story.

P–3. Barbot, Daniel. *Un Diente se Mueve* (A tooth moves). Illus. by Gian Calvi. Colección Ponte Poronte. Caracas: Ediciones Ekaré-Banco del Libro, 1981. 24pp. $5.55.

In this delightful story, Clarisse's tooth begins to wiggle. When the tooth comes out, Clarisse puts it under her pillow and dreams of Ratón Pérez, the equivalent of the tooth fairy in Spanish-speaking countries. Pérez the Mouse tells Clarisse about mouse life and how mice make jewels and ornaments from the teeth. Clarisse wakes up, the tooth is gone, and a coin is under her pillow in its place. Color illustrations by distinguished Brazilian Gian Calvi complement the text.

3–6. Barnet, Miguel, comp. *Los Perros Mudos: Fabulas Cubanas* (The mute dogs: Cuban fables). Illus. by Sergio Vesely. Madrid: Alfaguara, 1988. 136pp. pap. $5.95. ISBN: 84-204-4584-3.

Some of these stories from Cuban folklore can be used for storytelling or adapted for puppet shows. Although some are originally from Spain and others from Africa, all have been shaped by the Cuban experience. Black-and-white drawings illustrate the characters, mostly animals in how-and-why stories.

4–6. Bruni, Mary Ann Smothers. *El Sueño de Rosita.* Illus. by Thom Ricks. Trans. by Rogelio de Castro. San Antonio: TexArt Services, 1985. unp. $16.95. ISBN: 0-935857-02-8. (Dist. by Texas Monthly Press.*)

See Bruni's *Rosita's Christmas Wish* in the English Fiction section of this Bibliography.

K–4. Cueto, Mireya. *La boda de la ratita y más teatro-cuentos* (The mouse's wedding and more theater stories). Mexico City: Secretaría de Educación Pública, 1986. 94pp. $9.95. ISBN: 968-29-1145-1.

These easy plays from Mexico, which can be presented as puppet shows or performed by children, are a combination of Mexican culture and such universally loved stories as "The Blind Man and the Elephant." Several of the plays would be appropriate for Hispanic cultural celebrations. Directions and diagrams are provided for making puppets and for staging.

P–3. Darío, Ruben. *Margarita* (Margaret). 4th ed. Illus. by Monika Doppert. Colección Rimas y Adivinanzas. Caracas, Venezuela: Ediciones Ekaré-Banco del Libro, 1989. 46pp. $6.50. ISBN: 980-2570532.

Margarita, the dreamy princess, not only wishes upon a star but actually takes the heavenly body as her own. She is reprimanded by her father, who orders her to return the star. This delightful, brief story in verse form is a superb introduction to the writings of the great Nicaraguan poet. Exquisite, finely detailed line drawings augment the aesthetic quality of this treasure of a poetry book.

1–4. De la Colina, José. *El Mayor Nacimiento del mundo y sus Alrededores* (The largest nativity set in the world and its surroundings). 2d ed. Illus. by Elena Climent. Reloj de Cuentos Series. Colección del Jicote Arguendero. Mexico City: Centro de Información y Desarrollo de la Comunicación y la Literatura Infantiles (CIDCLI, SC), 1985. 32pp. $11.95. ISBN: 968-494-001-7.

This story incorporates the popular Mexican folk art tradition of constructing nativity scenes. *Tío* (Uncle) Catarino's favorite pastime is collecting objects useful for the construction of nativity sets. Each year, Tío Catarino constructs a bigger nativity scene, consuming first one room, then the entire house, until finally even the streets of the city become obstructed. The uncle dies, but one day the children receive a letter from him informing them that he has finally found the perfect place for his gigantic nativity scene—heaven.

1–4. De Paola, Tomie. *Nuestra Señora de Guadalupe.* Trans. by Pura Belpré. New York: Holiday House, 1980. 48pp. $14.95. ISBN: 0823-40372; 0823-404048, 0-8234-0374-2.

See de Paola's *The Lady of Guadalupe* in the English Fiction section of this Bibliography.

P–3. Feliciano Mendoza, Ester. *Nanas* (Nannies). Prologue by Margot Arce de Vasquez. Illus. by W. Clegg. Puerto Rico: Editorial Universitária, Universidad de Puerto Rico, 1985. 71pp. $8.00. ISBN: 0847-732002.

This is a reissue of a 1945 publication by the author, whose rhythmic lyrics radiate a delicate tenderness for the young child. The author has taken common children's folklore motifs and composed verses about them. The result is a highly creative work of art that emanates a spirit of deep love for children and childhood.

K–2. Fernández, Laura. *Mariposa* (Butterfly). Mexico City: Editorial Trillas, 1983. unp. $7.95. ISBN: 968-24-1555-1.

A butterfly wanted to fly to the sky and play with the wind. She was afraid to fly so high by herself, so she asked a boy to throw her a string when it was time to come down. After a wonderful flight, she was transformed into a beautiful kite (*papalote* in Spanish). At the end of the story, children are asked, "Did you know that the Aztec word for butterfly was papalotl?" This charming picture book is useful for introducing the origin of Nahuatl words into the Spanish vocabulary. Lovely color illustrations enhance the text.

K–3. _____. *Pájaros en la Cabeza* (Birds in my head). Mexico City: Editorial Trillas. 24pp. ISBN: 968-24-1554-3.

A little girl wakes up with bluebirds dancing in her head. They stay throughout the day, but at night they leave to sleep in their tree house. The little girl is sad, but she consoles herself with the knowledge that the birds live just outside her bedroom window. Fernández has formulated a story based on a quite popular folk expression. This book has won the Antoniorrobles prize, a children's literature award presented annually by IBBY-Mexico.

P–4. Gonzalez Diaz, Josemililio. *La niña y el cucubano: Poemas para los niños de Puerto Rico* (The girl and the firefly: Poems for the children of Puerto Rico). San Juan: Instituto de Cultura Puertorriquena, 1985. 75pp. $8.95. ISBN: 0-881-377-9.

The beauty and simplicity of these poems on childhood themes, the repetition with variations, and the play on words make this a good choice for sharing aloud.

5–8. Guifford, Douglas. *Guerreros, Dioses y Espíritus de la mitología de America Central y Sudamérica.* Illus. by John Sibbick. Trans. by Jose Luis Moreno. Madrid: Ediciones Anaya, 1984. 132pp. o.p.

See Guifford's *Warriors, Gods, and Spirits from Central and South American Mythology* in the English Fiction section of this Bibliography.

K–5. Guillén, Nicolás. *Por el Mar de las Antillas anda un Barco de Papel* (Through the waters of the Antilles floats a paper boat). Illus. by Horacio Elena. Salamanca, Spain: Loquez Ediciones, 1984. 34pp. $8.95. ISBN: 8-4853-34329.

This abridged version of thirty-three poems written by one of Cuba's best-loved poets also includes original verses for riddles and songs (without music) about animals and about children who pretend to be tiny animals. The equally imaginative illustrations complement the poet's intent of speaking from the heart to all island children.

4–6. Hinojosa, Francisco. *Al Golpe de Calcetín.* Illus. by Francisco González. Colección Espiral, Libros del Rincón SEP. Mexico City: Secretaría de Educación Pública, 1986. 55pp. ISBN: 968-29-1172-9.

In the early 1930s, a young newspaper boy inadvertently becomes involved with a group of sophisticated bank robbers. Descriptions of the bustle of life in Mexico City during those days are wonderfully incorporated into the exciting drama.

4–6. Isla, Carlos. *Los Líseres* (The tigers). Illus. by Felipe Saldarriaga. Mexico City: Centro de Información y Desarrollo de la Comunicación y la Literatura Infantiles (CIDCLI) and Consejo Nacional de Fomento Educativo (CONAFE), 1989. 38pp. $11.95. ISBN: 968-494-015-7.

In this Olmec legend from the village of Toztlán (now Santiago Tuxtla in the coastal state of Veracruz, Mexico), a fair-skinned baby is born with light hair, red eyes, and golden lashes. She is a phenomenon to the villagers, who begin to call her "corn-haired girl." One day, the girl is saved by a tiger during a volcanic eruption. As a result, the villagers name her the Virgin of the Volcano. Each year, a ritual dance is performed by local men who don costumes representing the tiger. The celebration takes place during the Feast of Santiago (St. James). The dance honors the Virgin of the Volcano and the tiger, but it is also a reminder of the clash of pre-Christian and Christian civilizations.

4–8. Jimenez, Juan Ramón. *Platero y Yo* (Platero and I). Edited with introduction, notes, and commentary by Ana Suarez Marmon. Spain: Biblioteca Didactica Anaya. $9.30.

In this classic Spanish children's novel, an endearing relationship develops between an old man and his beloved donkey, Platero. The old man converses with the animal, espousing its ideas and philosophies as both learn and share the beauty and sensibilities of life. This excellent edition with study notes, designed especially for classroom use, is particularly helpful as a discussion guide.

2–5. Keller, Christina, adapter. *La Capa del Morrocoy: Cuento Guajiro* (The cape of the Morrocoy: A Guajiro tale). Illus. by Kurusa. Caracas, Venezuela: Ekaré-Banco del Libro. 35pp. $7.95. ISBN: N/A.

In this etiological story set in the days when the animals took human form, Mushale (a *caricae*) steals the prettiest girls from the village and turns three of them into a butterfly, a bee, and a hummingbird. He meets his fate, however, when he encounters two less-than-friendly creatures who injure and disable him, reducing him to a giant turtle. Contrasting black-and-white and color illustrations using intricate geometric designs give the story an eerie sensation that is sure to hold readers to the dramatic conclusion.

3–6. Kurusa. *La Calle es Libre* (The streets are free). Illus. by Monika Doppert. Ediciones Ekaré, Colección Cascada. Mexico and Caracas, Venezuela: Banco del Libro and Secretaría de Educación Pública, 1986. unp. $10.95. ISBN: 968-29-1174-5.

With the overpopulation of the *barrios* in Caracas, the children's play space is becoming increasingly limited. But with the help of a local librarian, the children confront city hall, which promises a park but doesn't deliver. The neighborhood people then take over the task and build a safe park for the children to play in. Alternate black-and-white and color illustrations add to the text.

P–3. Lars, Claudia. *Escuela de Pájaros* (School of birds). Illus. by María Antonieta Ugarte. Coleción Cumiche. Costa Rica: Educa, 1986. 21pp. ISBN: N/A.

Lars, the well-known Salvadorian children's poet, has expanded on the themes of familiar nursery rhymes, creating more verses and rhymes with her own poetry.

4–8. Lyra, Carmen. *Cuentos de mi Tía Panchita* (Stories of my Aunt Francisca). 4th ed. San Jose: Educa. 1984. 152pp. $7.95. ISBN: 9977-23-135-4.

This collection of fairy tales, well known and loved in Costa Rica, is a rich source for storytelling. Almost half of the tales are *Tio Conejo* (Uncle Rabbit) stories.

4–6. Medero, Marinés. *Al Otro Lado de la Puerta* (At the other side of the door). Illus. by Gustavo Aceves. Colección Espiral, Libros del Rincón SEP. Mexico City: Secretaría de Educación Pública, 1986. 53pp. ISBN: 968-29-1171-0.

Ana, a young girl from a Creole family (Spaniards born in Mexico), listens from the next room as her father and his friends discuss the current state of affairs. As she becomes aware of the political turmoil in her country, Ana must face the reality of the injustice taking place in the mining town that is her home. Eighteenth-century Mexico comes to life in this historical novel.

5–8. Muria, Anna. *El Maravilloso Viaje de Nico Huehetl a Través de México* (The marvelous journey of Nico Huehetl through Mexico). Illus. by Felipe Davalos. Colección Narrativa Para Niños. Amecameca, Mexico: Editorial Amaquemecan, 1986. 116pp. $10.25. ISBN: 968-7205-19-9.

Nico sits in his classroom, listening to his teacher tell the story of Nils Helgerson's travels through Switzerland. The images evoked by the tale stimulate his own imagination and he wonders if he too could journey throughout Mexico on a beautiful Quetzal bird. His imaginary journey takes place instead on a golden-maned horse named Orovolante (Golden Flying One). Nico travels to the ends of the country, discovering a beauty he never knew existed, both in the panorama of the landscape and in the richness of the culture and the history. When he returns from his journey, business is as usual, and no one believes his story of what he has seen. However, when his teacher tries to explain the concept of *forever*—meaning past, present, and future—Nico fully understands. This story is excellent for older readers as well as for classroom read-aloud.

2–6. Palma, Marigloria. *Teatro Infantil* (Children's theater). San Juan: Instituto de Cultura Puertorriquena, 1985. 153pp. $7.50. ISBN: 0-86581-385-X.

Here are two collections of plays from Puerto Rico that children can present. These plays have a special humor and a richness of beauty and language that would lend them to cultural presentations.

2–5. Paz Ipuana, Ramon, reteller. *El Conejo y el Mapurite: Cuento Guajiro* (The rabbit and the skunk: A Guajiro tale). Adapted by Veronica Uribe. Illus. by Vicky Sempere. Caracas, Venezuela: Ediciones Ekaré-Banco del Libro, 1979. 36pp. $7.95.

Here is another etiological tale told by the Mapurite (Skunk), a wise character with such beady eyes that he is unable to see that he is being tricked by the rabbit. Eventually, however, he discovers the rabbit's deception and devises a trick that helps to explain why the rabbit's mouth and nose are forever trembling. Wonderfully contrasting black-and-white and color illustrations vividly portray the two characters at their ingenious best.

2–5. Perera, Hilda. *Cuentos Para Chicos y Grandes* (Stories for young and old). Illus. by Ana Bermejo. Valladolid, Spain: Miñon, 1976. 49pp. $7.50. ISBN: 8435501140.

This collection of short stories is the winner of the famed Prémio Lazarillo, a prize given for the best contribution to children's literature in Spain. Perera is a highly creative author who uses much humor in her stories. She also endows animals with the sensitivities normally attributed to humans, thus allowing animals to speak of the injustices that humans commit toward them.

4–8. _____. *Kike*. 5th ed. Col. barco de Vapor. Serie Naranja. Madrid: S.M., 1984. 123pp. $5.95. ISBN: 84-348-1288-6.

One of the few stories in Spanish about a new immigrant Hispanic family, this tells of four children (including teenagers) who come to the United States from Cuba. There are many similarities between their experiences and those of any immigrant child. The first-person narrative is told with much humor and empathy and in an idiomatic and often funny style.

1–3. Peterson, Aline. *El Papalote y el Nopal* (The kite and the cactus). Illus. by Heraclio Ramirez. Colección Reloj de Cuentos. Mexico: Centro de Información y Desarrollo de la Comunicación y la Literatura Infantiles (CIDCLI) and Consejo Nacional de Fomento Educativo (CONAFE), 1985. 38pp. $11.95. ISBN: 968-494-019-X.

A kite desires to fly higher than the birds in the sky, until one day a cloud of rain causes her to fall upon a cactus plant. The cactus, in its desire to please the kite and keep her from leaving, grants her wish to grow into a beautiful white flower. The kite, however, values her freedom to fly more than anything else. This modern story, written as a traditional etiological legend, is illustrated in deep colors that reflect the beauty of the Mexican landscape.

3–6. Remolina, Tere. *En Busca de la Lluvia* (In search of the rain). Cuentos Mexiquenses Series. Illus. by Alejandra Thomé. Amecameca, México: Editorial Amaquemecan, 1990. 57pp. $7.95. ISBN: 968-7205-27-X.

A young child leaves his home in a small village, seaching for water for his plant. His search becomes a journey that takes him to many interesting and unusual places and

teaches him about the sad condition of the environment, caused by the carelessness and callousness of humans and industry. The author has created realistic fiction with a thought-provoking ecology theme.

P–2. Robleda Moguel, Margarita. *Pulgas, el perro de Jose Luis* (Flea, Jose Luis's dog). Cuentos para pulgitas Series. Illus. by Maribel Suarez. Mexico City: Sistemas Tecnicos de Edicion (SITESA), 1990. unp. ISBN: 968-6394-70-2.

Little Jose Luis has much fun naming his dog "Flea" and the fleas "Dog" until the day his mother wants to get rid of the "fleas." When mother discovers the confusion, she explains to Jose Luis the logic in calling things by their appropriate name. The whimsical illustrations greatly enhance the telling of this story by the 1991 winner of the Juan de la Cabada Mexican Children's Literature Award. Other books in the series include *El Gato de las Mil Narices* (The cat with a thousand noses) based on a folklore rhyme, and *El Carrito de Monchito* (Monchito's car).

3–6. Robles Boza, Eduardo (Tío Patota). *La Abuela del Juicio* (The grandmother of wisdom). Illus. by Gloria Calderas Lim. Mexico City: Editorial Trillas, 1984. 24pp. $7.95. ISBN: 968-24-1767-8.

Four curious children want to know why an elderly woman carries an old trunk wherever she goes. They learn of the trunk's meaning in her life and are personally affected when they hear of her sudden death. Robles Boza, a renowned Mexican children's author and winner of the IBBY Hans Christian Andersen Award, has also written other stories in this series entitled *Los Cuentos de Tío Patota* (The stories of Uncle Bigfoot).

K–6. Walsh, Maria Elena. *Tutu Maramba*. 4th ed. Illus. by Vilar. Buenos Aires, Argentina: Editorial Sudamericana, 1976. 98pp. $9.95. ISBN: N/A.

This delightful poetry by Argentina's renowned children's author is guaranteed to make children everywhere laugh. Walsh's characters come alive through the words that she has so carefully chosen to describe their deeds. Two-tone pen-and-ink illustrations are equally hilarious and add further delight to her poetry. Other works by Walsh include *Manuelita* (1987), *La Reina Batata* (1987), and *El Reino del Reves* (1986). This volume is an excellent choice for oral Spanish-language development.

1–3. Yturbide, Teresa Castello. *Cuentos de Pascuala* (Pascuala's stories). Illus. by Carlos Palleiro. Foreword by Elena Poniatowska. Colección para leer con voz Alta. Mexico City: Consejo Nacional de Fomento Educativo (CONAFE), 1986. 62pp. $10.25. ISBN: 968-29-177-X.

Nine fairy stories and folktales originally published in 1945 are collected by the author under the pseudonym Pascuala Corona. The stories are classic folktales of European and Indo-European extraction, but, in the course of their telling by the *nanas* (nannies) to children in the days of old, they have incorporated the flavor of the Mexican spirit. Modernistic line drawings and woodcuts in two and three tones update these stories, which are excellent storytelling material.

4–6. Zak, Monica. *Radda min Djungel*. Illus. by Bengt-Arne Runnerstrom. Switzerland: Broom, 1987. *Salven Mi Selva*. Illus. by Bengt-Arne Runnerstrom. Mexico City: SITESA (Sistemas Tecnicos de Edición, 1989. $12.95. ISBN: 968-6048-24-3; pap. $7.95. ISBN: 968-604-23-5.

Omar is a bright, serious student who listens daily to the news. One day he hears the tragic story of the destruction of the rain forests in Mexico. When he discovers that there is only one rain forest left in the entire country, he begins a campaign to save it by first writing a letter to the President. He has the help and encouragement of his father, who prides himself on being attentive to the needs of his son, and together they share many exciting and dangerous adventures to accomplish their mission. This realistic narrative is based on the true story of an eight-year-old boy's quest to save Mexico's sole remaining rain forest in the Lacandona area. Color wash illustrations depict a modern Mexico shortly after the earthquake.

P–3. Zendrera, C., adapter. *Yaci y su Muneca: Cuento Popular de Brazil*. 2d ed. Illus. by Gloria Carasusan Ballve. Barcelona, Spain: Editorial Juventud, 1981. 16pp. $5.95. ISBN: 8426156045.

Yaci's mother threatens to take away the child's precious doll if she continues to disobey. Yaci, taking her mother's warnings literally, hides her doll at the edge of the river, but the rains wash the doll away and she cannot find it when the rains subside. Soft, pastel crayon drawings tenderly illustrate this popular Brazilian legend of how corn came to grow in a small village amidst the great forest. A simple yet useful craft idea, making a corn husk doll, is included.

NONFICTION

English

1–3. Brown, Tricia, *Hello Amigos*. Photographs by Fran Ortiz. New York: Holt, 1986. unp. $12.95. ISBN: 08050-0090-9.

A modern and realistic portrayal of a young Hispanic child living in the United States is presented in sharp black-and-white photographs by an award-winning photojournalist. Frankie, a Mexican-American child, shares with us his family, social, and cultural life in the Mission District of San Francisco. A glossary of the Spanish words Frankie uses is included, along with their pronunciation.

5–adult. Catalano, Julie. *The Mexican Americans*. Introduction by Patrick Moynihan. The Peoples of North America Series. New York: Chelsea House, 1988. $17.95. ISBN: 0-87754-857-9; 1989, 95pp. pap. $9.95. ISBN: 0-7910-0272-1.

In presenting many black-and-white photographs of such important figures as former New Mexico governors Jerry Apodaca and Toney Anaya and noted historian Ernesto Galarza, the author has produced an important historical resource. This book could easily serve as a useful supplement to the limited material currently available in textbooks on the history and accomplishments of Mexican Americans. However, reference to the fierce woman activist pictured on the cover, Ema Tenayuca, who led a strike of over 10,000 pecan shellers in the 1940s, is omitted. Other titles in the series include *Cuban Americans*, *The Central Americans*, and *The Dominican Americans*.

1–7. Garza, Carmen Lomas, with Harriet Rohmer. *Family Pictures/Cuadros de Familia*. Illus. by Carmen Lomas Garza. Trans. by Rosalma Zubizarreta. San Francisco: Children's Book Press, 1990. 32pp. $12.95. ISBN: 0-89239-050-6.

Beautiful, color illustrations evoke images of a South Texas childhood filled with the warmth of a loving family and many caring adults. Pictured are a family *tamalada* (the gathering where tamales are prepared for a special occasion), a day at South Padre Island, and an outing to the *feria* (fair) in nearby Reynosa, Mexico. The accompanying text describes the many pleasant gatherings and events. The illustrator is a nationally renowned Mexican-American artist known for the fine detail in her work. This excellent book will stimulate family discussions of traditions and customs past and present.

5–12. Harlan, Judith. *Hispanic Voters: A Voice in American Politics*. Photos. New York: Watts, 1988. 112pp. $12.80. ISBN: 0-531-10586-5.

Harlan clarifies the distinct subgroups of Hispanics and then synthesizes the key issues affecting Hispanics nationwide, namely immigration reform, bilingual education, voting rights, and single member districts. The author provides the historical background to the elections of such high-profile Hispanic figures as Former Mayor Henry Cisneros of San Antonio, Federico Pena of Denver, and former New Mexico governor Anaya. The work of the Southwest Voter Registration and Education Project headed by the late William Velasquez is also noted.

5–8. Haskins, James. *The New Americans: Cuban Boat People*. Hillside, N.J.: Enslow, 1982. 64pp. $12.95. ISBN: 0-8947-00595.

The author documents the plight of 25,000 Cuban refugees who were transported from the island of Mariel in what is now referred to as the Mariel airlift. Black-and-white news photos throughout add to the impact of the text.

K–3. Lewis, Thomas P. *Hill of Fire*. Illus. by Joan Sandin. I Can Read Book and Cassette Library Series. New York: Harper and Row, 1987. 59pp. pap. $3.50. ISBN: 0-06-44040-0.

Earth-tone brown and glowing orange watercolors depict the 1943 eruption of the volcano Paricutin. The eruption is witnessed by a farmer who complains of being bored with the uneventfulness of life in his small village in Mexico. The illustrations depict village farmers dressed in the peasant outfits typical of that time period.

5–8. Meltzer, Milton. *The Hispanic Americans*. Photographs by Morrie Campi and Catherine Neren. Crowell, New York: Crowell, 1982. 149pp. $13.95. ISBN: 0-690-04110-1; PLB. $13.89. ISBN: 0-690-04111-X.

Meltzer's succinct writing style is brief yet to the point. He dispels the myth of Hispanics as newcomers and outlines the three distinct struggles each subgroup of Hispanics has undergone in the United States. Two chapters are devoted to issues of importance to Hispanics: bilingual education and stereotyping. A superb bibliography will assist further reading and research.

5–adult. Morey, Janet, and Wendy Dunn. *Famous Mexican Americans*. Photos. New York: Cobblehill Books, 1989. $14.95. ISBN: 0-525-65012-1.

In this collective biography, readers will discover many prominent community leaders who have made substantial contributions in their respective fields. Among the nine men featured are Henry Cisneros, Luis Valdez, the late Willie Velasquez, and Edward James Olmos. Notable women include Blandina Cardenas Ramirez, former member of the U.S. Commission on Civil Rights during the Carter administration; and Vilma Martinez, former chief counsel of the Mexican-American Legal Defense and Education Fund.

3–6. Perl, Lila. *Piñatas and Paper Flowers: Holidays of the Americas in English and Spanish/ Piñatas y Flores de Papel: Fiestas de las Américas en Inglés y Español.* Illus. by Victoria de Larrea. Spanish version by Alma Flor Ada. New York: Clarion, 1983. 91pp. $12.95. ISBN: 0-89919-112-6; pap. $4.50. ISBN: 0-89919-155-X.

Two-tone pen-and-ink caricatures portray children and their families participating in civic and cultural celebrations. The bilingual text includes descriptions of the most popular celebrations from North America (including Mexico and the United States), South America, and Puerto Rico.

5–8. Pinchot, Jane. *The Mexicans in America.* Rev. ed. The In America Series. Minneapolis: Lerner, 1989. 95pp. $9.95. ISBN: 0-8225-0222-4; pap. $3.95. ISBN: 0-8225-1016-2.

A concise history of the Mexican-American people, from the Aztec civilization through the conquest to modern times, appears in this particularly useful text that provides essential information many textbooks gloss over or ignore. Another relevant title in the series is *The Puerto Ricans in America.*

3–6. Roberts, Maurice. *Cesar Chavez and La Causa.* Picture Book Biographies. Chicago: Children's Press, 1986. 31pp. $12.60. ISBN: 0-516-03484-7.

This biography updates the life story of one of America's most well-known Mexican-American leaders. Numerous recent family photographs portray a history of involvement in seeking justice for farm workers. Photographs of the first successful American consumer boycott of grapes are included. A chronological listing of significant events in the life of Chavez and in the history of the union, and an easy-to-read, large-print format add to the usefulness of this beginning biography for young readers. A Spanish-language edition is also available.

3–5. _____. *Henry Cisneros: Mexican American Mayor.* Picture Book Biographies. Chicago: Children's Press, 1986. 32pp. $3.95. ISBN: 0-516-03485-5.

Numerous black-and-white and brown-tone photographs of former San Antonio (Texas) Mayor Henry Cisneros tell the story of the first Hispanic mayor of one of the largest cities in America. Special focus is placed on the mayor's heritage, a value instilled by his grandfather. A time line highlights milestones in the life of this prominent national figure.

4–8. Santos, Richard G. *Diaros de Vacaciones/ Vacation Diaries.* Illus. by Jesus Maria "Chista" Cantu. Photographs by Cynthia Ann Santos and Deborah Ann Zamora. San Antonio: Richard G. Santos,* 1979. 46pp. $10.95. ISBN: N/A.

Two cousins, young Mexican-American girls, journey through the Southwest on their summer vacation, each keeping a travel diary and photographing the many historical places and cultural events they encounter. Both diaries are simply written yet nicely introduce to young readers the beauty of the culture and the land. Alphabetical lists of colloquial words used in the narrative and of the places visited add much to an informative and entertaining text.

4–6. _____. *Origin of Spanish Names/Como te Llamas y Porque te Llamas Asi.* Illus. by Humberto N. Cavazos. Photographs by Cynthia Ann Santos and Deborah A. Zamora. San Antonio: Richard G. Santos,* 1981.

The author, a historian, here provides a brief history of the Spanish language as well as a beginning etymology of Spanish names. An alphabetical listing of surnames as well as feminine and masculine first names is included. Children and adults alike will be fascinated to find the etymology of their name in this handsome bilingual volume. The black-and-white pen-and-ink sketches and the black-and-white photographs of archival material add authenticity to the historical perspective.

P–3. Schon, Isabel, collector and translator, with R. R. Chalquest. *Doña Blanca and Other Hispanic Nursery Rhymes and Games.* Minneapolis, Minn.: Denison, 1983. 46pp.

Many games popular with Hispanic children are recorded from the childhood memories of the author. Illustrated in simple, two-tone drawings, the bilingual text includes instructions for playing each game. This is a particularly good source for the Spanish text of popular games and rhymes.

4–6. Villacana, Eugenio. *Viva Morélia.* Illus. by Elsa Manriquez. New York: Evans, 1972. 63pp. $6.95. ISBN: 0-87131-098-8.

The many rituals and customs practiced in the state of Michoacán, Mexico, an area rich in the blending of Tarascan (Indian) and Spanish cultures, are seen here through the eyes of a child. Useful as an introduction to anthropological studies, the book includes a glossary of Spanish terms and their pronunciations.

Spanish

4–6. De Teresa, Claudia, and Antonio Reina. *Construcción del Templo Mayor de México Tenochtitlán* (Construction of the Major Temple of Mexico Tenochtitlán). Mexico: Aconcagua Ediciones y Publicaciones, 1986. unp. $10.50. ISBN: 968-6000-19-4.

In 1978, a crew from the city light company, working on an underground cable, dug directly underneath the *Zocalo* (square) area next to the Cathedral of Mexico City. They hit a piece of solid rock that turned out to be the statue of the goddess Cooyolxauhqui and, shortly after, discovered an entire buried city, all that remained after the fierce Spanish conquerors destroyed all traces of Aztec civilization. In this large-sized book in the style of David Macaulay's series on buildings, the authors accurately and precisely reconstruct the great detail and planning of that great city. A concise history of the Aztecs is included. Abundant, finely detailed pen-and-ink drawings help young readers visualize the reconstructed city. A vocabulary list is provided to help students define words specific to the names of the gods and goddesses of the period.

2–6. Gerson, Sara, and Shulamit Goldsmit. *Las culturas prehispanicas: Olmecas, Zapotecos,* *Mixtecos, Teotihuacanos, Toltecas* (Pre-Hispanic cultures). Cronito en la História Series. Mexico City: Editorial Trillas, 1987. 32pp. ISBN: 968-24-2310-4.

Rina and Ricardo, two modern-day Mexican children, learn the exciting history of their country with the help of Cronito, a talkative reporter who lives in books and hides behind the dates of history. Cronito makes history come alive for children by giving them eyewitness accounts of his experiences with such key figures as Quetzalcoatl and the other great gods. Lively, color illustrations of everyday activities in each culture enhance the book's effectiveness. Other books in the series include *El encuentro* (The encounter) and *La civilización maya* (Mayan civilization).

2–6. Grupo CUICA (Cultura Infantil como alternativa). *Día de muertos: Disfrázate y juega* (Day of the Dead: Dress in costume and play). Mexico City: SITESA (Sistemas Técnicos de Edición), 1988. 40pp. $3.95. ISBN: 968-6135-81-2.

This wonderful collection of crafts, games, and foods for the celebration of the Day of the Dead will help bring the tradition to life for children. Many illustrations and diagrams help the reader follow the instructions and get into the spirit of the holiday.

3–6. Jacob, Ester. *Como Leer un Códice* (How to read a codex). Illus. by Bruno Lopez. Mexico City: Editorial Trillas, 1987. $10.95. ISBN: 968-24-2354-6.

Written in the style of a museum guidebook, this volume is filled with brilliant, color reproductions of the picture writing taken from the ancient books (codices) of the Mexica Indians of Mexico. The simple, easy-to-follow text includes questions to stimulate reader responses.

3–6. *Las Tortugas del Mar* (The turtles of the sea). 3rd ed. Illus. by Felipe Dávalos. Serie Educación Ambiental. Mexico City: Consejo Nacional de Fomento Educativo (CONAFE), 1987. 47pp. $8.95. ISBN: 968-29-0261-4.

This informative book about the rare giant sea turtles found along the Mexican Pacific and Gulf coasts offers detailed illustrations of the reproductive process of turtles and the phenomenon of egg burying. The danger of extinction caused by other animals and humans is also discussed, as are the different classes of sea turtles and turtle by-products. Handsomely illustrated by the winner of the 1986 Ezra Jack Keats Award, the book provides an accompanying etiological legend about how the turtle came to have its shattered back.

Roberts, Maurice. *César Chávez y la Causa.* Chicago: Children's Press, 1986. 32pp. $9.95. ISBN: 0-516334840.

_____. *Henry Cisneros: Alcalde México-Americano.* Trans. by Roberto Franco. Chicago: Children's Press, 1988. 30pp. $9.95. ISBN: 0-5163-34859.

See the author's *Cesar Chavez and La Causa* and *Henry Cisneros: Mexican American Mayor* in the English Nonfiction section of this Bibliography.

4–6. Rojas Mix, Miguel. *La Tierra de Paloma: Pequena Historia de America Latina.* Vol I. (Paloma's land: Brief history of Latin America). De la Serpiente Emplumada al Tío Conejo (From the Plumed Serpent to Uncle Rabbit). Illus. by Gloria Uribe. Barcelona, Spain: Editorial Lumen, 1981. 119pp. $8.95. ISBN: 84-264-3038-4.

Paloma, the inquisitive daughter of the author, asks endless questions, which unveil a history of the Americas as explained to her by her father, a former university professor who is now a lawyer. Combining past and present settings, the book offers an ingenious way to introduce history to children.

1–3. Urrutia, Christina, and Marcial Camilo. *El Maíz* (The corn). Colección Piñata. Serie: La Flora. Illus. by Marcial Camilo. Mexico City: Editorial Patria/Fundación E. Gutman, 1981. 47pp. $9.95. ISBN: 968-39-0004-6.

Deep, rich colors vibrantly convey a typical day in the life of a village in Mexico where all family members participate in harvesting the corn. The festive communal gathering, during which the kernels are separated from the stalk and stored for future use, is also portrayed in the energetic illustrations of this book, one of a series on the flora of Mexico. Other series in this collection focus on art (puppetry, sounds, rhymes), materials (wool, paper, silk, sugar, chocolate, color mixing), social life (city and rural life, the market), stories and legends, the country, and the environment. Each book contains a one-page activity corner as well as information about the author and illustrator.

3–6. Yturbide, Teresa Castelo, and Monica Martin de Castillo. *El Niño Dulcero.* 2d ed. Illus. by Maribel Suárez. Mexico: Centro de Información y Desarrollo de la Comunicación y la Literatura Infantiles (CIDCLI) and CeCme, 1988. 40pp. $11.95. ISBN: N/A.

This nicely illustrated recipe book (for children with adult supervision) contains instructions for making seventeen traditional candies from various regions in Mexico. An excellent introduction gives a history of candy-making and selling, beginning with Hernando Cortés, who brought sugar cane to Mexico. Included is a recipe for making sugar-candy skulls for Day of the Dead celebrations.

MEDIA AUDIOVISUAL MATERIALS

English

P–3. Cruz, Manuel and Ruth. *A Chicano Christmas Story/Un Cuento Navideño Chicano.* Pasadena, Calif.: Bilingual Educational Services,* 1980. One book, one filmstrip, two cassettes.

See the authors' *A Chicano Christmas Story* in the English Fiction section of this Bibliography.

P–3. Hayes, Joe. *No Way, José; De Ningura Manera, José (A Story in Two Languages).* New Mexico: Trails West Publishing, 1986. unp. pap. $3.95. ISBN: 0-939729-00-8; cassette and book: $7.95. ISBN: 0-939729-01-6.

José the rooster has difficulty getting his animal friends to help him clean his beak so he can be presentable at the wedding of his Uncle Perico (parrot), until he stumbles across some ghosts in the graveyard who scare the animals into helping him. Hayes combines folktale motifs with popular clichés ("No way, José") in this cumulative story to create a modern, not-so-scary scary story. Appropriate for Halloween, the text is illustrated in two-tone reds.

P–3. Lewis, Thomas P. *Hill of Fire.* New York: Harper and Row, 1987. 64pp. $10.89. ISBN: 0-694-00175-9.

Lewis records the first-person account of a bored farmer who witnessed the marvelous eruption of the volcano Pericutín in Uruapán, Mexico, in the 1940s.

P–5. Paz, Suni. *Canciones para el recreo* (Children's songs for the playground). Folkways 7850. 1977. $9.95. Sound recording.

Some of the songs in this wonderful collection are from folklore while others were written by respected children's authors and set to music by Suni Paz. Included are songs from Argentina, Puerto Rico, and Chile.

Spanish

P–3. Diaz Roig, Mercedes, and Maria Teresa Miaja. *Naranja Dulce, Limón Partido: Antología de la Lírica Infantil Mexicana.* Illus. by Illiana Fuentes. Mexico: El Colegio de México, Centro de Estudios Linguisticos y Literarios, 1979. 150pp. $12.00. Cassette and book.

This excellent anthology, drawn primarily from interviews with primary sources conducted by students from the Colegio de México, is a panorama of rhymes, riddles, formulas, lullabies, songs, games, verses for piñata parties, and *villancicos* (Spanish Christmas songs). Informative end notes, an excellent glossary that provides the etymology of names as well as their current usage, a thorough bibliography, and a quick-reference index combine to make this a very useful work. The cassette has children singing, reciting, and chanting their favorite riddles.

Exquisite black-and-white pen-and-ink drawings handsomely illustrate the text.

P–3. Grupo CUICA (Cultura Infantil como alternativa, A.C.). *Mi Libro de Navidad: Cuentos, Canciones y Pasatiempos.* Sistemas Tecnicos de Edición, 1987. Cassette and book.

These bilingual (Nahuatl and Spanish) stories and riddles about Christmas-related themes include *villancicos*, the Christmas songs sung by the shepherds and originating in Spain. The cover of the activity book features a color illustration of a traditional star-shaped piñata. The activity book contains the text for the stories and riddles as well as crossword puzzles for quiet-time activities.

P–3. Orozco, Jose Luis. *Lírica Infantil con Jose Luis Orozco: Hispanic Children's Folklore.* 3 vols. Berkeley, Calif.: Arco Iris Records,* 1986. $10.00 each. Sound recording.

The Raffi of Hispanic children's entertainment, Orozco incorporates the well-known sounds of Mexican songs commonly heard at home or on the radio into his repertoire of songs that elicit children's active participation. Volume 2 is particularly useful for reenacting the traditional games of Hispanic folklore. A volume of sheer fun and enjoyment.

P–3. Puncel, Maria, and Suni Paz. *El Patio de mi casa y otras canciones infantiles* (The patio of my house and other children's songs). Newark, N.J.: Altea/Santillana, 1988. $11.95. Book and cassette.

_____. *Estaba la pajara pinta y otras rimas infantiles* (The spotted bird and other nursery rhymes). Newark, N.J.: Altea/Santillana, 1988. $11.95. Book and cassette.

_____. *Estaba la pastora y otras canciones infantiles* (There was the shepherdess and other children's songs). Newark, N.J.: Altea/Santillana, 1988. $11.95. Book and cassette.

_____. *Manana es domingo y otras rimas infantiles* (Tomorrow is Sunday and other nursery rhymes). Newark, N.J.: Altea/Santillana, 1988. $11.95. Book and cassette.

These books and cassettes make available, in quality recordings, the wonderful music of

Suni Paz, Argentine-American singer and composer. The books, published in Spain, have lovely, watercolor illustrations and make a very nice introduction to traditional Hispanic nursery rhymes and songs. The same titles are also available in Big Book (22″ by 15″) format for the teacher or librarian.

K–6. Vela, Irma Saldivar. *Bailes a colores.* (Dances to colors). Austin, Tex.: American Universal Art Forms Corporation.* $27.75. Kit.

K–4. Yurchenco, Henrietta. *Children's Songs and Games from Ecuador, Mexico, and Puerto Rico.* Princeton: Folkways FC 7854. 1963. $9.95. Sound recordings.

This two-record collection of traditional songs and games features children from each country singing or chanting without accompaniment. Notes and translations are provided, along with directions for playing the games. This is an excellent source for many of the best-known and much-loved games.

PROGRAMMING IDEAS

CINCO DE MAYO

Cinco de Mayo, the Fifth of May, celebrates people's desire to be free from foreign invaders. Shortly after Mexico's independence from Spain, civil war broke out. One faction called on Napoleon for help in overthrowing the government. The French, however, were defeated in the Battle of Puebla on May 5, 1862. The French army fled and the Mexicans kept control of the city. Cinco de Mayo is a national holiday in Mexico and is a special day for the celebration of Mexican-American culture in the United States. Many elementary schools throughout the United States designate May as Hispanic Heritage Month.

Storytelling

The telling of fairy tales and folktales from Mexican culture is an excellent way to introduce to children the rich heritage rooted in the oral tradition. The following titles are recommended for a special storytelling program:

Bierhorst, John. *The Hungry Woman: Myths and Legends of the Aztecs* (see p. 136).

Blackmore, Vivien. *Why Corn Is Golden: Stories about Plants.*[†2]

Brenner, Anita. *The Boy Who Could Do Anything and Other Mexican Folktales.*[†]

Kouzel, Daisy. *The Cuckoo's Reward: A Folktale from Mexico in Spanish and English/El Premio del Cuco: Cuento Popular de México en Español e Inglés.*[†]

Rohmer, Harriet. *The Legend of Food Mountain/ La Leyenda de la Montana de Alimento.*[†]

_____and Mary Anchondo, adapters. *How We Came to the Fifth World/Como Vinomos al Quinto Mundo.*[†]

Crafts

PIÑATAS

After the storytelling session, the children can create a small *piñata* (papier-mâché figurine) as shown in figure 1.

Materials
  Tissue paper in four or five bright colors
  Scissors
  Ribbon or string in bright colors
  Styrofoam or paper cups
  Celophane tape
  Candy or small toys (optional)

Directions
  1. Cut the tissue paper into strips approximately eight inches long and three inches wide. Cut two-inch fringes along the width of each strip. Use six to eight strips per piñata.
  2. Tape two styrofoam or paper cups together at the rims. (Add candy or toys before taping, if desired.)
  3. Overlap the strips of tissue paper, beginning at one end of the piñata and working in one direction only (either top to bottom or bottom to top). Remember, you are trying to create fullness with the fringes of the tissue paper strips.
  4. Loop the string and tape the two ends together in the center of the top of your piñata.

[2] Titles marked with a dagger (†) have complete annotations in the Bibliography for this chapter.

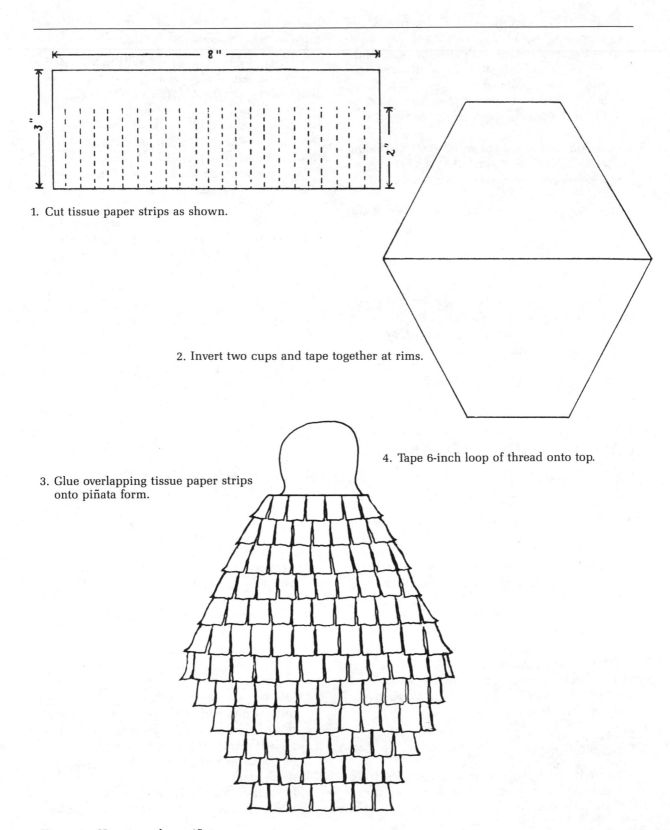

1. Cut tissue paper strips as shown.

2. Invert two cups and tape together at rims.

4. Tape 6-inch loop of thread onto top.

3. Glue overlapping tissue paper strips onto piñata form.

Figure 1.   How to make a piñata

PAPEL PICADO

Papel picado (cut paper) is a decorative craft in which elaborate designs are cut into square pieces of tissue paper (see figure 2). These colorful decorations can transform any area with a festive look.

Materials
Tissue paper cut in twelve-inch squares
String
Tape
Scissors
Glue

Directions
1. Depending on the age of the children, draw various designs onto a main pattern before beginning the project. Fold the pattern square in half and draw the design onto half of the tissue paper.
2. Cut out the inside shape of the design.
3. Open the folded square. When unfolded, the design will appear on the entire paper square.
4. Fold the top of the square one inch over a piece of string cut to whatever length you need and glue it.
5. As an alternative, overlay the open square onto a piece of construction paper of the same size but a complementary color, thus giving the design a frame.

For a more detailed description with illustrations for designing *papel picado*, see Salinas-Norman's *Indo-Hispanic Folk Art Traditions I*, pp. 20–21, and *Indo-Hispanic Folk Art Traditions II*, pp. 12–15 (see the Program Resources section).

References

Marcus, Rebecca B., and Judith Marcus. *Fiesta Time in Mexico.* Illus. by Bert Dodson. Champaign, Ill.: Garrard, 1974. ISBN: 0-8116-4953-9.

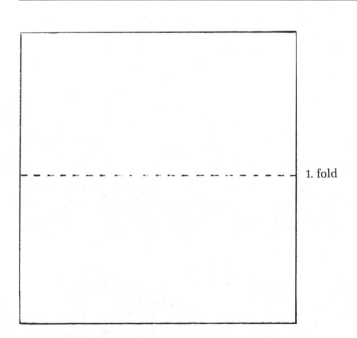

1. fold

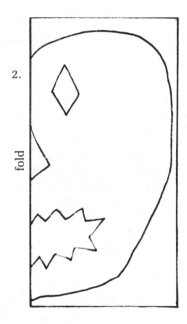

2.

fold

1. Fold 12″ by 12″ tissue sheet in half.
2. Draw skeleton design onto tissue paper and cut out.

Figure 2. Papel picado for the Day of the Dead

DAY OF THE DEAD/DIA DE LOS MUERTOS (November 1 and 2)

Day of the Dead is a ritual that honors a beloved deceased family member. The two-day ritual takes place on November 1 and 2, with November 1 set aside to honor all children who have died. Dia de los Muertos is firmly rooted in the belief that the souls of the dead return for a yearly visit. The primary custom associated with this celebration is the arranging of a special altar in memory of the deceased person. Another practice is to hold an all-night vigil in the cemetery, where the family shares favorite foods. The custom dates back to pre-Columbian times.

References

Garza-Lubeck, Maria, and Ana Maria Salinas. *Mexican Celebrations* (see Program Resources section).

Grupo CUICA (Cultura Infantil como alternativa). *Día de Muertos: Disfrázate y Juega.*[†]

Hinojosa, Francisco. *The Old Lady Who Ate People: Frightening Stories.*

Rohmer, Harriet, and Dorminster Wilson. *Mother Scorpion Country/La Tierra del la Madre Escorpion.*[†]

POETRY

The reading and recitation of poems by children are an excellent way to accelerate oral language development. In addition, learning nursery rhymes in another language introduces children to a different culture.

References

Darío, Ruben. *Margarita.*[†]

De Gerez, Toni. *My Song Is a Piece of Jade: Poems of Ancient Mexico in English and Spanish/Mi Cancion es un pedazo de Jade: Poemas del México Antiguo en Inglés y Español.*[†]

Jimenez, Juan Ramón. *Platero y Yo.*[†]

Pomerantz, Charlotte. *The Tamarindo Puppy and Other Poems.*[†]

Schweitzeer, Byrd Baylor. *Amigo.*

Walsh, Maria Elena. *Tutu Maramba.*[†]

HISPANIC CULTURE

Story Hour

MEXICAN THEME

These activities are suitable for preschool through 3rd grade.

A. Teach the folk song "Los pollitos dicen." Resources include Suni Paz's *Canciones para el recreo*[†] (sound recording), and Zwick and Cortes's *Rimas y Cancioncitas para Ninos* (see the Program Resources section).

B. Read the story or show the filmstrip of Thomas P. Lewis's *Hill of Fire.*[†] Introduce this as a historical book.

C. Teach the finger plays "Tortillitas para Mama" and "Chocolate" from *Rimas y Cancioncitas para Ninos* (Zwick and Cortes in Program Resources section), or from Margot Griego's *Tortillitas para Mama.*[†]

D. Show pictures from Carlos Somonte's *We Live in Mexico* (New York: Bookright, 1985) for an introduction to urban life in present-day Mexico.

E. Play a traditional singing game from the culture, such as "El lobo" or "El patio de mi casa" from the record *Children's Songs and Games from Ecuador, Mexico, and Puerto Rico*[†] by Henrietta Yurchenco.

For a Puerto Rican theme or one from another Latin American country, substitute other stories and songs from the Bibliography. For Puerto Rico, for example, you might use Richard Garcia's *My Aunt Otilia's Spirits/Los Espiritos de Mi Tía Otilia*[†] and games or songs from *Canciones para el recreo,*[†] or *Children's Songs and Games from Ecuador, Mexico, and Puerto Rico.*[†]

SPANISH THEME

Prepare the following puppet shows from Mireya Cueto's *La boda de la ratita y más teatro-cuentos:*[†] "Fabula del buen hombre y su hijo" (Fable of the good man and his son) and "La boda de la ratita" (Little Rat's wedding).

FIESTA NAVIDEÑA

The Christmas season in Mexico begins with the *posadas,* a nine-day vigil that reenacts the journey of Mary and Joseph to Bethlehem and their search for an inn. Each night from December 16 through December 24, friends and relatives gather at each other's homes to sing and recite ritual songs and prayers. For children, the posadas is a particularly exciting event because piñatas are enjoyed by all. The posadas officially begins the Christmas season, which continues with attendance at the midnight mass, called *la Misa de Gallo*, held on Christmas Eve—La Noche Buena, the Good Night. The "Pastorela," or shepherd's play, is also performed during this season. First presented in medieval Europe, this morality play served as a useful form of proselytizing and was brought to the New World by the Franciscans and the Augustinians. The season ends with the arrival of the Three Kings on Epiphany, January 6. The following titles are recommended for a Christmas season story hour:

Anaya, Rudolfo. *The Farolitos of Christmas: A New Mexico Christmas Story.*[†]

Bierhorst, John. *Spirit Child: A Story of the Nativity.*[†]

Bruni, Mary Ann Smothers. *Rosita's Christmas Wish.*[†]

Cruz, Manual and Ruth. *A Chicano Christmas Story/Un Cuento Navideño Chicano.*[†] Filmstrip, cassette, and book in English and Spanish.

"The Legend of the Poinsettia" in Sylvia Cavazos Pena's *Tun-Ta-Ca-Tun: More Stories and Poems in English and Spanish for Children.*[†]

Prieto, Mariana. *The Wise Rooster/El Gallo Sabio.*[†]

PROGRAM RESOURCES

Ada, Alma Flor, and Rosalma Zubizarreta. *Language Arts through Children's Literature: Using Children's Book Press Multicultural, Bilingual Books to Develop Critical Thinking and Creative Expression.* San Francisco: Children's Book Press, 1989. 74pp. $8.95. ISBN: 0-89239-046-8.

A teacher's manual designed to offer innovative approaches to the uses of multicultural books for children, this volume presents methods for applying critical thinking skills to the books published by Children's Book Press. Part I of the manual is comprised of

essays that present Ada's educational philosophy, based on the critical pedagogy of esteemed Brazilian educator Paulo Freire. While Part I presents useful classroom activities, Part II offers a brief description of each book and offers suggestions for what Ada calls a creative dialogue, a method designed to ensure that children understand what they are reading and explore the value in the content. This excellent resource is particularly useful for helping adults think differently about multicultural literature for children.

Garza-Lubeck, María, and Ana María Salinas. *Mexican Celebrations.* Austin: Institute of Latin American Studies, Univ. of Texas at Austin,* 1987. 54pp. $3.95. ISBN: 0-86728-019-0.

This useful resource features twelve Latin American cultural events, ranging from religious celebrations, such as the *Posadas* and the feast day of Our Lady of Guadalupe (Mexico's patron saint and the patroness of the Americas), to historic events, such as *Cinco de Mayo* (Fifth of May) and *Diez y Seis de Septiembre* (Sixteenth of September). Useful footnotes and a bibliography add to the text. Other teachers' manuals developed by the institute include Donna Dalferes's *The Gaucho: A Micro Course* (1977) and Kathryn F. B. Thompson's *Algunos Animales de Latino America: Some Animals of Latin America* (1977).

Salinas-Norman, Bobbi. *Indo-Hispanic Folk Art Traditions I/Tradiciones Artesanales Indo-Hispanas I.* Rev. ed. Albuquerque, N.Mex.: Pinata Publications,* 1990. 137pp. $15.00. ISBN: 0-934925-03-8.

———. *Indo-Hispanic Folk Art Traditions II/Tradiciones Artesanales Indo-Hispanas II.* Rev. ed. Albuquerque, N. Mex.: Pinata Publications,* 1990. 206pp. $15.00. ISBN: 0-934925-04-6.

Revisions of *Folk Art Traditions I* and *Folk Art Traditions II*, these excellent resources detail the many Christmas (vol. I) and Day of the Dead (vol. II) traditions practiced by Latin

American cultures. Each volume is filled with illustrated craft ideas and recipes, and provides the necessary historical background on the origin and practice of each tradition. The bilingual format adds to the usefulness.

Zwick, Louise Yarian, and Oralia Garza de Cortés. *Rimas y Cancioncitas para Ninos.* Illus. by Lilka Hornak Sorrels. Houston: Houston Public Library, 1984. 56pp. ISBN: N/A.

Particularly useful for a Spanish story hour program and designed for librarians and parents alike, this booklet contains nursery rhymes and songs in Spanish that stem from the oral tradition. Entries are arranged by type of rhyme as well as by season. Specific instructions for the finger plays are also included. A table of contents, an index, and musical arrangements for such popular songs as "De Colores" and the Pinata song add to the usefulness of this resource.

RESOURCES FOR ADULTS

Ada, Alma Flor. *A Magical Encounter: Spanish-language Children's Literature in the Classroom.* Compton, Calif.: Santillana, 1990.

Using a literature-based approach to classroom teaching, Ada, a distinguished educator and an expert on Spanish children's literature, provides an indispensable guide that combines the best of the theoretical framework of critical pedagogy. The book is filled with exciting ideas and activities that reflect Ada's creativity and that will challenge ESL teachers and librarians alike. Included is an excellent bibliography of children's books that can form a core collection of Spanish-language literature.

Allen, Adela Artola. *Library Services for Hispanic Children: A Guide for Public and School Librarians.* Phoenix, Ariz.: Oryx Press, 1987. 201pp. $29.50. ISBN: 0-89774-371-7.

This informative volume includes essays on the history of library services to Hispanics and on the related issue of evaluation of library services. A bibliography of resources for books in both English and Spanish as well as reference sources for adults working with

children form part of this valuable tool. It also contains a bibliography of software useful for Spanish-language or bilingual programs. A particularly insightful chapter by Mary Frances Johnson sheds much light on the selection and acquisition of materials in Spanish.

Cummins, Jim. "Bilingual Education and Anti-Racist Education." *Interracial Books for Children Bulletin 17,* nos. 3 and 4 (1986): 9–12.

This brief yet cogent article brings to light the various types of bilingual education programs that have proven effective in language acquisition theory. Many of these programs, however, are undermined by the politics of bilingual education policies implemented by local school boards. Written by an internationally recognized bilingual education researcher, this article will be useful for librarians wanting to comprehend the necessity and nature of bilingual programs.

Edmonds, Leslie. "The Treatment of Race in Picture Books for Young Children." *Book Research Quarterly* (Fall 1986): 31–41.

The author analyzed the themes and contents of children's books, including books on Hispanic culture, ranking the values commonly attributed to a specific culture.

"Hispanic Children's Literature." *Monographic Review/Revista Monografica,* * vol. 1, 1985 $4.50. ISBN: 0885-7512.

This monograph contains eleven articles that constitute an attempt to define the field of criticism of children's literature in Spanish. The articles are written by such noted scholars as Carmen Bravo-Villasante from Spain as well as such children's authors as Hilda Perera. Seven of the articles are in Spanish and no English translations are provided.

Myers, Walter Dean. "The Reluctant Reader." *Interracial Books for Children Bulletin 19,* nos. 3 and 4: 12–15.

The author, a noted writer of young adult and children's books, argues in this insightful article that, by providing culturally relevant materials to children, parents and teachers can motivate them to read books that are meaningful and that ultimately will stimulate them to become mature readers.

Moore, Opal, and Donnarae MacCann. "Paternalism and Assimilation in Books about Hispanics: Parts One and Two." *Children's Literature Association Quarterly* 12, nos. 2 and 3 (Summer and Fall, 1987).

In these excellent articles, the authors analyze the themes of paternalism and assimilation in eight books published between 1970 and 1980 with plot formulas that incorporate the "Anglo rescue" theme, one which the authors say reflects a larger sociopolitical reality.

Phaedrus: An International Annual of Children's Literature Research, vol. 10. New York: Columbia University, School of Library Service, 1984.

Chapter one of this volume, written by noted children's literature scholars from thirteen Latin-American countries, gives a panorama of the development of the literature. Each subsequent chapter is devoted to a specific Latin-American country, citing major historical works and including a bibliography. Missing from this volume, unfortunately, is an analysis of Hispanic children's literature in Mexico and the United States.

Ruiz, Deborah. "Children's Literature Booming in Mexico: A Review of the Most Recent Books." *Lector: The Hispanic Review Journal* 3, no. 6: 292–295.

Ruiz has produced a good reference source that looks at the renaissance of Spanish-language children's book publishing in Mexico. Ruiz provides brief reviews of the many authors currently being published and highlights the work of such noted Mexican authors as Eduardo Robles Boza (Tío Patota) and such illustrators as Laura Fernández and Felipe Dávalos, winner of the Ezra Jack Keats Award.

Zwick, Louise Yarian. "Cuentos y Canciones Infantiles: Recordings in Spanish for Children." *School Library Journal.* 35, no. 6 (Feb. 1989): 23–26.

In this bibliographic essay, Zwick discusses currently available disc recordings, cassettes, and book-and-cassette sets that are Hispanic culture specific.

_____ and Oralia Garza de Cortés. "Library Programs for Hispanic Children." *Texas Libraries* (Spring 1989): 12–16.

The authors outline specific books, themes, and ideas that can be incorporated into various types of library programs, such as a Spanish or bilingual story hour or special cultural and outreach programs. The authors point out that these are models of programs that work and are effective with Hispanic populations, and that will help to establish library-use traditions with Hispanic children and families. A helpful bibliography is included.

DISTRIBUTORS

Spanish-Language Children's Books

Bilingual Publications
270 Lafayette, Suite 705
New York, NY 10012
(212) 431-3500

Hispanic Books Distributors
1665 W. Grant
Tucson, AZ 85745
1-800-634-2124

Lectorum Books
137 W. 14th St.
New York, NY 10011
(212) 929-2833

Mariuccia Iaconi Book Imports
1110 Mariposa
San Francisco, CA 94107
(415) 255-8193

Other Materials

American Universal Art Forms Corp.
P.O. Box 2242
Austin, TX 78768

Arco Iris Records
P.O. Box 7428
Berkeley, CA 94707

Bilingual Educational Services
2514 South Grand Avenue
Los Angeles, CA 90007

Carolina Wren Press
P.O. Box 277
Carroboro, NC 27510

Institute of Latin American Studies
University of Texas at Austin
Sid Richardson Hall 1.310
Austin, TX 78712

Monographic Review/Revista Monografica
P.O. Box 8401 U.T. Permian Basin
Odessa, TX 79762-8301

Pan American Bookstore
4362 Melrose
Los Angeles, CA 90029

Paulist Press
997 Macarthur Blvd.
Mahwah, NJ 07430

Pinata Publications
200 Lakeside Drive
Oakland, CA 94612

Richard G. Santos
P.O. Box 29585
San Antonio, TX 78229

Texas Monthly Press
P.O. Box 1569
Austin, TX 78767

CHAPTER 5

Jewish Materials and Programs

by Enid Davis

If Judaism were a house, it would be a very old, very large apartment complex in the heart of a big city. Each apartment would hold a tenant symbolic of a country or time in which Jews lived and left their mark. Living in Apartment 1A, of course, would be the building superintendent, Abraham, the first Jew.

The lobby of this building would post the list of renters, and what an international directory it would be. These tenants' lives have spanned over 2,000 years of history worldwide, and their achievements—considering their small numbers and immense hardships—are awesome.

The hallways would echo with the sounds of many languages: Hebrew and Yiddish would be the major tongues, but you'll hear a good deal of English, especially if you are in the twentieth-century wing. And your nose will delight in the variety of cooking smells. Pass Queen Esther's door and you can sniff the *hamantashen* (filled pastry) baking in her royal oven. Pass Judah Maccabee's apartment and you'll grow faint with desire for potato pancakes.

If you are very quiet, you'll hear the sound of weeping from behind many doors. These tenants have lived under more furious führers than any other group of people. For example, put your ear against the door of Moses' mother when she had to hide her son from the Egyptians; Hannah's, when she lost her seventh and last son to King Antiochus of Syria; the doors of Jews belonging to the eras of the Inquisition and pogroms; Anne Frank's, Hannah Senesh's, and the six million tenants' who lost their lives because of Eastern European barbarity; and the doors of today's Soviet Jews.

Fortunately, you won't have to strain to hear the laughter, the talk, the music as well, because here are the homes of our great comedians, thinkers, and artists. You knew that Woody Allen, Sigmund Freud, Albert Einstein, Baruch Spinoza, and Stephen Sondheim lived here, didn't you? And so do countless others who have offered their gifts to the rest of the world.

As different as all these tenants are, their apartments share one thing in common—they have lots of bookshelves! And these bookshelves hold the books in this bibliography: books about the Hebrew language, history, Israel, people, legends, ritual, celebration, and identity. The books on this list are in fact only a small sampling of the books available about Jewish life for children, but they are among the best and most appropriate for the collections and programming activities of public schools and libraries.

Because this apartment house belongs to the people of the book, a lot of reading is done here, except when it's time for a holiday. That's when the weeping and the thinking stop and the celebrating begins. The books in this chapter reflect the joy of celebrating holidays with family and friends.

The children who live in this building, however, also belong to a larger community. They often feel that they live in two worlds, and they are resentful that society—the school, the shopping mall, the television set—does not recognize the existence of their Jewish selves. That is why it is important to bring these celebrations out of the books and into the classrooms and libraries. Jewish children need to know that their community recognizes Judaism as a legitimate part of American society. There is a lot of suppressed (and expressed) self-hatred that would evaporate if the library and school held out an acknowledging word to these minority youngsters.

It's time to enter the doors to this great dwelling and to meet some of the people who have shaped Judaism over the centuries. Welcome to a house in which the chief virtues are charity, justice, and education, where the sounds of laughter and prayer have miraculously survived centuries of persecution—and in which there will always be lots and lots of books!

BIBLIOGRAPHY

FICTION

P–3. Adler, David A. *The House on the Roof: A Sukkot Story.* Illus. by Marilyn Hirsh. Rockville, Md.: Kar-Ben, 1984. 32pp. pap. $4.95. ISBN: 0-930494-35-0.

When an urban grandfather builds a Sukkah (a makeshift hut decorated for the harvest holiday of Sukkot) for his grandchildren on his apartment roof, the landlady brings him to court. The old man explains the traditions behind the holiday to the judge, whose Solomonic verdict saves the Sukkah. This is a cheery tale with a bit of suspense and lots of colorful, cozy illustrations.

3–6. Chaikin, Miriam. Molly Series. Illus. by Richard Egielski. New York: Harper and Row.
Finders Weepers. 1980. 128pp. $12.89. ISBN: 0-06-021177-6.
Friends Forever. 1988. 128pp. PLB $11.89. ISBN: 0-06-021204-7; $11.95. ISBN: 0-06-021203-9.
Getting Even. 1982. 128pp. $12.89. ISBN: 0-06-021165-2.
I Should Worry, I Should Care. 1979. 103pp. $12.89. ISBN: 0-06-021174-1.
Lower! Higher! You're a Liar! 1984. 160pp. PLB $12.89. ISBN: 0-06-021187-3; $12.95. ISBN: 0-06-021186-5.

These five stories about a young girl growing up in Brooklyn during the 1940s often center around Jewish holidays and the family's growing fears of Nazism. Beverly Cleary's "Ramona" fans will enjoy meeting Molly, a sensitive, intelligent child who gets into predicaments reminiscent of everyone's childhood. Fun to read.

2–5. _____. Yossi Series. New York: Harper and Row.

How Yossi Beat the Evil Urge. Illus. by Petra Mathers. 1983. 64pp. $9.57. ISBN: 0-06-021184-9.
Yossi tries to be good.
Yossi Asks the Angels for Help. Illus. by Petra Mathers. 1985. 64pp. $11.95. ISBN: 0-06-021195-4.
Yossi loses money earmarked for Hanukkah gifts.
Yossi Tries to Help God. Illus. by Denise Saldutti. 1987. 80pp. PLB $11.89. ISBN: 0-06-021198-9; $11.95. ISBN: 0-06-021197-0.
Yossi's attempts to help his ailing sister backfire.

These stories are about an Orthodox Jewish boy whose ups and downs are flavored by his family's religious convictions. Children of all faiths will identify with these universal childhood themes, yet they will appreciate the uniquely Orthodox methods used by Yossi to get back into God's good graces. Each book is well written and fun to read aloud.

2–5. Cohen, Barbara. *The Carp in the Bathtub.* Illus. by Joan Halpern. New York: Lothrop, 1972. 48pp. $13.88. ISBN: 0-688-51627-0; New York: Kar-Ben, 1987. pap. $4.95. ISBN: 0-930494-67-9.

In the 1920s, two New York City children try to save Mother's recently purchased carp from being turned into gefilte fish, a Passover dish. The story offers good insight into the Jewish tradition of how and when to kill animals for food. Wonderful art nouveau-like illustrations and an easy-to-read text add some spice to this classic offering.

3–6. _____. *The Christmas Revolution.* Illus. by Diane DeGroat. New York: Lothrop, 1987. 96pp. $12.95. ISBN: 0-688-06806-5; Bantam, 1988. pap. $2.95. ISBN: 0-553-15642-X.

Cohen tackles a very sensitive issue to Jews—the celebration of Christmas in public schools. In this story a pair of twins react differently to the annual Christmas program: One sings a solo and one boycotts the production. This courageous book is smoothly written, has plenty of humor, and should start some wonderful discussions from both sides of the issue.

5–9. _____. *King of the Seventh Grade*. New York: Lothrop, 1982. 190pp. $13.95. ISBN: 0-688-01302-3.

Vic, a tough and troubled adolescent, does not want to attend Hebrew school in preparation for his Bar Mitzvah. He has an identity crisis, however, when the rabbi discovers that Vic's mother never converted to Judaism, thereby rendering him a non-Jew. Tackling other contemporary issues as well, Cohen creates an honest look at a troubled contemporary Jewish-American family. For a contemporary novel about intermarriage for this age group, see:

Barbara Cohen. *People Like Us*. New York: Bantam, 1989. 144pp. pap. $2.95. ISBN: 0-553-27445-7.

2–5. _____. *Molly's Pilgrim*. Illus. by Michael J. Deraney. New York: Lothrop, 1983. 32pp. $12.95. ISBN: 0-688-02103-4; PLB $12.88. ISBN: 0-688-02104-2; Bantam. First Skylark Series. 1990. pap. $2.75. ISBN: 0-553-15833-3.

Molly, a friendless Russian immigrant, is ridiculed when she brings her mother's version of a Pilgrim doll to school for a Thanksgiving assignment. Dressed as a Russian peasant woman, the doll initiates the lessons of how Thanksgiving originated from the Jewish harvest holiday Sukkot and that persecuted pilgrims continue to come to America from all over the world. The award-winning film based on this poignant story is available through Phoenix Films.*[1]

K–6. _____. *Yussel's Prayer: A Yom Kippur Story*. Illus. by Michael Deraney. New York: Lothrop, 1981. 32pp. $12.88. ISBN: 0-688-00461-X.

Yussel, an illiterate cowherder, must work on Yom Kippur, so he offers his prayers on a reed pipe at the end of the day. When the rabbi feels this music, he is able to close services, for until then the congregation's prayers were tainted with secular concerns and were not holy. The book emphasizes a Jewish value: When it comes to pleasing God, sincerity, not status, will open the gates of heaven. Beautiful sepia line drawings complement the story.

P–3. Davis, Enid. *The Five Maccabees Tough*. Illus. by the author. Available from Enid Davis.* 1984. 12pp. pap. $3.95.

In this modern folktale created by a children's librarian especially for Hanukkah story times, the Maccabee brothers must pass the giant of King Antiochus before they can clean up the synagogue after their victory. Audiences will chuckle at the similarity to the story of "Three Billy Goats Gruff," as the Maccabees outwit their enemy with mops and buckets. This nonsexist story is adaptable for various types of presentations.

P–3. _____. *Latke Lad: A Hanukkah Tale to Serve with Your Potato Pancakes*. Illus. by the author. Available from Enid Davis.* 1981. 12pp. pap. $3.95.

In the folktale tradition of the Gingerbread Boy, a potato pancake uses the symbols of Hanukkah to save himself from three greedy animals on his way to join Judah Maccabee's army. Used as a feltboard tale, for a puppet show, for creative dramatics, or as a read-aloud, this humorous, versatile story with beguiling line drawings will delight young audiences.

P–4. Freedman, Florence B. *Brothers: A Hebrew Legend*. Illus. by Robert Andrew Parker. New York: Harper and Row, 1985. 40pp. $11.89. ISBN: 0-06-021872-X.

Two Israeli brothers inherit land from their father and continue to share with each other during bad times. "How good it is for brothers to live together in friendship" are the

---

[1]Complete addresses for all sources marked with an asterisk (*) can be found in the Resources section at the end of this chapter.

words learned at their father's knee. Parker's vivid stylistic watercolor sketches beautifully complement this brief, soul-satisfying, and award-winning book.

P–3. Goffstein, M. B. *My Noah's Ark*. Illus. by the author. New York: Harper and Row, 1978. 32pp. $13.95. ISBN: 0-06-022022-8.

With succinct text and minimal line drawings, Goffstein portrays an old woman whose toy ark and its animals have been her companions through a long, full life. This bedridden grandmother describes how her father's voice boomed like God's as he constructed the ark for his daughter. As the old woman finds comfort in this symbol of her religious beliefs and of her father's caring, one feels the might of both myth and love.

K–3. Goldin, Barbara Diamond. *Just Enough Is Plenty: A Hanukkah Tale*. Illus. by Seymour Chwast. New York: Viking, 1988. pap. $12.95. ISBN: 0-670-81852-6.

Cheerful Mama says there is always enough to go around, but young Malka, an Eastern European *shtetl* child, is worried that Hanukkah won't be the same since Papa's business is doing poorly. When a stranger comes to their door, however, the family cannot turn him away. Imagine their surprise and joy the next (gift-laden) morning when Malka and her kin suspect him of being no other than the prophet Elijah. Stunning folk-art paintings transport the modern reader to the old village and its snowy landscape in this holiday treat.

K–6. Hirsh, Marilyn. *Joseph Who Loved the Sabbath*. Illus. by Devis Grebu. New York: Viking, 1986. 32pp. pap. $11.95. ISBN: 0-670-81194-7.

Based on a Talmudic story, this tale is about a man who inherits his greedy master's lands due to his own faithful observance of the Jewish Sabbath. A smooth text and humorous, colorful illustrations show Joseph observing the weekly holiday by feasting, relaxing, and studying the Torah. Older readers will not only relish Joseph's ironic road to riches but also begin to appreciate how rejuvenating a day of rest can be.

P–3. _____. *Potato Pancakes All Around: A Hanukkah Tale*. Illus. by the author. Philadelphia: Jewish Publication Society of America, 1982. 34pp. pap. $6.95. ISBN: 0-8276-0217-0, 604.

This humorous story about a peddler who gets some teamwork going while preparing a batch of latkes (potato pancakes, a traditional Hanukkah treat) is reminiscent of the folktale "Stone Soup." Getting the residents to cooperate (each has her own favorite recipe) is half the battle—and half the fun. Illustrated in warm golds and browns, this story will be gobbled up by latke lovers everywhere.

4–7. Kerr, Judith. *When Hitler Stole Pink Rabbit*. Illus. by the author. New York: Putnam, 1972. 191pp. $8.95. ISBN: 0-698-20182-5; Dell. 1987. pap. $3.25. ISBN: 0-440-49017-0.

Young Anna leaves all her belongings behind when her family flees Nazi Germany for France, Switzerland, and England. The story, based on the author's life, is a tribute to the Jewish family, for as long as Anna has them, Hitler cannot hurt her. An excellent introduction to the Holocaust with well-drawn historic events and engaging characters playing against an international backdrop.

3–6. Kushner, Arlene. *Falasha No More: An Ethiopian Jewish Child Comes Home*. Illus. by Amy Kalina. New York: Shapolsky, 1986. 58pp. $9.95. ISBN: 0-933503-43-1.

Avraham Fereday, an Ethiopian Jewish boy, has come with his family to find freedom in Israel. His father explains that, once they arrive, they will be like one people. Avraham, however, is distressed to learn that his African ways are very different from those of his classmates. His customs will interest the young reader who will understand the need to accept and appreciate everyone's unique culture and contributions. For a similar title, see:
Jonathan Kendall. *My Name Is Rachamim*. New York: Union of American Hebrew Congregations, 1987. $7.95. ISBN: 0-8074-0321-0, 123925. Grades 2–3.

5–9. Lasky, Kathryn. *Night Journey*. Illus. by Trina Schart Hyman. New York: Viking, 1986.

pap. $12.95. ISBN: 0-670-80935-7; Puffin. 152pp. pap. $4.95. ISBN: 0-14-032048-2.

Teenage Rachel is tired of sitting with her ailing great-grandmother until the old woman starts to remember her childhood in Russia, a childhood darkened by raids against Jewish homes and forced conscriptions into the czar's army. Nana Sashie's description of the escape plans she organized and carried out at the age of nine will mesmerize the reader. Fine writing and characterization make Sashie's history come to life.

6–10. Levitin, Sonia. *The Return*. New York: Atheneum, 1987. 224pp. $13.95. ISBN: 0-689-31309-8; Fawcett. 1988. pap. $2.95. ISBN: 0-449-70280-4.

In this unique account, a dangerous journey is undertaken by a Beta Israel (Ethiopian Jew) out of her beloved village to a new life in Israel. Older readers will appreciate this novel about Desta, a teenage girl, and her hair-raising escape with her siblings: One brother is murdered before her eyes. Much research has gone into the description of the tribe's political situation and customs in this rich offering.

5–9. Levoy, Myron. *Alan and Naomi*. New York: HarperCollins, 1977. 176pp. $12.89. ISBN: 0-06-023800-3; 1987. pap. $3.50. ISBN: 0-06-440209-6.

The author weaves a touching story of a New York boy's attempts to heal the emotional scars of a young French refugee who has witnessed the beating death of her father by the Nazis. Unfortunately, Alan's work is undermined by an anti-Semitic scene that takes place before the two friends. The book's memorable quality is the well-developed relationship between a boy who lives only for baseball and a girl who does not want to live at all.

K–5. _____. *The Hanukkah of Great-Uncle Otto*. Illus. by Donna Ruff. Philadelphia: Jewish Publication Society of America, 1984. 47pp. $10.95. ISBN: 0-8276-0242-1.

Great-Uncle Otto is old and disabled; he even needs help holding onto his hot cup of tea. But Joshua, his young nephew, loves Otto

for his stories of Hanukkahs past and of life in Germany "before Hitler came with his ugly, lunatic hate." When Joshua helps Otto build a menorah like the one he had as a boy, the old man is rejuvenated, and the family enjoys a grand celebration. Tenderly told and nicely illustrated with black-and-white drawings, this story makes a good read-aloud.

4–7. Lowry, Lois. *Number the Stars*. Boston: Houghton, 1989. 160pp. $12.95. ISBN: 0-395-51060-0; Dell. 1990. pap. $3.50. ISBN: 0-440-40327-8.

The 1989 Newbery Award went to this title about ten-year-old Annemarie Johansen, who joins the Danish Resistance when the Nazis threaten the life of her best friend, Ellen Rosen. This is a well-told, adventurous tale that reveals the goodness of a nation and also demonstrates to young readers that Jewish lives were precious in one small, brave corner of the world. For an exciting story about a young Jewish heroine's bravery in the Danish Resistance, see:

Carol Matas. *Lisa's War*. New York: Scribner's, 1989. 128pp. $12.95. ISBN: 0-684-19010-9; Scholastic. 1991. pap. $2.75. ISBN: 0-590-43517-5. Grades 5–8.

P–3. Miller, Deborah Uchill. *Only Nine Chairs: A Tall Tale for Passover*. Illus. by Karen Ostrove. Rockville, Md.: Kar-Ben, 1982. 40pp. pap. $4.95. ISBN: 0-930494-13-X.

This clever rhyming tale, with exuberant drawings, is about inviting nineteen people for the Passover *Seder* (dinner) but only owning nine chairs. The narrator imagines everyone sitting on one chair in each other's laps and reading the prayer book through a periscope. In addition to recognizing Seder customs, all children will be able to identify with the seating problems created whenever a large family gathers.

4–7. Ofek, Uriel. *Smoke over Golan: A Novel of the 1973 Yom Kippur War in Israel*. Trans. by Israel I. Taslitt. Illus. by Lloyd Bloom. New York: Harper and Row, 1979. 192pp. $12.89. ISBN: 0-06-024614-6.

Young Eitan, who lives on a farm in the Golan Heights near the Syrian border, is unintentionally left alone when war breaks out. It is he who helps rescue an injured Israeli soldier and captures a Syrian spy. This is a fast-paced, lively novel about a resourceful lad who must fight the very people with whom he has become friends. For other award-winning adventure novels in which Jewish boys survive the Holocaust, see:

Uri Orlev. *The Island on Bird Street.* Trans. by Hillel Halkin. New York: Houghton, 1984. 176pp. $13.95. ISBN: 0-395-33887-5, 5-92515. Grades 5–9.

Yuri Suhl. *Uncle Misha's Partisans: The Story of Young Freedom Fighters in Nazi-Occupied Europe.* New York: Shapolsky, 1988. 211pp. pap. $7.95. ISBN: 0-933503-23-7. Grades 5–10.

5–8. Orgel, Doris. *The Devil in Vienna.* New York: Dial, 1978. 246pp. $8.95. ISBN: 0-8037-1920-5; Puffin. 1988. pap. $4.95. ISBN: 0-14-032500-X.

Rich in detail about everyday life in Vienna during the late 1930s, Orgel's scene is set for the dissolution of a girlhood friendship and the crumbling of a civilized society. A Jewish child and a Nazi's daughter have been friends since they started school, and not even Hitler (the devil himself) can come between these two adolescents. This book has proved to be a favorite among all readers.

2–8. Peretz, Isaac Leib. *Even Higher.* Retold by Barbara Cohen. Illus. by Anatoly Ivanov. New York: Lothrop, 1987. 32pp. o.p.

A skeptical visitor to the village of Nemirov aims to discover where the rabbi goes during the Jewish New Year after the villagers claim he visits with God. Actually, he goes to help the poor, and because charity is high on the Jews' priority list, the rabbi does, indeed, go higher than heaven. Illustrated with colorful paintings in the Russian tradition, this Hassidic folktale makes you feel good inside.

K–6. Pinkwater, Daniel. *The Frankenbagel Monster.* New York: Dutton, 1986. unp. $9.95. ISBN: 0-525-44260-X.

Local bagelmaker Harold Frankenbagel creates a monster—a renegade bageloid who

terrifies the neighborhood—in this silly but satisfying story with computer-generated illustrations. Jewish children will recognize the bagel as part of their culture and they, as well as non-Jewish children, will love this tale. Serve with cream cheese and get a grant for the lox.

3–6. Schnur, Steven. *The Narrowest Bar Mitzvah.* Illus. by Victor Lazzaro. New York: Union of America Hebrew Congregations, 1986. 48pp. pap. $5.95. ISBN: 0-8074-0316-4, 123923.

Schnur tells the story of Alex's Bar Mitzvah, held in his grandparents' unusual six-foot-wide house. This home, which resembles an ark, saves the day, for the synagogue floods the night before the event and all the food and decorations are ruined. The story entertainingly probes the real meaning of the Bar Mitzvah celebration, and the competent black-and-white drawings depict a warm family life.

P–3. Schwartz, Amy. *Mrs. Moskowitz and the Sabbath Candlesticks.* Illus. by the author. Philadelphia: Jewish Publication Society of America, 1983. 32pp. pap. $6.95. ISBN: 0-8276-0231-6.

Old Mrs. Moskowitz feels depressed in her new apartment until some Sabbath candlesticks stir fond memories, and she is able to unpack, tidy up, and cook a wonderful dinner for her family. With humor and warmth (expressed both in the words and in the soft, pencil drawings), Schwartz reveals how tradition can rejuvenate all of us. Not a bad choice to share with youngsters recovering from a move themselves!

P–6. _____. *Yossel Zissel and the Wisdom of Chelm.* Illus. by the author. Philadelphia: Jewish Publication Society of America, 1986. 32pp. $9.95. ISBN: 0-8276-0258-8.

Meet Yossel Zissel, Judaica's legendary Chelmite, who convinced his noodleheaded neighbors to leave their village and populate the rest of the world. Everyone will enjoy Yossel's unique method of investing the bags of gold inherited from his Warsaw uncle.

Humorous black-and-white sketches of Chelm add to the great fun.

6–12. Schwartz, Howard, selected by. *Elijah's Violin and Other Jewish Fairy Tales.* Illus. by Linda Heller. New York: HarperCollins, 1985. 320pp. pap. $10.95. ISBN: 0-06-091171-9.

These thirty-six stories, derived from many eras, lands, and sources, are a fine introduction to the subject of Jewish folklore. The stories have all the familiar trappings of fairy tales—castles, kings, love, and quests—but also include religious themes. Interestingly, this collection includes some Jewish versions of several Grimm Fairy Tales. An equally fine volume is the sequel, *Miriam's Tambourine: Jewish Folktales from Around the World.* New York: Free Press, 1987. $24.95. ISBN: 0-02-929260-3.

7–up. Serwer-Bernstein, Blanche. *Let's Steal the Moon: Jewish Tales, Ancient and Recent.* Illus. by Trina Schart Hyman. Boston: Little, Brown, 1970. Reprint. New York: Shapolsky, 1987. 96pp. pap. $6.95. ISBN: 0-933503-27-X.

These eleven stories from the Middle East and Eastern Europe are an entertaining addition to the diversity of Jewish folktales. They feature such legendary giants as the Golem, Hillel, King Solomon, the wise men of Chelm, and, surprisingly, Napoleon. The lively tales express the Jews' love for learning, justice, and freedom, and are illustrated with the expressive faces for which Hyman is famous.

P–6. Shulevitz, Uri. *The Treasure.* Illus. by the author. New York: Farrar, Straus and Giroux, 1979. 32pp. $13.95. ISBN: 0-374-37740-5; 1986. pap. $3.95. ISBN: 0-374-47955-0.

Iridescent colors paint breathtaking scenes of the Eastern European countryside in this folktale about poor old Isaac who travels far to seek riches, only to find them in his own home. Brief and poetic, the tale reinforces the Jewish beliefs in following your dreams, in learning from others (it's the palace guard who sends Isaac home to his treasure), and in charity, for Isaac's wealth pays for the new synagogue.

6–12. Siegal, Aranka. *Upon the Head of the Goat: A Childhood in Hungary, 1939–1944.* New York: Farrar, Straus and Giroux, 1981. 214pp. $14.95. ISBN: 0-374-38059-7.

_____. *Grace in the Wilderness: After the Liberation, 1945–1948.* New York: Farrar, Straus and Giroux, 1985. 220pp. $13.95. ISBN: 0-374-32760-2.

Excellent writing and a powerful tribute to the dignity of the Jewish family stand out in this story of the slow but ceaseless destruction of the Hungarian Jewish community. This fictionalized personal memoir of Piri Davidowitz will stay in the mind of the reader for a long time. The first of the two volumes is a Newbery Honor Book.

3–8. Simon, Solomon. *The Wise Men of Helm and Their Merry Tales.* Illus. by Lillian Fische. West Orange, N.J.: Behrman, 1942. pap. $6.50. ISBN: 0-87441-125-4.

_____. *More Wise Men of Helm and Their Merry Tales.* Illus. by Stephen Kraft. West Orange, N.J.: Behrman, 1979. pap. $6.50. ISBN: 0-87441-126-2.

Travel to the silliest imaginary village on earth—Helm, Poland, a place that symbolizes humankind's irrational thinking in Eastern European Jewish folklore. For example, imagine a group of civic leaders who punish a greedy lobster by trying to drown it. It reminds one of the time an American legislative body had to finish passing laws by midnight and, when they failed to do so, simply turned the chamber clock back. Helm logic. For more fun, see:
Miriam Chaikin. *Hinkl and Other Shlemiel Stories.* New York: Shapolsky, 1987. 96pp. $10.95. ISBN: 0-933503-15-6; pap. $6.95. ISBN: 0-933503-37-7. Grades 3–12.

3–12. Singer, Isaac Bashevis. *Naftali the Storyteller and His Horse, Sus, and Other Stories.* Illus. by Margot Zemach. New York: Farrar, Straus and Giroux, 1976. 144pp. $13.95. ISBN: 0-374-35490-1; 1987. pap. $3.50. ISBN: 0-374-48487-6.

_____. *When Shlemiel Went to Warsaw and Other Stories.* Illus. by Margot Zemach. New York: Farrar, Straus and Giroux, 1969. 128pp. $13.95. ISBN: 0-374-38316-2; 1986. 161pp. pap. $3.50. ISBN: 0-374-48365-5.

_____. *Zlateh the Goat and Other Stories.* Illus. by Maurice Sendak. New York: Harper and Row, 1966. 96pp. $15.95. ISBN: 0-06-025698-2; 1984. pap. $4.95. ISBN: 0-06-440147-2.

Singer has made an enormous contribution to the field of Jewish folktales retold for children. Many of his stories take place in Chelm, the imaginary Polish village inhabited by *shlemiels* (fools). Singer embroiders characterization and fine writing upon the simple fabric of these nineteenth-century Eastern European stories.

3–9. _____. *Stories for Children.* New York: Farrar, Straus and Giroux, 1984. 338pp. $16.95. ISBN: 0-374-37266-7. pap. $7.95. ISBN: 0-374-46489-8.

This anthology of more than thirty stories collected from previously published titles for children includes folk stories as well as autobiographical pieces about life in Warsaw. Humorous, poignant, and reflective of the values and vicissitudes of Jewish existence, these tales will keep alive the memories of Jewish family life in Eastern Europe for generations to come. See the Nonfiction section of this bibliography for additional Singer titles.

3–6. Snyder, Carol. Ike and Mama Series. Illus. by Charles Robinson. New York: Putnam.
Ike and Mama and the Block Wedding. 1979. 81pp. $7.95. ISBN: 0-698-20461-1.
Ike and Mama and the Once-in-a-Lifetime Movie. 1981. 96pp. o.p.
Ike and Mama and the Seven Surprises. 1985. 160pp. o.p.
Ike and Mama and Trouble at School. 1983. $12.95. ISBN: 0-698-20570-7.

This award-winning series features a pair of likable protagonists living in the Bronx in the 1920s. Ike's life reflects the boyhoods of Jewish Americans living in that era. The warmhearted, humorous stories are reminiscent of Sydney Taylor's All-of-a-Kind Family series.

3–7. Sussman, Susan. *There's No Such Thing as a Chanukah Bush, Sandy Goldstein.* Illus.

by Charles Robinson. Niles, Ill.: A. Whitman, 1983. 40pp. $7.95. ISBN: 0-8075-7862-2.

In this book that explores the problems Jewish children face during the Christmas season, a wise grandfather tries to explain how Robin can still enjoy the Christian holiday without adopting it as her own celebration. His argument is complicated by Sandy, who is Jewish but is allowed, nonetheless, to have a tree. Many Jewish children will eagerly listen to and identify with this contemporary tale.

5–10. Yolen, Jane. *The Devil's Arithmetic.* New York: Viking, 1988. 160pp. pap. $12.95. ISBN: 0-670-81027-4; Puffin. 1990. pap. $3.95. ISBN: 0-14-034535-3.

When Hannah, a young teenager from New Rochelle, New York, nonchalantly opens the door of her grandparents' apartment for the prophet Elijah (a Passover custom), she stumbles into hell: Poland, 1942. Yolen has written a frightening and stirring time travel account of life in a Nazi concentration camp. A macabre, Jewish version of "Back to the Future," this story deeply personalizes the Holocaust, as does *The Diary of Anne Frank.*[†2] Yolen, a talented writer and an imaginative storyteller, has written one of the most effective accounts of the Holocaust I have ever read.

K–6. Zemach, Margot. *It Could Always Be Worse.* Illus. by the author. New York: Farrar, Straus and Giroux, 1990. pap. $4.95. ISBN: 0-374-43636-3.

A poor family man, desperate to bring peace and quiet to his one-room hut, is advised by the rabbi to board a succession of barnyard animals. When the animals are finally released, his hovel feels like heaven. The confidence in the rabbi's wisdom and power to work ironic miracles mark this as a Yiddish folktale. Exhuberant, comical watercolor drawings create a spectacular setting for the story. For another enjoyable treatise on the theory of relativity, see:
Marilyn Hirsh. *Could Anything Be Worse?* New York: Holiday House, 1987. 32pp. pap. $5.95. ISBN: 0-8234-0655-5.

[2] Titles marked with a dagger (†) have complete annotations in the Bibliography for this chapter.

NONFICTION

2–6. Abells, Chana Byers. *The Children We Remember*. Photos. New York: Greenwillow, 1986. 48pp. $9.95. ISBN: 0-688-06372-1.

Sweet and tormented children's faces replace statistics in this photographic essay on the effects of Nazism on Jewish children. Along with black-and-white photographs from the archive of Yad Vashem, the Holocaust museum in Jerusalem, the brief text shows the Nazis turning the everyday lives of youngsters into nightmares. Through their ordeals, the children are depicted as helpers: sharing food, aiding the elderly, and bearing their grief with dignity.

2–6. Adler, David A. *The Number on My Grandfather's Arm*. Photos by Rose Eichenbaum. New York: Union of American Hebrew Congregations, 1987. 28pp. $7.95. ISBN: 0-8074-0328-8, 103641.

When her grandfather absentmindedly rolls up his sleeves to wash dishes, a seven-year-old girl questions the numbers tattooed on his arm. This leads to a dialogue on the Holocaust in which the child assures Grandpa that the shame of the numbers belongs on the Nazis, not on him. When they return to the kitchen, he rolls up his sleeves and they finish the task. Sensitive photographs deepen the poignancy.

P–3. _____. *A Picture Book of Hanukkah*. Illus. by Linda Heller. New York: Holiday House, 1982. 32pp. $13.95. ISBN: 0-8234-0458-7; pap. $5.95. ISBN: 0-8234-0574-5.

This is a brief but informative account of the history of Hanukkah, charmingly retold for young children. Attractive stylized drawings in orange, gold, and green have a warm holiday glow, and the book is short enough to share during a class visit to the library. For a similar treatment, see:
David Adler. *A Picture Book of Passover*. New York: Holiday House, 1982. 32pp. $13.95. ISBN: 0-8234-0439-0; pap. $5.95. ISBN: 0-8234-0609-1.

6–12. Atkinson, Linda. *In Kindling Flame: The Story of Hannah Senesh*. *1921–1944*. New York: Lothrop, 1985. 224pp. $14.95. ISBN: 0-688-02714-8.

This is a fascinating, award-winning account of a young woman who had the soul of a poet and the nerve of a Rambo. Senesh joined a Zionist group in Palestine after facing discrimination in Hungary. During World War II, she volunteered to parachute into Occupied Europe to rescue Jews. She was soon captured, tortured, and murdered by the Nazis. Using diaries, letters, poetry, and photographs, the author chisels a fine memorial to a true heroine.

P–4. Brinn, Ruth Esrig. *Let's Celebrate: Fifty-Seven Jewish Holiday Crafts for Young Children*. 1977. 72pp. pap. $4.95. ISBN: 0-930494-02-4.
_____. *More Let's Celebrate*. 1985. 72pp. o.p.

Kar-Ben Copies has published these two craft books based on Jewish holidays. Filled with attractive projects that are fun and easy to make, the books are wonderful resources for parents, teachers, and librarians.

3–7. Brodsky, Beverly. *The Story of Job*. Illus. by the author. New York: Braziller, 1986. 40pp. $14.95. ISBN: 0-8076-1142-5.

The author presents a dramatic retelling of the Bible story in which a wealthy, righteous man becomes the subject of an experiment conducted by God and Satan. The testing of Job's faith is played against a vibrant, almost feverish, background of luminous watercolor paintings. This compelling version succeeds both as a dramatic reading and as a discussion starter.

2–7. Burstein, Chaya. *The Jewish Kids Catalog*. Illus. by the author. Philadelphia: Jewish Publication Society of America, 1983. 224pp. pap. $12.95. ISBN: 0-8276-0215-4.

Everything you ever wanted to know about Judaism can be found in this vastly entertaining book: snippets of history, folklore, recipes, rituals, bibliographies, crafts, foreign-language skills (Hebrew and Yiddish), holidays, etc. This hefty, award-winning volume is enhanced by amusing cartoon drawings and black-and-white photographs.

2–7. _____. *A Kid's Catalog of Israel*. Illus. by the author. Philadelphia: Jewish Publication Society of America, 1988. 288pp. $12.95. ISBN: 0-8276-0263-4.

Similar in format and style to her award-winning *The Jewish Kids Catalog*, this upbeat, informative introduction to Israeli history, culture, languages, crafts, recipes, geography, and music will provide hours of learning fun for children.

2–5. Cashman, Greer Fay. *Jewish Days and Holidays*. 2d ed. Illus. by Ilona Frankel. New York: Adama Books, 1986. 64pp. $9.95. ISBN: 0-915361-58-2.

Knockout pictures in vivid colors and charming designs accompany a short but informative text on the history and customs associated with eleven holidays. This is a perfect book for someone who wants a brief definition of the holidays.

4–12. Chaikin, Miriam. *Exodus*. Illus. by Charles Mikolaycak. New York: Holiday House, 1987. 32pp. $14.95. ISBN: 0-8234-0607-5.

With a biblical cadence, Chaikin retells the story of Exodus, from Moses' birth to his triumphant march to Israel. The full-page, full-color paintings are majestic and sensual, featuring close-ups of men who star in the narrative. This contrast between an exalted text and a very human cast of players makes for a dramatic and intense reading experience.

3–8. _____. Jewish Holiday Series. New York: Ticknor and Fields.
Ask Another Question: The Story and Meaning of Passover. 1986. 96pp. $13.95. ISBN: 0-89919-281-5.
Light Another Candle: The Story and Meaning of Hanukkah. 1987. 80pp. pap. $4.95. ISBN: 0-89919-057-X.
Make Noise, Make Merry: The Story and Meaning of Purim. 1986. 96pp. pap. $4.95. ISBN: 0-89919-424-9.
Shake a Palm Branch: The Story and Meaning of Sukkot. 1986. 80pp. $12.95. ISBN: 0-89919-254-8; pap. $4.95. ISBN: 0-89919-428-1.
Sound the Shofar: The Story and Meaning of Rosh HaShanah and Yom Kippur. 1986. 96pp. $13.95. ISBN: 0-89919-373-0; pap. $5.95. ISBN: 0-89919-427-3.

These well-written and appealingly illustrated books contain a good amount of information on the history, customs, and religious rituals behind the holidays.

5–10. _____. *A Nightmare in History: The Holocaust, 1933–1945*. Boston: Houghton, 1987. 128pp. $14.95. ISBN: 0-89919-461-3.

Chaikin traces the history of anti-Semitism from biblical times through the Nazi era. She describes Hitler's plans to annihilate European Jewry, focusing on the Warsaw Ghetto and the Auschwitz-Birkenau concentration camp. A chapter covers present-day memorial sites and customs. The explicit text contains many black-and-white photographs as well as selections from diaries and eyewitness accounts.

P–3. Cohen, Floreva G. *My Special Friend*. Photos by George Ancona. New York: Board of Jewish Education, 1986. pap. $5.95. ISBN: 0-88384-102-9.

Expressive black-and-white photographic portraits and a brief text tell the story of Jonathan, a retarded boy, who is given the honor of leading the singing at a synagogue service. Children will see such Jewish ceremonial objects as the Torah, the *tallit* (prayer shawl), and the *kippah* (skull cap). Moreover, they will beam, along with the entire congregation, at Jonathan's success.

3–9. Cowan, Paul, and Rachel Cowan. *A Torah Is Written*. Photos by Rachel Cowan. Philadelphia: Jewish Publication Society of America, 1986. 32pp. $12.95. ISBN: 0-8276-0270-7.

The Jews may be the people of the book, but prayers are read from a handwritten scroll that contains the first five books of the Bible, called the Torah. Here, we see the enormous skill, preparation, and concentration needed to transcribe Torah scrolls, and we learn what materials, tools, and procedures go into this creation. The Cowans' book is unique and handsomely produced.

5–10. Cowen, Ida, and Irene Gunther. *A Spy for Freedom: The Story of Sarah Aaronsohn.* Jewish Biography Series. New York: Lodestar, 1984. 176pp. $14.95. ISBN: 0-525-67150-1.

Aaronsohn's story reads like an action-packed novel. The child of settlers in Palestine at the turn of this century, she rejected the traditional female role to become a spy for the British against the Turkish oppressors. The book contains romance, intrigue, and adventure, but ends unhappily with Sarah's capture, torture, and suicide. The authors have produced a well-researched and exciting portrayal of a committed Zionist.

4–7. Davidson, Margaret. *The Golda Meir Story.* Rev. ed. New York: Macmillan, 1981. o.p.

This lively biography emphasizes Golda's childhood and is filled with anecdotes and personal details. Children will enjoy meeting this strong-willed child, already a political genius by age ten, who grew up to be Israel's first woman prime minister. For slightly younger readers, see:
David Adler. *Our Golda: The Story of Golda Meir.* Illus. by Donna Ruff. New York: Viking, 1984. 64pp. pap. $11.95. ISBN: 0-670-53107-3; Puffin. Women of Our Time Series. 1986. pap. $3.95. ISBN: 0-14-032104-7. Grades 2–7.

P–3. De Paola, Tomie. *Queen Esther: A Bible Story Book.* Illus. by the author. New York: Harper and Row, 1987. 40pp. pap. $8.95. ISBN: 0-06-255540-5.

The author tells a simple version of the story of the Jewish queen who saved the Persian Jews from the wicked prime minister Haman. The clear illustrations in lovely colors and interesting designs will attract the eye of the youngest listener, and the story is brief enough for a holiday story time. For more detailed retellings, see:
Ruth Brin. *The Story of Esther.* Old Testament Bible Stories. Illus. by H. Hechtkopf. Minneapolis: Lerner, 1976. 32pp. $6.95. ISBN: 0-8225-0364-6. Grades 1–6.
Miriam Chaikin. *Esther.* Illus. by Vera Rosenberry. Philadelphia: Jewish Publication Society of America, 1987. $9.95. ISBN: 0-8276-0272-3. Grades 1–6.

3–8. Drucker, Malka. Jewish Holidays Books Series. Illus. with drawings and black-and-white photographs. New York: Holiday House.
Hanukkah: Eight Nights, Eight Lights. 1980. 96pp. $14.95. ISBN: 0-8234-0377-7.
Shabbat: A Peaceful Island, 1983. 95pp. o.p.
Sukkot: A Time to Rejoice. 1982. o.p.

Less historic in perspective than Miriam Chaikin's holiday titles,[†] Drucker's books emphasize the contemporary celebration, along with related recipes, games, and crafts. Her writing is inspired and personal.

P–3. Feder, Harriet K. *It Happened in Shushan: A Purim Story.* Illus. by Rosalyn Schanzer. Rockville, Md.: Kar-Ben, 1988. pap. $3.95. ISBN: 0-930494-75-X.

This creatively illustrated Purim story is humorously retold in rebus form. Children will enjoy participating in the lilting, Yiddish refrain, "Of course not! Of course not! Of course!" as the storyteller asks questions that move the modernized Bible tale along. This handsomely produced paperback will prove popular both at home and at story times.

2–8. Fisher, Leonard Everett. *The Wailing Wall.* Illus. by the author. New York: Macmillan, 1989. 32pp. $14.95. ISBN: 0-02-735310-9.

The Wailing Wall is all that is left of the Jewish people's First and Second Temples. As Fisher's text and drawings relate, the wall has witnessed many battles from the time of the First Temple's construction in 961 B.C. (A battle of the sexes is taking place today.) Emphasizing the history of the wall (and of the Jews) to A.D. 70, Fisher writes an informative, succinct narrative and paints bold black-and-white pictures as solid and dramatic as the history of the wall itself.

5–12. Frank, Anne. *Anne Frank: The Diary of a Young Girl.* Trans. by B. M. Mooyaart. New York: Doubleday, 1967. Reprint. 312pp. $21.95. ISBN: 0-385-04019-9.

Anne's diary, discovered after she died in the Bergen-Belsen concentration camp, has become a world classic. Her writing astounds youngsters in several ways: Her finding refuge in an attic with family and friends is extra-ordinary, but equally powerful is her faith in humanity; her awakening love for another political prisoner, Peter; and her feelings of adolescent discontent toward her parents.

3–9. Freeman, Grace R., and Joan G. Sugarman. *Inside the Synagogue*. Rev. ed. Photos by Ronald Mass and others. New York: Union of American Hebrew Congregations, 1984. 64pp. pap. $6.00. ISBN: 0-8074-0268-0, 301785.

Tour a synagogue in this large paperback with full-page black-and-white photographs. Text and photos reveal the history of the Jewish temple, its place in the religious community, and a variety of the sacred objects used in the services. The authors provide a comprehensive, easy-to-understand introduction to Judaism's house of worship.

2–5. Ginsburg, Marvell. *Tattooed Torah*. Illus. by Jo Gersham. New York: Union of American Hebrew Congregations, 1983. 32pp. $6.95. ISBN: 0-8074-0252-4, 104030.

This introduction to the Holocaust for young children is based on the true story of the discovery and restoration of a small Torah from Brno, Czechoslovakia. The Torah, tattooed with a number (like its worshipers) and held prisoner in a Czech warehouse, is finally rescued by an American. Its deliverance to an American synagogue symbolizes the survival of the Jewish people.

K–4. Hirsh, Marilyn. *The Hanukkah Story*. Illus. by the author. New York: Hebrew Publishing Co., 1977. 32pp. pap. $4.95. ISBN: 0-88482-761-5.

Judah Maccabee and his men sweep across Hirsh's colorful and lively landscape to reveal the miracle of Hanukkah: that a small army could defeat the great might of the Syrian King Antiochus. The illustrations depict the costumes and architecture of the period (165 B.C.E.).

P–3. _____. *I Love Hanukkah!* Illus. by the author. New York: Holiday House, 1984. 32pp. $12.95. ISBN: 0-8234-0525-7; pap. $5.95. ISBN: 0-8234-0622-9.

_____. *I Love Passover!* Illus. by the author. New York: Holiday House, 1988. 32pp. o.p.

Two titles for the young child describe the customs of these two holidays from a youngster's perspective: family gatherings, special foods, and traditional games and festivities. The bright pictures will carry in a group setting, and the books are brief enough for preschool story times.

K–6. Hutton, Warwick. *Adam and Eve: The Bible Story*. New York: Macmillan, 1987. 32pp. $13.95. ISBN: 0-689-50433-0.

_____. *Jonah and the Great Fish*. New York: Macmillan, 1984. 32pp. $13.95. ISBN: 0-689-50283-4.

_____. *Moses in the Bulrushes*. New York: Macmillan, 1986. 32pp. $13.95. ISBN: 0-689-50393-8.

Hutton's award-winning books interpret Bible stories through the use of dramatic and beautifully executed watercolor illustrations. His prose is brief and dignified, and his paintings complement the mood of his stories.

P–1. Kahn, Katherine J., illus. Four colorful toddler board books contain the scenes and symbols of Jewish celebrations for the youngest participants. Published by Kar-Ben Copies, 1986. 12pp. $4.95 each.

Rainbow Candles: A Chanukah Counting Book by Myra Shostak. ISBN: 0-930494-59-8.
Let's Build a Sukkah by Judyth Groner and Madeline Wikler. ISBN: 0-930494-58-X.
My First Seder by Judyth Groner and Madeline Wikler. ISBN: 0-930494-61-X.
The Purim Parade by Judyth R. Saypol and Madeline Wikler. ISBN: 0-930494-60-1.

1–6. Kipness, Levin. *Aleph-Bet*. 2d ed. Illus. by Rev Raban. New York: Adama Books, 1987. $9.95. ISBN: 0-915361-8.

Calligraphy and verse introduce the Hebrew alphabet and language in this artistic picture book originally printed in Berlin in 1923. The letters are lavishly illustrated in gold and jewel-like colors, and the poetry is presented both in Hebrew and in English. This beautifully executed title reflects the truth that Hebrew is a sacred language to the Jews.

6–12. Koehn, Ilse. *Mischling, Second Degree: My Childhood in Nazi Germany.* New York: Greenwillow, 1977. 240pp. $12.88. ISBN: 0-688-84110-4.

Because one of her grandparents was Jewish, Ilse's parents divorce in order to protect their daughter from the Nazis. Thus begins Ilse's suffering. Raised as a reluctant Hitler Youth, she witnesses the atrocities that the Nazis deliver even upon their own sons and daughters. Unforgettable.

2–8. Kuskin, Karla. *Jerusalem, Shining Still.* Illus. by David Frampton. New York: HarperCollins, 1987. 32pp. $13.95. ISBN: 0-06-023548-9; PLB $13.89. ISBN: 0-06-023549-7.

Kuskin offers a poetic and informative account of 4,000 years of Jerusalem's history. From the rocky hills surrounding the city to the pebble David used to slay Goliath, the author uses the imagery of the stone to describe the endless stream of conquerors, builders, and believers that Jerusalem has attracted. Exquisite woodcuts in jewel tones depict the city as a magical, mystical place. This is a fine read-aloud choice.

3–8. Livingston, Myra Cohen, ed. *Poems for Jewish Holidays.* Illus. by Lloyd Bloom. New York: Holiday House, 1986. 32pp. $13.95. ISBN: 0-8234-0606-7.

Sixteen poems, most commissioned for this anthology by contemporary American writers, are well crafted and diverse in mood and style. The full-page, black-and-white drawings are lovely and reverent, evoking images of Orthodox Judaism.

6–12. Meltzer, Milton. *Never to Forget: The Jews of the Holocaust.* New York: Harper and Row, 1976. 217pp. $13.89. ISBN: 0-06-024175-6.

This unique account of the Holocaust focuses on the human experience of its victims and villains. While not avoiding in any way the horrible truths that emerge from diaries, letters, poetry, and other firsthand accounts,

Meltzer does not dwell solely on the horrors. Even in this hell, we are offered glimpses of special people and of moments in which love and kindness prevail.

For another powerful title that uses firsthand accounts and photographs of the victims and survivors, see:

David A. Adler. *We Remember the Holocaust.* New York: Holt, 1989. 144pp. $16.95. ISBN: 0-8050-0434-3. Grades 5–12.

Other highly readable accounts of Jewish history by Meltzer include:

The Jewish Americans: A History in Their Own Words, 1650–1950. New York: Crowell, 1982. 192pp. $13.89. ISBN: 0-690-04228-0. Grades 6–adult.

The Jews in America: A Picture Album. Philadelphia: Jewish Publication Society of America, 1985. 169pp. $12.95. ISBN: 0-8276-0246-4. Grades 5–10.

Rescue: The Story of How Gentiles Saved Jews in the Holocaust. New York: Harper and Row, 1988. 224pp. $13.95. ISBN: 0-06-024209-4; PLB $13.89. ISBN: 0-06-024210-8. Grades 6–12.

World of Our Fathers: The Jews of Eastern Europe. New York: Farrar, Straus and Giroux, 1974. 256pp. o.p. Grades 6–adult.

4–7. Metter, Bert. *Bar Mitzvah, Bat Mitzvah: How Jewish Boys and Girls Come of Age.* Illus. by Marvin Friedman. New York: Houghton, 1984. 64pp. pap. $4.95. ISBN: 0-89919-292-0.

Metter explains the history, ritual, and customs associated with the religious service that welcomes the 13-year-old boy and girl into the adult Jewish congregation. The text is appropriate for all children. For a more historic look at this ceremony, see:

Howard Greenfeld. *Bar Mitzvah.* Illus. by Elaine Grove. New York: Holt, 1981. 32pp. o.p.

K–6. Nathan, Joan. *The Children's Jewish Holiday Kitchen.* New York: Schocken, 1987. 144pp. $10.95. ISBN: 0-8052-0827-5.

In this fun- and fact-filled cookbook centering around ten Jewish holidays, Nathan invites parents and children into her kitchen to learn about the holidays, traditional foods, and recipes that both can create together. Teachers and librarians will pick up some easy craft and cooking ideas for programs. The book is nicely formatted and organized, and the spiral binding allows it to lie flat on table or counter when cooking.

P–3. Pomerantz, Barbara. *Bubby, Me and Memories*. Photos by Leon Lurie. New York: Union of American Hebrew Congregations, 1983. 32pp. $6.95. ISBN: 0-8074-0253-2, 104025.

This award-winning photographic essay, with full-page black-and-white photographs and a brief text, reassures the grieving child and introduces some Jewish mourning customs. "Our immortality is in the memories we leave behind," the foreword declares, and in this book a little girl shares her fond memories of a much-loved grandmother. This sensitive treatment is not limited to a Jewish audience.

K–6. Postman, Frederica. *The Yiddish Alphabet Book*. Illus. by Bonnie Stone. P'Nye Press, 1979. Reprint. New York: Adama, 1988. $12.95. ISBN: 1-55774-029-1.

Take an alphabetical journey to childhoods blessed with a candle-lighting *bo'be* (grandmother), a tallis-wearing *zey de* (grandfather), and the lovely lace *sha bas* (Sabbath) cloth in this basic introduction to the Yiddish language. Artist Bonnie Stone's striking, finely detailed illustrations in black, white, and burnt sienna face each page of text. In addition, fine calligraphy and an English transliteration and translation of each Yiddish word complete this handsome, lovingly produced volume.

5–10. Reiss, Johanna. *The Upstairs Room*. New York: Crowell, 1987. 196pp. $12.95. ISBN: 0-690-85127-8; PLB $12.89. ISBN: 0-690-04702-9. HarperCollins. 1987. 192pp. pap. $2.95. ISBN: 0-06-447043-1.

_____. *The Journey Back*. New York: Crowell, 1976. 128pp. $12.95. ISBN: 0-690-01252-7; HarperCollins. 1987. 224pp. pap. $2.95. ISBN: 0-06-447042-3.

Young Annie, along with her older sister, finds a cramped refuge from the Nazis in the attic of a Christian family of Dutch farmers.

The sequel describes her visit back to these brave people. Children of all faiths need to realize that there were Christians who risked their lives to save their Jewish neighbors during the Holocaust era. These books are popular for recreational reading as well as biography assignments.

K–6. Schwartz, Lynne Sharon. *The Four Questions*. Illus. by Ori Sherman. New York: Dial, 1989. 40pp. $15.95. ISBN: 0-8037-0600-6; PLB $15.89. ISBN: 0-8037-0601-4.

Monkeys and elephants with *yarmulkes* (skull caps), whales and horses bellowing *oye vey*—it takes a moment to get used to these colorful, batik-like paintings using an array of expressive animals to depict the Seder (the Passover meal) and the four questions about the meal traditionally asked by the youngest child present. This book is an exotic feast itself and a lovely interpretation of the freedom from slavery and persecution that Passover symbolizes. See also Sherman's dramatic and stylized paintings of Hanukkah in:
Amy Ehrlich. *The Story of Hanukkah*. New York: Dial, 1989. PLB $14.89. ISBN: 0-8037-0616-2; $14.95. ISBN: 0-8037-0615-4. Grades K–4.

4–12. Singer, Isaac Bashevis. *A Day of Pleasure: Stories of a Boy Growing Up in Warsaw*. Photos by Roman Vishniac. New York: Farrar, Straus and Giroux, 1986. 160pp. pap. $3.95. ISBN: 0-374-41696-6.

These nineteen stories about Isaac Singer's boyhood in Warsaw, Poland, are told with humor and skill. The author's Jewish world was destroyed under the Nazi regime but will live on forever in his entertaining memoir and in Vishniac's priceless black-and-white photographs. Read this one aloud. For an informative biography of Singer, see:
Paul Kresh. *Isaac Bashevis Singer: The Story of a Storyteller*. Jewish Biography Series. New York: Lodestar Books, 1984. 192pp. $13.95. ISBN: 0-525-67156-0. Grades 5–12.

5–12. Sofer, Barbara. *Kids Love Israel, Israel Loves Kids: A Travel Guide for Families*. Rockville, Md.: Kar-Ben, 1988. 256pp. pap. $11.95. ISBN: 0-930494-73-3.

The author lives in Jerusalem with her five children and has a thorough knowledge of both the sights of Israel and the travel needs of families. She provides a practical guide with information on transportation, food, lodging, tours, parks, beaches, camps, special holidays and holy days, and advice on how to plan this great adventure.

P–6. Spier, Peter, illus. *Noah's Ark*. New York: Doubleday, 1977. 44pp. PLB $15.00. ISBN: 0-385-09473-6; pap. $13.99. ISBN: 0-385-2730-8; 1981. 48pp. pap. $6.95. ISBN: 0-385-17302-4.

"The Flood," a lean and clever poem by seventeenth-century poet Jacobus Revius, serves as an introduction to Spier's hilarious yet poignant retelling. The colorful cartoon-like drawings invite readers to examine the detailed description of ark life. Panoramic views of the desolate ark contrast with the noisy and mischievous antics of the animals, enabling the reader to appreciate Noah's awesome challenge. For an attractive retelling for the younger child, see:

Tomie de Paola. *Noah and the Ark*. Illus. by the author. New York: Harper and Row, 1984. 40pp. $12.95. ISBN: 0-86683-699-3; pap. $5.95. ISBN: 0-86683-690-3. Grades P–2.

3–7. Taubes, Hella. *The Bible Speaks*. Trans. by Lolla Bloch. Illus. by Dan Bar-Giora. 3 vols. New York: Bloch, 1974. $14.95 each. ISBN: 0-686-76831-0.

In this appealing trio of oversized books printed on heavy stock, the retellings are succinct and inviting, and the reteller does not hesitate to insert her own opinion on certain important matters. A nonsexist attitude, bold black-and-white drawings, and a text that reads well aloud make for a very attractive set. Other excellent anthologies of Bible stories for this grade range include:

Walter de la Mare. *Stories from the Bible: From the Garden of Eden to the Promised Land*. New York: Knopf, 1961. Reprint. Winchester, Mass.: Faber and Faber, 1985. 418pp. pap. $5.95. ISBN: 0-571-11086-X.

Lore Segal. *The Book of Adam to Moses*. Illus. by Leonard Baskin, New York: Knopf, 1987. 144pp. $14.99. ISBN: 0-394-96757-7;

Schocken. 1989. pap. $11.95. ISBN: 0-8052-0961-1.

5–12. Volavkova, Hana, ed. *I Never Saw Another Butterfly: Children's Drawings and Poems from Terezin Concentration Camp, 1942–1944*. Trans. by Jeanne Nemcova. Illus. by the children. New York: Schocken, 1987. pap. $6.95. ISBN: 0-8052-0598-5.

It is sobering to experience poems and drawings created by children in Nazi concentration camps. Read, for example, these lines by young Franta Bass: "When the blossom comes to bloom/The little boy will be no more." Moreover, these poems continue to speak of love, kindness, and hope. This powerful book is already a classic in children's Judaica.

P–3. Zwerin, Raymond A., and Audrey Marcus. *But This Night Is Different: A Seder Experience*. Illus. by Judith Gwyn Brown. New York: Union of American Hebrew Congregations, 1981. 48pp. pap. $10.95. ISBN: 0-8074-0032-7, 102561.

Young children will enjoy learning about the ritualistic Passover meal (the Seder) as they pour over the big, colorful watercolor pictures and listen to the traditional question "Why is tonight different from all other nights?" repeated like a chant on every page. This is a good choice both for religious school story times and for public library collections.

PROGRAMMING IDEAS

HANUKKAH

Hanukkah falls in the month of December and celebrates the Jewish triumph over the Syrian King Antiochus, who tried to outlaw Judaism (175–165 B.C.E.). The heroes in this historic event are Judah Maccabee and his four brothers, who led a small band of Jewish rebels to victory over an enormous Syrian army.

The Hanukkah festival celebrates the rededication of the Temple in Jerusalem, which had been desecrated by the enemy. Hanukkah has become an important holiday to American Jews largely because of its proximity to Christmas. It represents an alternative holiday for Jewish children to celebrate.

The materials and activities in this program guide are appropriate for children in preschool through third grade, and can be presented in all types of schools and libraries.

Explaining Hanukkah to the Audience

BACKGROUND READING FOR ADULTS

Chaikin, Miriam. *Light Another Candle: The Story and Meaning of Hanukkah.*[†]
Drucker, Malka. *Hanukkah: Eight Nights, Eight Lights.*[†]
Hirsh, Marilyn. *The Hanukkah Story.*[†]

CUSTOM AND HISTORY BOOKS TO SHARE ALOUD WITH CHILDREN

Adler, David A. *A Picture Book of Hanukkah.*[†]
Ehrlich, Amy. *The Story of Hanukkah.*[†]
Hirsh, Marilyn. *The Hanukkah Story.*[†]
_____. *I Love Hanukkah!*[†]

Tales to Adapt for Storytelling and Dramatics

Davis, Enid. *Latke Lad.*[†]
_____. *The Five Maccabees Tough.*[†]
Hirsh, Marilyn. *Potato Pancakes All Around.*[†]
Shofar.[*] This attractive, high-quality children's magazine contains articles, stories, puzzles, and so forth on contemporary American Jewish life. The magazine is a good resource for holiday programming.
Singer, Isaac Bashevis. *Zlateh the Goat and Other Stories.*[†]

Creative Dramatics

To explain the custom of lighting a candle a night for eight nights, have the children create a "living *menorah*" (a candle holder). Library footstools are the nine candle holders and the children are the candles, each holding a brightly colored cardboard flame.

Pretend it's the eighth night of Hanukkah and all the candles are standing in the holders being "lit" by the ninth helper candle as prayers are sung in Hebrew. Then explain how Hanukkah candles disappear rather quickly, and watch the children enjoy "melting" off the stools and back to their seats.

One recommended recording for this activity is Shimon and Ilana's *Chanukah Songs for Children* (Elite Records, 214–58 Whitehall Terrace, Queens Village, NY 11427, $9.98).

Finger Plays

Look for finger plays with themes involving candles, spinning tops, and presents. Here are two I adapted:

Candles and Latkes
(Tune: "Ten Little Indians")

One yellow, two yellow, three yellow candles,
Four yellow, five yellow, six yellow candles,
Seven yellow, eight yellow, nine yellow candles
Flickering gaily on Hanukkah night.

One yummy, two yummy, three yummy latkes,
Four yummy, five yummy, six yummy latkes,
Seven yummy, eight yummy, nine yummy latkes,
Candles and latkes, what a wonderful sight!

Have You Ever Seen a Dreidel?
(Tune: "Have You Ever Seen a Lassie?")

Have you ever seen a dreidel spin this way and
that way? (fingers spin)
Have you ever seen a dreidel spin this way and
that?
Spin this way and that way, (turn your body
around)
And this way and that way,
Have you ever seen a dreidel spin this way and
that?

Filmstrips and Movies

See the Resources section at the end of this chapter for publishers' catalogs containing filmstrips and videos based on Hanukkah customs and themes. For example, Miller-Brody has some wonderful adaptations of Isaac Singer's stories on filmstrips.

Crafts and Cooking Ideas

Brinn, Ruth Esrig. *Let's Celebrate;*[†] *More Let's Celebrate.*[†]
Nathan, Joan. *The Children's Jewish Holiday Kitchen.*[†]

LUCKY DREIDEL CHARM NECKLACE

The dreidel is a toy top with four sides, each bearing a Hebrew letter. If the dreidel lands on the letter *gimel*, the spinner takes all the pennies or nuts from the pot. It is traditional to play with the dreidel during Hanukkah. The lucky dreidel charm necklace is not a traditional craft but, rather, an easy project and good program souvenir (see figure 1).

Materials
  Construction paper
  Crayons or colored markers
  Yarn
  Hole puncher

Directions
  1. Dreidel shapes can be precut or made by the children and cut out.
  2. Draw the Hebrew letter *gimel* on the dreidel.
  3. Punch a hole in the top of the dreidel.
  4. Slip the yarn through and tie the ends in a knot.
  5. Wear the lucky charm when you play the dreidel game at the program or later at home.

Inexpensive dreidels can be purchased at synagogue gift shops. Instructions on how to play dreidel games and craft ideas on making dreidels can be found in Chaya M. Burstein's *The Jewish Kids Catalog.*[†]

Games

Drucker, Malka. *Hanukkah: Eight Nights, Eight Lights*[†] (see dreidel games).

Using the symbols of Hanukkah—the menorah, the dreidel, and Judah Maccabee—adapt traditional children's games, for example, pin the candle on the menorah.

PASSOVER

Passover is a springtime holiday that celebrates the Jews' liberation from Egyptian bondage. The story is told in Exodus. Passover is celebrated at home during a special, ritualistic meal called the Seder. The Seder follows the Haggadah, a prayer book, which contains the story of Exodus along with prayers and songs.

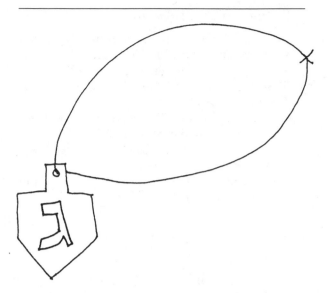

Figure 1. This lucky dreidel charm always lands on the winning *gimel*.

Special foods, such as matzah, are eaten during the week-long holiday, and foods that contain yeast are forbidden.

The theme of freedom is closely associated with Passover by Jews and other cultures; indeed, Harriet Tubman, the heroine of the Underground Railroad, is called the "Black Moses" by her people.

The materials and activities in this program are appropriate for children in preschool through third grade and can be presented in all types of schools and libraries.

Explaining Passover to the Audience

BACKGROUND READING FOR ADULTS

Chaikin, Miriam. *Ask Another Question: The Story and Meaning of Passover.*[†]
Kustanowitz, Shulamit, and Ronnie Foont. *A First Haggadah.* Illus. by Ronnie Foont. New York: Hebrew Publishing Co., 1980. 64pp. $6.95. ISBN: 0-88482-766-6.

CUSTOM AND HISTORY BOOKS TO SHARE ALOUD WITH CHILDREN

Adler, David. *A Picture Book of Passover.*[†]
Hirsh, Marilyn. *I Love Passover!*[†]
Schwartz, Lynne Sharon. *The Four Questions.*[†]

Stories to Read Aloud

Hutton, Warwick. *Moses in the Bulrushes.*[†]

Marcus, Audrey, and Raymond A. Zwerin. *But This Night Is Different: A Seder Experience.*[†]

Miller, Deborah Uchill. *Only Nine Chairs: A Tall Tale for Passover.*[†]

Peretz, I. L., and Uri Shulevitz. *The Magician.* Illus. by Uri Shulevitz. New York: Macmillan, 1985. 32pp. $11.95. ISBN: 0-02-782770-4. Grades K–4.

A magician (Elijah) provides a poor couple with a Passover feast.

Tales to Adapt for Storytelling and Dramatics

A. Tell the story of Exodus, highlighting the ten plagues. This would be appropriate for children in grades 1 and up. The narrative ends tragically with the death of firstborn Egyptian children, revealing how oppressors can become victims of their own punishments.

B. "One Little Goat" is a traditional accumulative rhyme about a father bartering a small goat. It can be found in most Haggadahs and in Passover anthologies and can be retold as a feltboard story. Marilyn Hirsh's picture-book version (New York: Holiday House, 1979) is out-of-print.

Finger Plays

Visiting Israel
by Enid Davis

When you go to Israel,
There are lots of things to do: (count on fingers)
Ride a camel on the desert, (riding motion)
Shake the sand out of your shoe; (tap bottom of shoe)
You can climb the great Masada, (climbing motion)
That's a ruin very steep, (stretch out arms lengthwise)
You can visit an old Temple
Where the people laugh and weep. (dab tear from eye)
It's a lovely place to visit,
With its beaches in great motion; (roll arms)
But it's awfully hot in Israel, (wipe sweat from forehead)
So bring your suntan lotion! (dab on lotion)

Matzah Ball
by Enid Davis

Mama made a matzah ball (form ball with hands)
And put it in a pot, (drop in pot)
She stirred it and she stirred it,
'Til it was nice and hot. (stirring motion)
She poured some in a little dish, (pouring motion)
The one with pretty roses, (cup hands)
And promised if I ate it up, (eating motion)
I'd be as wise as Moses! (point to yourself)

Crafts and Cooking Ideas

Brinn, Ruth Esrig. *Let's Celebrate;*[†] *More Let's Celebrate.*[†]

Nathan, Joan. *The Children's Jewish Holiday Kitchen.*[†]

Games

During the Seder meal, an adult hides a piece of matzah, which he or she will buy back from the child who finds it. Therefore, hide-and-seek games can be used during this program.

The symbols and themes of Passover are Moses, the Ten Plagues, the Red Sea, the Seder, Jerusalem, Israel, the prophet Elijah, spring, and freedom. Adapt traditional children's games to fit these themes; for example, change "London Bridge Is Falling Down" to a Red Sea adventure:

The Red Sea is falling down, falling down, falling down.
The Red Sea is falling down,
My dear children.
Hurry up, we're coming through, coming through, coming through.
Hurry up, we're coming through,
My dear Moses.

Trust me. They'll love it!

PURIM

Purim is a late-winter holiday that falls several weeks before Passover and celebrates a queen's victory over the wicked Persian prime minister Haman. The queen, of course, is the Biblical heroine Esther.

Purim is celebrated with a great deal of noise and merriment, with people masquerading as the story's protagonists. Such gaiety during the dreary days of late winter makes Purim a tempting holiday to celebrate at story time!

The materials and activities in this program are appropriate for children in preschool through third grade and can be presented in all types of schools and libraries.

Explaining Purim to the Audience

BACKGROUND READING FOR ADULTS

Chaikin, Miriam. *Make Noise, Make Merry: The Story and Meaning of Purim.*[†]

CUSTOM AND HISTORY BOOKS TO SHARE ALOUD WITH CHILDREN

Brin, Ruth. *The Story of Esther.*[†]
Chaikin, Miriam. *Esther.*[†]

Suggested Program Framework

Introduce the stories found here or Jewish or Persian folktales by saying that Queen Esther enjoyed entertaining her husband by bringing storytellers to the castle. The king would direct Esther to begin the festivities with these words:

Queen Esther, Queen Esther, bring in the jester!

Crown two children and seat them on library thrones. Have the king announce these words as the court (the audience) joyfully repeats the chant after him.

Stories to Read or Dramatize

De Paola, Tomie. *Queen Esther: A Bible Story Book.*[†]
Feder, Harriet K. *It Happened in Shushan: A Purim Story.*[†]
   Enlarge the pictures in this rebus version or put the kids in costumes and have the audience call out their names as you read the book.

Filmstrips and Movies

"Purim for Little Children." New York: Union of American Hebrew Congregations, $18. Fifty-seven frames that capture the merriment of Purim. Guide and script included.
"A Purim Costume for Shoshanah." New York: Union of American Hebrew Congregations,

$18. An Israeli fairy tale with a Cinderella theme. Guide and script included.

A Feltboard Song

It is a Purim tradition to read the Bible story of Esther (the Megillah) and to boo loudly whenever Haman's name is pronounced. Here's an adaptation of the song "B-I-N-G-O" that my audiences have enjoyed.

1. Make five black felt squares. With a brightly colored felt letter glued on each square, spell out *HAMAN*. On the reverse side of the squares spell out *BOOO!* (one character per square).
2. Arrange the squares vertically on the feltboard.
3. To the tune of "B-I-N-G-O," sing:

   There was a man and he was bad and Haman was his name, oh . . .
   H-A-M-A-N, H-A-M-A-N, H-A-M-A-N, and Haman was his name, BOO!

4. Turn over the *H* square and reveal the *B*. Now sing:

   There was a man and he was bad and Haman was his name, oh . . .
   BOO!-A-M-A-N, BOO!-A-M-A-N, BOO!-A-M-A-N, and Haman was his name, BOO!

5. Continue to substitute "Boo!" for all the letters in Haman's name, until all the squares are turned and you've spelled out *B-O-O-O-!*

Finger Play

Haman is identified by his three-cornered hat. In fact, his hat has inspired the classic dainty hamantashen, a triangular pastry with a fruit filling. Use the traditional finger play "My Hat It Has Three Corners."

My hat it has three corners,
Three corners has my hat,
If it did not have three corners,
It would not be my hat.

Craft and Cooking Ideas

Brinn, Ruth Esrig. *Let's Celebrate; More Let's Celebrate.*[†]
Nathan, Joan. *The Children's Jewish Holiday Kitchen.*[†]

MAKE A MEGILLAH!

The Old Testament story of Queen Esther is traditionally read aloud at synagogue services from a scroll called a *Megillah*. After the children have been told this tale, they can draw the leading characters on paper, roll up the picture, and tie it with a ribbon (see figure 2). The scroll can be untied upon reaching home and the story on the Megillah can be told to parents and friends.

Materials

White parchment paper, 8 inches by 10 inches
Crayons or markers
Blue ribbon

Directions

Program leaders can draw the four characters on a large piece of paper for the children to copy, or the youngsters can make up their own pictures. Roll up the completed pictures and tie with blue ribbons.

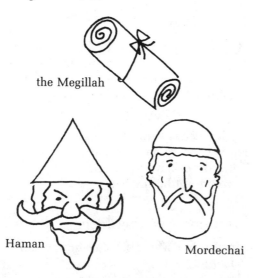

King Ahashverus   Queen Esther

the Megillah

Haman   Mordechai

Figure 2. Leading characters from the story of Queen Esther, traditionally read from a Megillah

RESOURCES

Children's Judaica

Coalition for Alternatives in Jewish Education
468 Park Ave. S.
New York, NY 10016
(212) 696-0746

Devoted to innovative learning.

Davis, Enid. *A Comprehensive Guide to Children's Literature with a Jewish Theme.* New York: Schocken, 1981. 177pp. o.p.

A compilation of over 500 annotated, critical reviews and resources with a detailed subject index.

Jewish Book Council
15 East 26th St.
New York, NY 10010
(212) 532-4949

Subscribe to its *Jewish Book World* to keep up with new children's Judaica. Free.

Jewish Book News
Book News Inc.
303 W. 10th St.
New York, NY 10014

Jewish book reviews and more. Published twice a year, $4 per issue.

Jewish Education Service of North America
730 Broadway
New York, NY 10003-9540
(212) 529-2000

Information and evaluation of Jewish publications, conferences, education, and library service.

Jewish Music Council
15 E. 26th St.
New York, NY 10010
(212) 532-4949

Catalog and information on Jewish music.

Posner, Marcia. *Juvenile Judaica: The Jewish Values Book Finder.* Association of Jewish Libraries, 122 E. 42nd St., New York, NY 10168. 1985.

A critical evaluation of children's books in the English language.

Distributors, Publishers, and Producers of Books and Media

Aviv Judaica Imports
Brooklyn, NY 11219

Children's stickers, puzzles, games with a Jewish theme. Order through synagogue gift shops or Jewish bookstores.

Board of Jewish Education of Greater New York
426 W. 58th St.
New York, NY 10019
(212) 245-8200

Offers a variety of children's films and filmstrips, records and cassettes, and books.

Caedmon
10 E. 53rd St.
New York, NY 10022
(212) 207-7000

Recordings based on fine, popular children's literature with a Jewish theme.

Children's Television Workshop
1 Lincoln Plaza
New York, NY 10023
(212) 595-3456

Five "Sesame Street in Israel" videos. $34.95 each.

Enid Davis
64 Dior Terrace
Los Altos, CA 94022

Ergo Media Video Catalog
P.O. Box 2037
Teaneck, NJ 07666
(201) 692-0404

Over 50 educational and recreational videos on Jewish subjects.

Jewish Educational Toys
P.O. Box 469
Brooklyn, NY 11225

Puzzles with Hebrew letters, etc.

Kar-Ben Copies, Inc.
6800 Tildenwood Lane
Rockville, MD 20852
(301) 984-8733
Toll free: (800) 452-7236

Publishes books, special holiday calendars, and other material with child appeal to celebrate the Jewish holidays.

Ktav Publishing House
900 Jefferson St.
Hoboken, NJ 07030
(201) 963-9524

Holiday records, books, toys, decorations, maps, and wall charts.

Miller-Brody Productions
Div. of Random House, Inc.
400 Hahn Rd.
Westminster, MD 21157
(301) 848-1900

Producers of quality recordings, filmstrips, and cassettes based on children's literature.

Shapolsky Publishers
136 W. 22nd St.
New York, NY 10011
(212) 633-2022

A publisher and distributor of Jewish children's literature, records, and videos.

Shofar
43 Northcote Drive
Melville, NY 11747

Subscription: $14.50.

Tara Publications
29 Derby Ave.
Cedarhurst, NY 11516

Distributor of a wide selection of music and songbooks for adults and children.

Union of American Hebrew Congregations
838 Fifth Ave.
New York, NY 10021
(212) 249-0100

Offers a large variety of educational audiovisuals, filmstrips, and videos on all aspects of Jewish life.

World Tone Music, Inc.
230 Seventh Ave.
New York, NY 10011
(212) 691-1934

Offers Israeli folk dance music, instructional dance books, and Hebrew and Yiddish folk songs.

CHAPTER 6

Native American Materials and Programs

by Elaine Goley

The selections in this chapter were chosen to provide children with culturally valid and accurate information on Native American cultures. Although some worthy books have not been included because of space limitations, a concerted effort has been made to eliminate books that present stereotypes of Native Americans. It is especially important to reject those stereotypes in books for children because young readers often are not aware of the inaccuracies or might, if they are Native Americans, be hurt or offended by them.

Stereotypes of Native Americans are, unfortunately, part of the national popular culture in the United States. Many movies, television programs, books, magazine advertisements, and even common sayings continue to portray Native Americans, both historically and currently, as a monolithic group with decidedly negative personal traits. These negative portrayals continue to permeate literature for young people. The stereotypes of Native Americans that books and other media have created are strong images that cannot easily be corrected. For this reason, we as educators should first reeducate ourselves. We should sensitize ourselves and children to the cultural dignity, worth, and values of all minority ethnic groups. It is only through real understanding of other groups and individuals that we can help children understand the world around them and, ultimately, themselves.

In addition, we must be sensitive to stereotypes of Native Americans in storytelling and craft programs for children. It is important to introduce ethnic information to children in ways that are positive, accurate, sensitive, and humane.

Cultural validity connotes not only accuracy in conveying information but also accuracy in reflecting the dreams, hopes, fears, and suffering of a people. For too long, American history has been told only from a white, European perspective. A child's self-esteem and personal dignity, which are essential to survival in a world of adversities, are developed only through understanding. Learning to respect other cultures and values as represented in children's books can help lead to this understanding.

Mythology and legend can also provide keys to understanding the great mysteries of life. The questions Who am I? Who made me? What is the purpose of life? are frequently answered in the mythologies and legends of various ethnic cultures. The insights children can gain from such stories often help them deal with the trials and disappointments encountered in life. By absorbing the values of various cultures through legend, folklore, and mythology, young people, it is hoped, achieve understanding of others. As a Native American saying tells us, true understanding comes not from the mind but from the heart.

BIBLIOGRAPHY

FICTION

K–3. Baylor, Byrd. *Hawk, I'm Your Brother.* New York: Scribner's, 1976. 48pp. $13.95. ISBN: 0-684-14571-5.

The subtlety of Peter Parnall's illustrations evokes the quiet and profound nature of this story. An Indian child perceives nature as his culture perceives it—as part of the continuum of life. The themes of this eloquent book are the regenerative cycle of life and the interdependency of all living things. The spirit of the book is true to the Native American ideas of harmony with nature and the joy the human spirit shares with animals.

K–3. De Paola, Tomie. *The Legend of the Bluebonnet. An Old Tale of Texas.* New York: Putnam, 1983. 32pp. $13.95. ISBN: 0-399-20937-9. pap. $5.95. ISBN: 0-399-20938-7.

This legend, based on a Comanche tale, explains how the Bluebonnet, a Texas wildflower, came to be. De Paola's vibrant, full-color illustrations use the earth tones of the Texas hill country and the blues and pinks of the Texas skies. The author diligently researched the origins of the tale and found its many variants. The legend is told with the dignity and reverence common to Native American mythology.

K–3. _____. *The Legend of the Indian Paintbrush.* Sandcastle Series. New York: Putnam, 1988. 40pp. $13.95. ISBN: 0-399-21534-4.

Award-winning author-illustrator de Paola retells the beautiful Indian legend of the Indian Paintbrush, a wildflower common in Texas and Wyoming. The spirit of de Paola's text and the beauty of his illustrations capture reverently and profoundly this Native American legend of the Indian boy who paints the great deeds of his people on animal skins. The illustrations, in the muted earth tones of the southwest and the brilliant colors of the southwestern sunset, evoke the mystery and magic of Native American mythology.

5–8. George, Chief Dan. *My Heart Soars.* Vancouver: Hancock House, 1989. 96pp. pap. $7.95. ISBN: 0-88839-231-1.

Chief Dan George describes the experience of being a Native American who lives in two cultures. His poetry and prose reflect the deepest sorrows and greatest joys of Native American peoples. The themes of harmony with nature and love of fellow humans are evoked by Chief George's powerful verbal images, and the drawings reflect the dignity and grace of traditional Indian cultures.

3–5. Goble, Paul. *Buffalo Woman.* New York: Bradbury, 1984. 32pp. $13.95. ISBN: 0-02-737720-2.

Goble's hauntingly beautiful full-color illustrations bring this legend of the Great Plains Indians to life. The themes of this tale are the kinship of humans and nature, and the redeeming power of love. The illustrations and text evoke the magic of the oral storytelling traditions of these people.

6–8. Highwater, Jamake. *ANPAO: An American Indian Odyssey.* Philadelphia: Lippincott, 1977. 256pp. $13.95. ISBN: 0-397-31750-6; New York: Harper and Row, 1983. pap. $8.95. ISBN: 0-06-131986-4.

The powerful stone lithographs of Native American artist Fritz Scholder illuminate the story of Anpao, whose exploits have been passed down through the Native American oral tradition. The story follows Anpao from youth to manhood, and bears themes and elements from traditional Indian folklore.

3–6. _____. *Moonsong Lullaby.* New York: Lothrop, 1981. 32pp. $14.95. ISBN: 0-688-00427-X.

The lullaby is inspired by the Native American lore and traditions of Highwater's Blackfoot and Cherokee ancestors. The theme of this haunting work, harmony with nature, is common in Native American folklore and culture. The text is enhanced by beautiful and moving photographs.

5–8. O'Dell, Scott. *Black Star, Bright Dawn.* Boston: Houghton, 1988. 144pp. $14.95. ISBN: 0-395-47778-6.

Bright Dawn lives between two cultures: that of the white settlers and her own Eskimo heritage. Her search for identity takes the form of all great quests: She enters the 1,000-mile Iditarod dogsled race. Her courage and convictions are tested as she and her lead dog, Black Star, who is mostly wolf, fight for their lives. Bright Dawn is aided by the skills of her Eskimo culture and by her lead dog's instincts.

5–8. _____. *Island of the Blue Dolphins.* New York: Houghton, 1960. 161pp. $13.95. ISBN: 0-395-06962-9.

This Newbery Award book, based on an historical incident, depicts the struggle of a young Indian girl who is stranded on an island off the coast of California for many years. Her triumph over loneliness, the elements, and the death of her brother is possible because of her inner strength of spirit and the skills of her Indian culture. The motifs of Native American culture—harmony with nature, dignity, strength of spirit, and resourcefulness—are eloquently presented.

5–8. _____. *Streams to the River, River to the Sea: A Novel of Sacagawea.* Boston: Houghton, 1986. $14.95. ISBN: 0-395-40430-4; New York: Fawcett, 1987. pap. 176pp. $3.50. ISBN: 0-449-70244-8.

O'Dell brings the Shoshone girl Sacagawea to life in this sensitively written novel. Sacagawea served as a guide for the Lewis and Clark Expedition to map the Northwest. Her facility with languages and her knowledge of the land and the customs of the Shoshone people were crucial to the success of the expedition. The author used the journals of Lewis and Clark as background for the novel, the spirit and language of which are true to Indian customs and spirit.

2–6. Ortiz, Simon. *The People Shall Continue.* San Francisco: Children's Book Press, 1988. 24pp. $12.95. ISBN: 0-89239-041-7.

The author, a Native American (Ancoma) poet, has written this history of Native American peoples in the rhythmic, eloquent style of Native American legend. In simple language, Ortiz weaves the epic story of Native Americans from the creation to the present. The story embraces the traditional tribal values that Native Americans share—reverence for life and the land. The colorful illustrations help us understand the messages of Native American history, values, and culture.

4–8. Sneve, Virginia Driving Hawk. *Jimmy Yellow Hawk.* New York: Holiday House, 1972. 76pp. o.p.

In the old days, a Sioux boy earned his name by doing a courageous deed. Jimmy is growing up on a modern Sioux reservation where his life is full of adventure and courageous deeds are still possible. A rodeo and a pow wow are described as Jimmy participates in the customs and rituals of his tribal culture.

5–8. Speare, Elizabeth George. *The Sign of the Beaver.* Boston: Houghton, 1983. 144pp. $12.95. ISBN: 0-395-33890-5.

Thirteen-year-old Matt, left alone to guard his family's cabin in the wilderness, survives his lonely vigil with the help of an Indian boy. From the boy, Matt learns Indian survival skills and comes to appreciate the customs of the Beaver Clan. Finally, he understands the Indians' struggle to keep their culture alive as their land is invaded by white people.

NONFICTION

K–3. Aliki. *Corn Is Maize: The Gift of the Indians.* A Let's-Read-and-Find-Out Science Book. New York: Crowell, 1976. 40pp. PLB $13.89. ISBN: 0-690-00975-5.

One of the Let's-Read-and-Find-Out Science Books, this volume explains in simple text and clear, color illustrations how Native Americans planted, cultivated, harvested, and used corn. The origin of corn, its propagation, and the contributions it has made through the ages to Native American cultures as well as to others are explored.

5–9. Ashabranner, Brent. *Children of the Maya*. New York: Putnam, 1986. 96pp. $14.95. ISBN: 0-399-21707-X.

The plight of the modern Native American refugee from Central America is examined in this story of modern Mayan refugees from Guatemala who settle in Indiantown, Florida. Photos of the Mayans and interviews with them and those who help them vividly present the effects of the violence in their native country and the ways in which the refugees adjust to life in the United States.

5–8. Bealer, Alex W. *Only the Names Remain: The Cherokees and the Trail of Tears*. Boston: Little, Brown, 1972. $14.95. ISBN: 0-316-08520-0.

With an easy, narrative style and excellent black-and-white illustrations, the author eloquently recounts the tragic Trail of Tears forced march and its effects on Native American tribal culture. Bealer clearly presents the history of Cherokee-White relations in the United States.

5–8. Beck, Barbara L. *The Ancient Maya*. New York: Watts, 1983. 72pp. $10.40. ISBN: 0-531-04529-3.

History, trade, religion, writing, and the arts are all discussed in a well-written text as the author explores the rise and collapse of the Mayan civilization. Black-and-white illustrations show the ruins of Mayan cities as well as artifacts, and a chart of Mayan time periods and one of Mayan numbers and symbols are included.

5–8. _____. *The Aztecs*. New York: Watts, 1983. 72pp. $10.40. ISBN: 0-531-04522-6.

The rise of Aztec society, the Aztec calendar, Aztec arts, and the Spanish conquistadores are all described in this concise volume. Black-and-white photographs and illustrations of the Codex illuminate Aztec life in Central America. Important archaeological sites are highlighted and illustrated.

5–8. _____. *The Incas*. New York: Watts, 1983. 72pp. $10.40. ISBN: 0-531-04528-5.

Architecture, religion, science, and the arts are highlighted as the author continues her exploration of Native Central and South American cultures. The origins of the Peruvian Incas and their technological skills are described. Black-and-white illustrations of art, archaeological sites, and modern Incan life are included.

K–6. Behrens, June. *Powwow: Festivals and Holidays*. Ethnic and Traditional Holidays Series. Chicago: Children's Press, 1983. 32pp. $14.60. ISBN: 0-516-02387-X. pap. $3.95. ISBN: 0-516-42387-8.

This book describes the gatherings of Native American families of many tribes as they celebrate their culture through competitions in dancing as well as arts, crafts, games, and songs. Color photographs document these events as well as the body painting and costumes that are an important part of this cultural celebration.

4–8. Bierhorst, John. *A Cry from the Earth: Music of the North American Indians*. New York: Four Winds, 1979. o.p.

Music is an essential element in all Indian cultural life. It is used for every activity, including babysitting, mourning the dead, and controlling the weather. This book presents the music of Northwest Coast Indians, Great Basin Indians, and many others. The songs reflect the melodic and rhythmic ingenuity of Indian music while the text explains Indian music and introduces each type of song. The lyrics and music are enhanced by photographs and maps.

5–8. Bleeker, Sonia. *The Cherokee Indians of the Mountains*. New York: Morrow, 1952. o.p.

The author's easy, narrative style enhances her description of the history and customs of the Cherokee as she presents everyday village life for young people in the nineteenth century. The text explores marriage customs, nature rites, ball games, hunting, and shamans. Of particular interest is the author's discussion of Sequoia, the chief who developed a written language for the Cherokee and who was instrumental in the writing of the Cherokee constitution.

4–8. Boy Scouts of America. *Indian Lore*. New Brunswick, N.J.: The Scouts, 1959. 90pp. pap. $1.85. ISBN: 0-8395-3358-6.

In this volume of the Boy Scout Merit Badge series, North American Indian tribes are arranged by geographic region. The history and culture of each tribal group are covered, including housing, village life, family life, clothing, religion and mythology, arts and crafts, and warfare and weapons. There is also a chapter on authentic Indian games. Black-and-white illustrations of clothing, tools, and houses enhance the text. Crafts and program ideas can be garnered from this book as well as from other merit badge books on leatherwork, basketry, and pottery.

5–8. Crosher, Judith. *The Aztecs*. Peoples of the Past Series. Morristown, N.J.: Silver Burdett, 1977. o.p.

Numerous color illustrations and photographs emphasize such aspects of Aztec culture as sacred games, clothing, arts, and daily life. Maps and reproductions illustrate the history and geography of the Aztecs as well as the effects of the Spanish Conquest on Aztec culture. A chronological chart compares Aztec cultural development with that of other groups.

5–8. Fichter, George S. *How the Plains Indians Lived*. New York: David McKay, 1980. $10.95. ISBN: 0-679-20683-3.

After a short description of each Plains Indian tribe in the first chapter, Fichter goes on to discuss the effect of the White prairie farmers and buffalo hunters on Indian life. The text highlights the sign language of the Plains Indians as well as their beliefs, customs, games, and sports.

3–5. Fradin, Dennis. *The Pawnee*. A New True Book. Chicago: Children's Press, 1988. 48pp. $14.60. ISBN: 0-516-01155-3. pap. $4.95. ISBN: 0-516-41155-1.

This book covers the history, culture, and mythology of the Pawnee people. One chapter is devoted to the importance of the buffalo to Pawnee life—from food to ritual. Another chapter describes the loss of Pawnee traditional tribal lands to white people. Period photographs and illustrations as well as contemporary color photographs help to illuminate Pawnee history and culture.

4–8. Freedman, Russell. *Buffalo Hunt*. New York: Holiday House, 1988. 52pp. $16.95. ISBN: 0-8234-0702-0.

Freedman eloquently describes the importance of the buffalo to Native American mythology and culture as he notes the reverence that Native Americans have for the animal that provided their sustenance. The buffalo was worshiped as a sacred animal with mystical powers and the buffalo hunt was surrounded by ritual and mystery. Even the Milky Way was created by the buffalo according to Indian legend. Buffalo dreams contain magic and mystical qualities. Freedman describes the simultaneous demise of the buffalo and of traditional Native American culture in the West.

5–8. _____. *Indian Chiefs*. New York: Holiday House, 1987. 160pp. $16.95. ISBN: 0-8234-0625-3.

This picturesque history book includes the biographies of Red Cloud, Satanta, Quanah Parker, Washakie, Chief Joseph, and Sitting Bull. Full-page period photographs, maps, and reproductions of paintings by Remington and others make the book a unique resource. The book eloquently recounts the nineteenth-century struggle of Native Americans to preserve their vanishing lands and culture.

4–8. Gates, Frieda. *North American Indian Masks: Craft and Legend*. New York: Walker, 1982. 64pp. $8.95. ISBN: 0-8027-6462-2. PLB $9.85. ISBN: 0-8027-6463-0.

This book describes the mythology of ritual masks as well as their uses in Native American societies. Instructions for making facsimilies of the Southwest Kochina masks as well as the masks of the Eastern Iroquois, the Northwest Coast Indians, the Alaskan Eskimos, and others are included. Easy directions for constructing the masks are clarified with photographs, illustrations, and diagrams. The book will be useful both in developing culturally valid craft programs and in providing essential information on the ritual uses of masks in the context of Native American mythology.

4–8. Glubok, Shirley. *The Art of the Southwest Indians*. New York: Macmillan, 1971. 48pp. o.p.

One of a series of books written by Glubok on the art of various ethnic groups and cultures, this volume explains motifs in Native American artwork, artifacts, and clothing and their importance in the context of Native American mythology and culture. Beadwork, leatherwork, pottery, dwellings, and silver items found in various museums and private collections are reproduced in black-and-white photographs.

5–7. Hanlan, Judith. *American Indians Today: Issues and Conflicts*. New York: Watts, 1987. o.p.

Many of the problems that Native Americans face today—poverty, malnutrition, illness, discrimination, and unemployment—are eloquently presented in this book. The author describes the economic and political problems of Native American peoples in the historical context of the unjust treatment they have received from white governments and society. The court battles Indian tribes have fought and continue to fight for their land and sovereignty are described as well as the Native Americans' search for their lost cultural identity.

5–8. Hofsinde, Robert (Gray Wolf). *Indian Costumes*. New York: Morrow, 1968. 96pp. $11.88. ISBN: 0-688-31614-X.

This book presents the three basic types of North American Indian dress: everyday, war, and ceremonial. The author describes the clothing of the Apache, Blackfoot, Crow, Iroquois, Navaho, Northwest Coast, Ojibwa, Pueblo, Seminole, and Sioux tribes. Black-and-white illustrations of each costume are included.

5–8. _____ . *Indian Sign Language*. New York: Morrow, 1956. 96pp. $12.88. ISBN: 0-688-31610-7.

This concise presentation describes and illustrates over two hundred signs. In researching these signs, the author used Winnebago and Sioux chiefs as his authorities. The manuscript was further verified by an ethnologist at the Smithsonian Institution. This language, one of the original uses of codes and ciphers, fascinates the uninitiated.

4–8. Hughs, Jill. *Aztecs*. New York: Gloucester Press, 1986. o.p.

This book relates the history of the Aztec culture of Central America and Mexico. Color illustrations indicate what life was like for the Aztec five hundred years ago. Their temples, costumes, and rituals are illustrated and described in clear, simple text. The Aztec calendar and a discussion of their astronomical skills are included.

4–8. *The Indian Texans*. San Antonio: Univ. of Texas Institute of Texan Cultures, 1982. o.p.

This is one of a series of pamphlets published by the institute on the many ethnic groups that have contributed to the heritage of Texas. The book begins with the native peoples of prehistoric Texas and describes the tribes, their culture, and their interactions with European settlers. The great Comanche chief Quanah Parker is depicted, and period photos and engravings of prominent Native Americans and artifacts illuminate Native American daily life.

3–5. Lepthien, Emilie U. *The Choctaw*. A New True Book. Chicago: Children's Press, 1987. 48pp. $14.60. ISBN: 0-516-01240-1. pap. $4.95. ISBN: 0-516-41240-X.

This history of the Choctaw people includes their education, religion, treaties, culture, and government. Full-color illustrations enhance the simple, large-print text. The contemporary life and culture of the Choctaw are also presented, and the book includes a glossary of Choctaw words.

3–5. _____ . *The Seminole*. A New True Book. Chicago: Children's Press, 1985. 45pp. $14.60. ISBN: 0-516-01941-4. pap. $4.95. ISBN: 0-516-41941-2.

Printed in clear, large type with both color and black-and-white photographs and illustrations, this book describes the history of the Seminole Indians of Florida as well as life on the modern reservation. The book covers the wars led by Osceola for the independence of his people, their journey to Oklahoma, and the life of the small group who remain in the Florida Everglades.

6–8. McIntyre, Loren. *The Incredible Incas and Their Timeless Land*. Washington, D.C.: National Geographic Society, 1975. 199pp. o.p.

The history of the Inca Empire during its expansion in the fifteenth and sixteenth centuries is brought to life in this authoritative work written and photographed by a man who lived in Peru for twenty years. The well-written text illuminates the religion and daily life of the Incas as well as the invasion of the Conquistadores.

3–5. McKissack, Patricia. *The Apache*. A New True Book. Chicago: Children's Press, 1984. 48pp. $14.60. ISBN: 0-516-01925-2. pap. $4.95. ISBN: 0-516-41925-0.

Color photographs and illustrations help to bring the history and culture of the Apache to life. The book describes the origins of the Apache tribes—the Hohokam and Anasazi and, later, the Zuni and Papago, Hopi, and Pueblo tribes that migrated to the southwestern United States. Later, the *Apachu*, or "enemies," invaded these lands. Seven groups— Navajo, Chiricahua, Lipan, Western Apache, Mescalero, Jicarilla, and the Kiowa-Apache— comprised the Apache nation. Later the Navajo became an independent tribe. Leaders, beliefs, hunting, and wars are described, and the final chapter discusses the present-day life of the Apache.

3–6. _____. *Aztec Indians*. New True Books. Chicago: Children's Press, 1985. 48pp. $14.60. ISBN: 0-516-01936-8. pap. $4.95. ISBN: 0-516-41936-6.

In this history of Mexico's Aztecs, the author covers the rise of Aztec culture, mythology, language, counting, the Aztec calendar, everyday life, merchants, craftsmen, the no-

bility, arts and sciences, and the final days of the empire. The large type and clear presentation are augmented by color photographs and illustrations, and a glossary is included.

3–5. _____. *The Maya*. New True Books. Chicago: Children's Press, 1985. 45pp. $14.60. ISBN: 0-516-01270-3. pap. $4.95. ISBN: 0-516-41270-1.

McKissack provides a concise and well-written history of the Mayan people of Central America, including their customs, art, music, dance, religion, warfare, and calendar. The final chapter describes Mayan life in the modern world. Color photographs and maps as well as a glossary add to the text.

5–8. Mangurian, David. *Children of the Incas*. New York: Four Winds, 1979. 73pp. o.p.

In this photo essay, the author describes the everyday life of a contemporary Incan family living in an isolated village in the highlands of Peru. The text and black-and-white photographs illustrate the life of deprivation and hard work these people must endure to survive in this harsh environment. The book focuses on a loving family and their oldest son, who is determined to leave the village to get an education in the city.

4–8. May, Robin. *Plains Indians of North America*. Original People Series. Vero Beach, Fla.: Rourke, 1987. 48pp. $15.33. ISBN: 0-317-60597-6.

The history of the Plains Indians, as well as their cultural decline and rebirth, is described here. Color photographs and illustrations are included along with a map showing the distribution of Indian tribes of North America.

3–5. Morrison, Marion. *Indians of the Andes*. Original People Series. Vero Beach, Fla.: Rourke, 1987. 48pp. $15.33. ISBN: 0-86625-260-6.

Morrison clearly and succinctly reviews the history, from the fifteenth century to the present, of the Aymara, Quechua, Uru-Chipaya, and Inca peoples, whose culture and language survive today in the Andean regions. Clear maps and color photographs emphasize aspects of modern life and culture. A glossary of Spanish and Indian words complements the text.

6–8. Nabokov, Peter, ed. *Native American Testimony: An Anthology of Indian and White Relations. First Encounter to Dispossession.* New York: Crowell, 1978. ISBN: 0-690-01313-2.

The words of Native Americans eloquently document their perspective on the conflict between the white and Indian cultures. The entries present the human aspects of the clash between these cultures and reveal the human price that is paid when one culture attempts to annihilate another.

3–6. Osinski, Alice. *The Nez Perce.* New True Books. Chicago: Children's Press, 1988. 48pp. $14.60. ISBN: 0-516-01154-5. pap. $4.95. ISBN: 0-516-41154-3.

The demise of traditional Nez Perce culture and the tribe's vanishing homeland are documented as the people struggle against the dominance of white culture and the inevitable Indian wars. The history, culture, mythology, and art of this Idaho tribe are brought to life with color photos and reproductions of period illustrations and artifacts. Chief Joseph spoke for his people when they were freezing and starving to death: "Our Chiefs are killed," he said. "From where the sun now stands, I will fight no more forever."

3–5. _____. *The Sioux.* New True Books. Chicago: Children's Press, 1984. 48pp. $14.60. ISBN: 0-516-01929-5. pap. $4.95. ISBN: 0-516-41929-3.

How the Sioux migrated to the Great Plains, the seven council fires, Sioux ponies, camp circles, the buffalo, the Great Spirit, the fight to preserve their way of life, and the modern Sioux all are touched on in this well-written text. The large type and simple presentation as well as the color illustrations and photos make this an appealing book for younger readers.

4–8. Porter, Frank W. *The Nanticoke.* Indians of North America Series. New York: Chelsea House, 1987. 104pp. $17.95. ISBN: 1-55546-686-9.

In this first volume of a series on the Indian tribes of North America, photographs, maps, and illustrations effectively illuminate the history of the Nanticoke Indians of the Chesapeake Bay. A list of Indian place names (translated) and a chart of prehistoric peoples of the Middle Atlantic states are included. The last chapter updates the book with color photos and illustrations of contemporary life for the tribe members, including a traditional pow wow.

4–8. Smith, J. H. *Eskimos: The Inuit of the Arctic.* Original People Series. Vero Beach, Fla.: Rourke, 1987. 48pp. $15.33. ISBN: 0-86625-257-6.

Smith does a fine job of reviewing for young readers the history and culture of the Inuit people of Greenland and other Arctic regions. Inuit life before and after Europeans explored and colonized these regions is discussed in clear, simple text. A glossary of Inuit words and the Inuit alphabet plus color photographs and illustrations complement the text.

6–8. Stuart, Gene S. *The Mighty Aztecs.* Crump, Donald J., ed. Special Publications Series 16: No. 2. Washington, D.C.: National Geographic Society, 1981. 200pp. $7.95. ISBN: 0-87044-362-3; LB $9.50. ISBN: 0-87044-367-4.

An examination of archaeological sites and everyday contemporary life highlights this study of the Aztec culture of Mexico. Color photographs and illustrations help bring the Aztec world to life for the young reader. Ancient customs are compared with those of the descendants of the Aztecs, for, although their empire was destroyed, their art and culture survive.

5–8. Tannenbaum, Beulah and Harold E. *Science of the Early American Indians.* New York: Watts, 1988. 96pp. $10.40 ISBN: 0-531-10488-5.

The authors explore the scientific achievements of pre-Columbian Native American tribes. Archaeological discoveries reveal the astronomical and technological skills of these tribes before European invaders destroyed their culture. Topics covered include medicine, fire making, cooking, architecture, astronomy, language, calendars, number systems, pottery, weaving, and weapons.

4–8. Weiss, Harvey. *Shelters: From Tepee to Igloo*. New York: Crowell, 1988. 80pp. $10.95. ISBN: 0-690-04553-0; PLB $12.89. ISBN: 0-690-04555-7.

From the open, thatched platforms of the Seminole Indians to the stone dwellings found in Machu Picchu, the author illustrates and describes the tepees, igloos, and adobe dwellings of Native American cultures as well as dwellings common to other cultures.

MYTHS AND LEGENDS

K–3. Bierhorst, John. *Doctor Coyote: A Native American Aesop's Fables*. New York: Macmillan, 1987. 48pp. $15.95. ISBN: 0-02-709780-3.

Bierhorst, one of the most authoritative experts on Native American mythology, has collected the Aztec legends of Coyote, the trickster. These legends are reminiscent of the cautionary tales of ancient Greece and Rome.

6–8. _____. *The Hungry Woman: Myths and Legends of the Aztecs*. New York: Morrow, 1984. 148pp. $10.95. ISBN: 0-688-02766-0.

These stories are based on the Aztec narratives recorded in the sixteenth century after the Spanish conquest of Mexico. The themes of these myths include the creation of the world, the rise and fall of Aztec cities, the founding of Mexico, and the exploits of Montezuma. The last segment of the book contains myths and legends that were told after the Spanish conquest.

5–8. _____. *In the Trail of the Wind: American Indian Poems and Ritual Orations*. New York: Farrar, Straus and Giroux, 1971. 224pp. $6.95. ISBN: 0-374-33640-7; 1987. pap. $4.95. ISBN: 0-374-43576-6.

The powerful images and language of these evocative poems, songs, and chants lift the human spirit and give us a glimpse of the sorrow and joy in the Indian heart. Subjects range from the creation, the deer, home, and war to love, death, dreams, and omens and prophecies. The tribe of origin, as well as the source, is given for each selection, and a glossary of tribes, cultures, and languages adds to the text.

6–8. _____. *The Mythology of North America*. New York: Morrow, 1985. 272pp. $13.00. ISBN: 0-688-04145-0; pap. $6.95. ISBN: 0-685-09410-3.

This authoritative volume arranges the myths and legends by geographic region and by folk motif. Bierhorst sees these myths—myths that are kept alive through the oral storytelling tradition of these peoples—as an inheritance from the past that reflects the fears and hopes of each tribal culture as well as their stewardship of the land and the unseen powers that guide them. Maps and illustrations expand the text.

6–8. _____. *The Mythology of South America*. New York: Morrow, 1988. 256pp. $15.95. ISBN: 0-688-06722-0.

Gathering myths from the various geographical regions of South America, Bierhorst explores the central themes—the rise of civilizations and how they came to be. In South America, priority has been given to the preservation of Indian cultures. As a result, many are still intact—languages are still spoken and the folklore and rituals are still practiced. The trickster tales are among the many in this fascinating volume.

5–8. _____. *The Naked Bear: Folktales of the Iroquois*. New York: Morrow, 1987. 144pp. $14.95. ISBN: 0-688-06422-1.

The first folktales collected in North America were from Iroquois tribes. The Iroquois culture survives today in New York State and Canada, and sixteen stories of the Six Nations of the Iroquois are presented here. Bierhorst has been careful to preserve the character of the Iroquois storytelling language. The motifs are common in Iroquois folktales, ranging from animal tricksters to monsters.

P–2. _____. *Spirit Child: A Story of the Nativity.* Illus. by Barbara Cooney. New York: Morrow, 1990. pap. $4.95. ISBN: 0-688-09926-2.

Bierhorst discovered this fifteenth-century Aztec version of the Nativity story while researching an Aztec-English dictionary. The story was recited in the Aztec language to the accompaniment of drums. The legend, here beautifully illustrated in the vibrant earth tones and blues of the Mexican landscape and sky, is a blending of Aztec legends, the Bible, and medieval European legends.

4–8. _____. *The Whistling Skeleton: American Indian Tales of the Supernatural.* New York: Four Winds, 1984. 128pp. $13.95. ISBN: 0-02-709770-6.

These Indian myths were collected by George Bird Grinnell in the nineteenth century. Grinnell lived with the Pawnee and participated in their storytelling and buffalo hunts. He also befriended the Blackfoot and Cheyenne Indians in the 1880s and 1890s and learned their languages and stories. These myths deal with the supernatural but also reflect the real world of marriage customs, hunting, warfare, and domestic life.

6–8. Burland, Cottie. *North American Indian Mythology.* The Library of the World's Myths and Legends. New York: Peter Bedrick Books, 1985. 144pp. $22.50. ISBN: 0-87226-016-X.

Burland, a British Museum staff member and scholar of the mythology of the North American Indians, describes the mythology of tribal groups in each geographic region of North America. The chapters cover tribal life, crafts, and festivals as well as mythology. Black-and-white and color photos and illustrations of costumes, masks, and other items central to the mythology of these peoples add much to the text.

4–8. Feather Earring, Monica. *Prairie Legends.* Indian Culture Series. Billings, Mont.: Council for Indian Education, 1978. $2.95. ISBN: 0-89992-069-1.

These four legends, identified as versions told by specific tribes, are related by Native Americans who have studied Indian mythology. The book is illustrated by an Indian artist and is authentic in language and content. This is one of over eighty publications on Indian culture and mythology published by this nonprofit group, which provides culturally relevant reading materials for children.

5–8. Gifford, Douglas. *Warriors, Gods and Spirits from Central and South American Mythology.* World Mythologies Series. New York: Schocken, 1987. 132pp. $16.45. ISBN: 0-8052-3857-3.

The introductory chapter describes the origins of Native American tribes and their colonization of Central and South America over 10,000 years ago. The importance of the environment is evident in the folklore of the forest and river people. The legends and myths of the Aztecs and Incas are arranged by geographic region. The skillful, full-page, color illustrations depict the symbols identified with the characters and events of each myth.

P–2. Goble, Paul. *The Great Race of the Birds and Animals.* New York: Bradbury, 1985. 32pp. $13.95. ISBN: 0-02-736950-1.

This legend comes to us from the Cheyenne and Sioux mythologies. In the old days, the buffalo and other animals had magnificent powers. Humans gained power over the animals by winning the great race, run near the Black Hills of what is now South Dakota. The valley below the hills was called the *race track* by the Indians, and the earth was red from the blood of the many runners who died of exhaustion. Humans were given power over all the animals but were also made the guardians of all creatures. The power thus carried responsibilities. This theme is common to Native American myths and carries a powerful message, not only to Indian culture but to all humans. Goble's color illustrations add power and mystery to the myth.

3–5. _____. *Her Seven Brothers.* New York: Bradbury, 1988. 32pp. $13.95. ISBN: 0-02-737960-4.

Goble's bold, colorful illustrations reinforce the mystery and magic of the Cheyenne legend about the creation of the Big Dipper. He uses Native American motifs to decorate the tepees and clothing, while birds, flowers, and butterflies represent the Indian theme of harmony with nature.

5–8. Guard, Jean, and Ray A. Williamson. *They Dance in the Sky: Native American Star Myths.* New York: Houghton, 1987. 130pp. $13.95. ISBN: 0-395-39970-X.

Native American legends explaining the constellations are presented for each tribe or tribal group. Each chapter contains a list of Native American star signs with their corresponding constellations in Western mythology. A glossary of Native American names, a bibliography, and an index are included. These tales are replete with the magic of people who change into animal forms and monsters who roam the earth freely, and the author's rich, evocative style preserves the tradition of a people whose culture survives without a written language.

4–8. Hoffman, Mrs. Albert, and Dorra Torres. *Cheyenne Short Stories: A Collection of Ten Traditional Stories of the Cheyenne.* Billings, Mont.: Council for Indian Education, 1977. $2.95. ISBN: 0-89992-057-8.

These legends are told both in English and in the Cheyenne language. The alphabet used is the typewriter version of the Cheyenne Bilingual Alphabet, which is used in programs on the Northern Cheyenne Reservation.

K–3. *Iktomi and the Boulder: A Plains Indian Story.* Retold and illus. by Paul Goble. New York: Orchard, 1988. 32pp. PLB $14.99. ISBN: 0-531-08360-8; $14.95. ISBN: 0-531-05760-7; 1991. pap. $4.95. ISBN: 0-531-07023-9.

This is a picture-book version of a Sioux legend about a character found in all Native American mythologies. He is clever and has magical powers, but he is also proud and stupid, both a liar and a mischief maker. Goble's superb illustrations painted in natural tones reflect his lifelong study of Native American mythology and art. He effectively

captures the authenticity of the language and message of this myth.

2–5. McDermott, Gerald. *Arrow to the Sun: A Pueblo Indian Tale.* New York: Viking, 1974. 48pp. pap. $14.95. ISBN: 0-670-13369-8.

A Pueblo Indian tale illustrated in bold, strong colors and designs, this book won the Caldecott Medal. The author relates the story in an uncluttered, dignified style that skillfully embodies the spirit and profound nature of Native American mythology and art.

4–8. Marsh, Jessie. *Indian Folk Tales from Coast to Coast.* Indian Culture Series. Billings, Mont.: Council for Indian Education, 1978. $2.95. ISBN: 0-89992-068-3.

The legends included here were selected and evaluated by an Indian editorial committee. The stories, which represent common themes in Indian mythology, include "The Golden Cranes"; "How the Indians Came to Own Horses"; "The Seven Brothers Who Turned to Stone"; "The White Trail in the Sky"; "The Enchanted Stag"; and "The Skunk and the Purple-Clawed Monster."

4–8. Rohmer, Harriet, adapter. *The Legend of Food Mountain: La Leyenda del Montana del Alimento.* San Francisco: Children's Book Press, 1982. 24pp. $12.95. ISBN: 0-89239-022-0.

A bilingual legend adapted from the Chimalpopocatl Codex, this is one of several pictographic manuscripts recorded by native priests after the Spanish conquest of Mexico. This Mayan creation myth, which explains the origins of the earth and the human race, is the story of the conflict between Quetzalcoatl, who civilized the world, and the warlike rain god Tlaloc. The legend reflects the Mayan tradition of respect for all of nature, which is the source of life. It also represents the cycles of nature, the seasons, birth and death, and conservation, which must be observed in order for the earth to replenish itself and sustain life.

4–8. Tall Bull, Henry, and Tom Weist. *Cheyenne Legends of Creation.* Indian Culture

Series. Billings, Mont.: Council for Indian Education, 1972. $2.95. ISBN: 0-89992-025-X.

These legends, handed down from generation to generation through the oral storytelling tradition, represent the oldest surviving oral literature of North America and are still part of Cheyenne culture. They are among the oldest legends told by the Northern Cheyenne tribes. Here, they are told and illustrated by Native Americans who are living repositories of this ancient culture.

4–8. _____. *The Rolling Head: Cheyenne Tales.* Indian Culture Series. Billings, Mont.: Council for Indian Education, 1971. o.p.

Tales about rolling heads are common in the mythology of many Plains Indian tribes. This is the favorite of all the Cheyenne legends told today. The second tale in this volume, "Falling Star," is based on a version recorded by George Bird Grinnell in the early part of this century. The story deals with the communal hunts that took place before the coming of Europeans and the horse. A glossary of Indian words adds to the text. The title story in this volume involves ritual sacrifice and the consumption of human flesh and is not suitable for young children.

5–8. Wood, Marion. *Spirits, Heroes and Hunters from North American Indian Mythology.* World Mythologies Series. New York: Schocken, 1987. 156pp. $16.45. ISBN: 0-8052-3792-5.

This collection of Native American animal myths is beautifully illustrated to emphasize their magical quality. The myths contain archetypes common to these cultures, depicting religious beliefs as well as the hardships of the daily lives of these nomadic hunters. The selections show the effects of the environment on the mythology. An introductory chapter recounts the history and origins of North American tribes.

PROGRAMMING IDEAS

It is of great concern to educators and others who work with children that cultural authenticity be maintained and stereotypes be eliminated in any activity that presents Native American culture. The following activities have been used successfully to introduce authentic Native American culture to children.

DWELLINGS

Students can construct models of traditional Native American dwellings using clay, sand, leather, or canvas on a plywood base. Native American art and designs can be incorporated into this project. Several books are available that describe various styles and construction methods for traditional Native American houses. Museum exhibits and dioramas can also be used as models.

POTTERY

Some simple modeling clay and a book describing traditional clay-working techniques are all you need to present an exciting hands-on workshop that will delight children of all ages—and their parents, too. You can demonstrate how to make pinch pots as well as the slab and coil methods of construction. Have the children practice each technique and allow them to take their creations home.

FOODS

Native American foods and traditional cooking can be demonstrated using an electric frying pan or outdoor cooking equipment. Recipes for popcorn, corn pudding, Indian fry bread, roasted ears of corn and many other delicious foods can be found in Native American cookbooks.

SAND PAINTING

Sand painting is done by the Southwest Indians in ceremonial kiva purification rituals. Put some plain sand in a covered jar, add food coloring, and shake. Children can duplicate traditional designs found in books or they can create their own designs. Although traditional sand paintings are swept away after the rituals are performed, workshop participants can take theirs home simply by making the paintings on cardboard covered with glue.

STRING GAMES

String games have been played by children for hundreds of years. Most of these games are Native American in origin. All you need is a ball of butcher's string or yarn and a book of string games to keep children fascinated for hours.

CULTURAL DISPLAYS

Prints of contemporary and historical Native American figures can be used in conjunction with artifacts, such as baskets and pottery, to create informative displays. Visual displays impart an immediacy to the study of a culture and can engender greater understanding and respect. Native American artifacts are readily available in North America, and prints that include biographical information are available from audiovisual suppliers.

SPEAKERS AND PERFORMERS

Many states and cities have tribal and cultural organizations that will provide speakers or performers for programs on Native American literature, art, music, and dance.

PROGRAMMING RESOURCES

The following resources contain suggestions for programming ideas that will enhance understanding of traditional Native American cultures through arts and crafts. Before presenting Native American programming to children, it is necessary to understand and appreciate the cultures. It is also important to present the cultures authentically, avoiding stereotypes and racism. In addition to the titles listed here, the Native American Public Broadcasting Consortium publishes a catalog of video programs covering every aspect of Native American traditional culture, including the arts and crafts of various tribes (see the following section, Audiovisual Materials).

BOOKS

Barry, John W. *American Indian Pottery: An Identification and Value Guide.* Florence, Ala.: Books Americana, 1984. 213pp. pap. $22.95. ISBN: 0-89689-047-3.

Bernstein, Bonnie, and Leigh Blair. *Native American Crafts Workshop.* Carthage, Ill.: Fearon Teacher Aids, 1982. pap. $8.95. ISBN: 0-8224-9784-0.

Dittert, Alfred E., Jr., and Fred Plog. *Generations in Clay: Pueblo Pottery of the American Southwest.* Flagstaff, Ariz.: Northland Publishing, 1980. 156pp. pap. $17.95. ISBN: 0-87358-270-5.

Hartman, Russell P., and Jan Musial. *Navajo Pottery: Traditions and Innovations.* Flagstaff, Ariz.: Northland Publishing, 1987. pap. $12.95. ISBN: 0-87358-430-9.

Harvey, Virginia I. *The Techniques of Basketry.* Seattle: Univ. of Washington Press, 1986. 132pp. pap. $14.95. ISBN: 0-295-96415-4.

Highwater, Jamake. *Arts of the Indian Americas: North, Central and South: Leaves from the Sacred Tree.* New York: HarperCollins, 1985. 320pp. pap. $22.50. ISBN: 0-06-430135-4.

Newman, Sandra C. *Indian Basket Weaving: How to Weave Pomo, Yurok, Pima, and Navajo Baskets.* Flagstaff, Ariz.: Northland Publishing, 1984. 108pp. pap. $9.95. ISBN: 0-87358-112-1.

Turnbaugh, Sarah P., and William Turnbaugh. *Indian Baskets.* West Chester, Pa.: Schiffer, 1986. 264pp. $45.00. ISBN: 0-88740-055-8.

AUDIOVISUAL MATERIALS

Anti-Defamation League of B'nai B'rith
Dept. M-89
823 United Nations Plaza
New York, NY 10017
(212) 490-2525

The league publishes a filmstrip set called *The American Story* that describes twelve families from different ethnic groups, one of which is Native American.

Cloud Associates
P.O. Box 39016
Phoenix, AZ 85069

The company distributes learning kits designed by the Heard Museum in Phoenix. Available in levels 2–6 for $267.66 each, the kits combine print and audiovisual materials (color slides, overhead transparencies, and cassette tapes of Indian music, chants, and Native American interviews).

Creek Nation Communication Center
P.O. Box 580
Okmulgee, OK 74447

The center has a series of videotapes on Creek life that can be duplicated for a nominal charge and your own blank tape.

Folkways Records
Available from Rose Records
214 South Wabash Avenue
Chicago, IL 60604

Folkways has a collection of ethnographic recordings of the folk and ritual music of Native American and other cultures. This collection was recently given to the Library of Congress.

National Geographic Society
Educational Services
Department 88
1145 17th Street NW
Washington, DC 20036

(301) 921-1200
(800) 638-4077

The society has filmstrips and videotapes on Native American culture.

Native American Public Broadcasting
Consortium
Box 83111
Lincoln, NE 68501-3111
(402) 474-3522

The consortium's catalog is available on request.

Passamaquoddy-Maliseet Bilingual Program
Nisi-Latuwewakon
P.O. Box 295
Perry, ME 04667

Troll Associates
Instructional Materials
100 Corporate Drive
Mahwah, NJ 07430
(201) 529-4000
(800) 526-5289

The company carries several filmstrips on Native American groups.

CHAPTER 7

Persian Materials and Programs

by Shahla Sohail Ghadrboland

Children's literature in Iran began with stories told aloud and passed from one generation to another. In early times, there were books that children could read or that were read to them, but these books were not written especially for them. Among the most popular of those books was the *Kilīlih-va-Dimnih*, a collection of Indian folktales translated into Persian during the twelfth century. Toward the end of the nineteenth century, more attention was given to the production of literature just for children. Between 1930 and 1950, more Persian authors began writing for children. Many traditional folktales were collected and retold in formats for children, and children's books in English and other European languages were translated. During the 1940s, Persian periodicals began including special sections for children, and the first children's magazine, *Kiyhān-i-Bachihā* (Children's Kiyhan), was published in 1955. Three years later, the first library with a suitable collection for children was established in Teheran.

The establishment in 1965 of the Institute for Intellectual Development of Children and Young Adults (IIDCYA) marked a turning point for Persian children's literature. The IIDCYA set up cultural and educational centers, including libraries, to promote learning among children and young adults. The centers were designed to encourage young people to learn and to appreciate reading. There are currently about 250 such centers and libraries, including mobile libraries, in cities and rural areas. In addition to publishing books and nonbook materials, IIDCYA sponsors book selection and discussion programs, film making, art programs, and book exhibitions.

During the 1970s, publication of materials for children increased substantially and more attention was given to the quality of children's books, both in content and format. The many social, political, and economic changes brought about by the Islamic revolution in 1979 caused substantial modifications in children's books. Among the most notable are the following:

1. Islamic culture has become a prominent feature in children's literature.
2. The war between Iran and Iraq (1980–1988) became a popular theme in children's and young adult fiction between 1980 and 1988.
3. The number of imaginary stories (except folktales) and science fiction titles has decreased.
4. The percentage of translations, particularly of fiction, has decreased. (Most scientific books, however, are still being translated.)

For this bibliography, books were selected according to their availability, relationship to Persian culture, and quality. I have had access to many Persian children's books published in Iran, including some out-of-print titles. Although an attempt was made to avoid out-of-print titles, some are included. Because of Iran's recent economic problems, books tend to go out-of-print rapidly. The scarcity of paper also contributes to this problem.

Persian children's books published in the United States can be ordered directly from the publishers or purchased from book dealers. However, due to the present unusual currency fluctuation, prices for the books published in Iran are not included. The best way to obtain Iranian books in the United States is through book dealers.

BIBLIOGRAPHY

FICTION

English

5–9. Mehdevi, Anne. *Parveen.* New York: Knopf, 1969. 177pp. o.p.

In 1920, sixteen-year-old Parveen leaves her mother's home in Chicago to visit her father, a patriarch of a large estate in Khurāsān, Iran. It is hard at first for Parveen to adjust to her new life and the Persian customs, but when she meets Javād, a young Persian landlord who has been educated in England, things change for her. The two take secret rides at dawn and dig for historical treasures. As the days go by, Parveen discovers the charm and beauty of her new country. This fascinating story about Persian life in the early twentieth century comes alive through the author's skillful style.

7–adult. Picard, Barbara Leonie. *Tales from Ancient Persia.* New York: Z. Walck, 1972. 208pp. o.p.

Here are twenty-four stirring epic legends from the *Shāhnāmih* of Firdawsī, skillfully retold in English. These exciting tales are about love, vengeance, battles between good and evil, and the daring deeds of Rustam, the hero of Shāhnāmih. There are no illustrations. The *Shāhnāmih*, or "Book of Kings," consists of 60,000 verses by Firdawsī, the great epic poet of the tenth century.

2–6. Scott, Sally. *The Magic Horse.* New York: Greenwillow, 1985. unp. o.p.

In older times in Persia, a wizard brings before a king and his son a flying horse made of ebony. He asks for the princess's hand in exchange, but she angrily refuses the offer. The prince sits on the horse and is flown to other lands where he meets a princess and falls in love with her. When he brings the princess back with him, the wizard steals her. In retelling this Persian fairy tale, the author has created an enchanting book that is hard to resist. Detailed and refined illustrations, inspired by Persian miniatures, can take readers to the land of flying carpets.

1–4. Stanley, Diane. *Fortune.* New York: Morrow Junior Books, 1990. 32pp. $12.95. ISBN: 0-688-07210-0.

In old times in Persia, a young farmer named Omar wanted to get married but did not have enough money to support a wife. Taking the advice of his betrothed, he went to the market to seek his fortune. Using all his money, he bought a dancing tiger and made his fortune. As a rich man, Omar decided to marry the king's daughter but discovered to his surprise that the tiger was the prince whom the princess loved. With lively narration and colorful and detailed illustrations inspired by Persian miniatures, the author has created a book that children will adore.

3–6. Walkstein, Diane. *The Red Lion.* New York: Crowell, 1977. unp. o.p.

Long, long ago in Persia, it was customary for young princes to fight a furious red lion to prove their bravery and become king. Prince Azgīd, who is afraid of lions, runs away on the eve of his coronation. Yet everywhere he goes, he has to face a lion. Color illustrations, inspired by traditional Persian miniatures, add an appropriate flavor to the story.

Persian

P–3. Āmilī, Hamīd. *Khālih Sūskih* (Lady beetle). Tihrān: Dādjū, 1977. unp. o.p.

Khālih Sūskih is a beetle who leaves her hometown to go to Hamadān to find a husband. On her way she meets some men who ask for her hand, but she does not like them. They are rude and unkind. Finally she meets Āqā Mūshih (Mr. Mouse) and falls in love with him. This old and popular folktale is presented with color photos of beautiful, handmade puppets.

P–3. Āzād, M. *Qissih-yi Tawqī* (The tale of Tawqī). Tihrān: Kānūn (Kānūn-i Parvarish-i

143

Fikrī-yi Kūdakān va Nujavānān [The Institute for Intellectual Development of Children and Young Adults]), 1983. 28pp.

A little bird named Tawqī finds a cotton ball and is told by his father to have it made into a new dress for the New Year. Tawqī takes the cotton ball to the spinner, the weaver, the dyer, and finally to the tailor. Based on an old folktale, this story is made into a beautiful and amusing poem. Elaborate full-color illustrations add warmth to the delightful tale. A bilingual edition of this book is available from Mazda Publishers*[1] ($4.95. ISBN: 0-939214-15-6).

3–adult. _____. *Zāl va Sīmurgh* (Zāl and Sīmurgh). Tihrān: Kānūn, 1972. 24pp. o.p.

Sām, the hero of seven lands and the king of Zābulistan, longs for a boy to be his successor. When Zāl, his son, is born, his hair is completely white, like a very old man. Sām, disappointed and angry, commands that he be taken away to the mountains and left there to die. But Sīmurgh, the mythical bird, finds the child and raises him to be a hero. Years later, Sām dreams of Zāl and, filled with shame, starts to search for him. The author has retold this touching tale from the *Shāhnāmih* in a sensitive text while retaining its essence. Elaborate and fascinating illustrations bring this classic to life.

4–adult. Āzar Yazdī, Mihdī. *Qissih-hā-yi Khūb Barā-yi Bachih-hā-yi khūb* (Nice stories for nice children). 13th ed. 8 vols. Tihrān: Shikūfih, 1987.

This collection of old Persian tales consists of some masterpieces of Persian poetry and literature, retold for children. The author has used simple language while maintaining the themes, values, and essence of the originals. Black-and-white drawings add an appropriate flavor to each tale.

2–7. Bahār, Mihrdād. *Bastūr*. Trans. by Mansūr Alyshmīr. Costa Mesa, Calif.: Mazda, 1983. unp. $4.95. ISBN: 0-939214-17-2. Also available in English.

Long, long ago, Persians and Tūranians were bitter enemies. In one of their battles, Zarīr, the commander of the Persian army and the mightiest warrior, is killed by Bīdaraf, the sly wizard of Tūran. Full of sorrow and anger, Bastūr, the seven-year-old son of Zarīr, kills Bīdaraf with the help of his father's horse and defeats the entire Tūran army. A touching tale of the *Shāhnāmih* of Firdawsī, retold simply and skillfully. Colorful illustrations depict the atmosphere of epic tales of old Persia.

5–adult. Bātmānglīj, Muhammad and Najmīyih. *Afsānih-yi Zāl* (The wonderful story of Zaal). Washington, D.C.: Mage, 1985. unp. $18.50. ISBN: 0-934211-01-9.

This is a slightly different version of *Zāl and Sīmurgh*[2] written in elegant text in both English and Persian. Colorful, subtle illustrations by Franta, a Czech artist, complement the text.

2–6. Bihrangī, Samad. *Uldūz va Arūsak-i-sukhangū* (Uldūz and the talking doll). Tihrān: Donyā, 1979. 60pp.

After discovering that her doll is able to talk, Uldūz treasures her as a friend. Uldūz is also afraid that her mean stepmother might take the doll away. One summer night, the doll turns herself, Uldūz, and Uldūz's friend Yashar into doves. The three of them fly to the woods where they watch the dolls' festival. They have some exciting adventures, but the stepmother, angry and suspicious of what has happened, destroys the talking doll.

Samad Bihrangī (1939–1968), a teacher and author of many remarkable children's books, believed that children's literature should look toward a more dynamic life based on the fight against oppression and the search for freedom. Most of his stories were inspired by Turkish folktales from Āzarbāyjān. His best book, *The Little Black Fish* (1967), translated into English and other languages, won the Gold Medal at the 1969 Bologna International Book Exhibition.

---

[1] Complete addresses for all sources marked with an asterisk (*) can be found in the Vendors section at the end of this chapter.

[2] Titles marked with a dagger (†) have complete annotations in the Bibliography for this chapter.

3–adult. Burhān, Ibn-i Yūsif. *Kaiumars, Nukhustīn Shāh-i Jahān* (Kaiumars, the first king of the world). Trans. by Ahmad Iranī. Glendale, Calif.: Vartan, 1987. unp. o.p.

In the old times in Persia, there was a kind-hearted man named Kaiumars. Because he loved and helped the people, he was chosen as the leader, or the king. The occasion of his coronation was celebrated as *Nuruz*. Everyone had a happy life until the Black Devil and the demons came and the battle began between good and evil. This is the first story of the *Shāhnāmih*, retold in Persian and translated to English. The story is retold in a simple way and can be used to familiarize young readers with the *Shāhnāmih* stories. Color illustrations catch the highlights of the story.

P–1. *Davīdam-u-Davīdam* (I ran and I ran). 4th ed. Tihrān: Kānūn, 1985. 28pp.

"I ran and I ran. I reached the top of a mountain. I saw two ladies. One of them gave me a piece of bread and the other gave me some water." So begins this popular nursery rhyme. Beautiful color illustrations add more fun to the book.

K–adult. Farjām, Farīdih. *ʿAmū Nurūz* (Uncle Nuruz). Trans. by Ahmad Jabbāri. Costa Mesa, Calif.: Mazda, 1983. unp. $4.95. ISBN: 0-939214-14-8. Also available in English.

Uncle Nurūz, the symbol of spring, comes to town on the first day of spring, the Iranian New Year, to bring happiness and freshness to the people. Everybody is anxious to see him. But the old woman, or winter, who waits for him every year falls asleep when he arrives. This popular folktale, retold in a refined yet simple text, can be used as a holiday book. Color illustrations are included.

P–2. _____. *Mīhmān-hā-yi Nākhāndih* (The uninvited guests). 7th ed. Tihrān: Kānūn, 1983. 24pp.

A kind old woman lives in a tiny house. One rainy night a sparrow appears at the door seeking shelter. Then a crow, a cat, a dog, a donkey, and a cow come one at a time to ask for the old woman's help. When morning comes, the animals make breakfast and ask the old woman to let them stay so they can help with the housework. This popular Persian folktale is retold in a sensitive text, and the playful, color illustrations create an appropriate setting for the story.

2–7. Ibrāhīmī Nadir. *Bārān, Āftāb va Qissih-yi Kāshī* (Rain, sunshine and the story of tile). 3rd ed. Tihrān: Shikūfih, 1985. 24pp.

Mosaic tile making is an old art in Iran. This book tells how mosaic tile making started in Kāshān, one of the cities of Iran. Exquisite color illustrations with Persian motifs vividly bring out the charm and beauty of the story.

4–9. Kashkūlī, Mahdukht. *Rasm-i Mā Sahm-i Mā* (Our tradition, our share). Tihrān: Fātimī, 1984. 38pp.

These five short stories, based on the traditions of tribal life in southern Iran, beautifully depict the simple life and customs of the people. Beautiful watercolor illustrations add more charm to the sensitive text.

K–4. Kasrā'ī, Sīāvash. *Baʿd Az Zimistān Dar Ābādī-yi Mā* (After the winter in our village). 6th ed. Tihrān: Kānūn, 1983. 24pp.

When spring and *Nurūz*, the Persian New Year, are late, everyone in the village wonders why. The morning breeze brings the message that the swallow, or the spring messenger, has been wounded on her way and is not able to move. Umīd Alī and some other villagers agree to go and take care of her until she can fly again. Bright, colorful illustrations accompany the poetic yet easy-to-read text.

P–1. Lutfī, Kīānūsh. *Yikī Būd Yikī Nabūd* (There was one and there wasn't one). Tihrān: Sharīfī, 1982. unp.

Under the blue dome, everybody has a job—the dog is a butcher, the cat is a grocer, the mouse is a spinner, and so on. This is a new version of an old Persian nursery rhyme. Color illustrations add to the text.

P–1. _____. *Gandum-u Kī Mīkhurih?* (Who eats the wheat?) Tihrān: Sharīfī, 1982. unp.

Who eats the wheat? The mouse. Who eats the mouse? The cat. So this popular nursery rhyme continues in a cycle. Color illustrations covering two-thirds of the pages also depict the nursery rhyme in an amusing way.

P–3. Malikī, Kīānā. *Kadū-yi Qil Qilzan* (The rolling pumpkin). Tihrān: Sipīdih, 1988. unp.

On the way to her daughter's house, an old woman confronts a wolf, a tiger, and a lion. The hungry animals want to eat her, but she convinces them to wait until she returns from her daughter's house with more meat. When the time comes, the daughter hides her in a hollowed pumpkin and rolls her back so the animals are outwitted. Color illustrations accompany the retelling of this old Persian folktale.

4–adult. Murādī Kirmānī, Hūshang. *Qissih-hā-yi Majīd* (Stories of Majīd). 5 vols. Tihrān: Sahāb, 1979–88.

Majīd, the poor boy, lives with his grandmother. They are sincere, kind, and happy together. These five volumes are a series of short stories about their simple life and the events they are confronted with. In a beautiful writing style, the adventures of the finely wrought characters are sensitively depicted with vitality and humor. Murādī Kirmānī has written several other books for children and young adults and has won national and international prizes.

5–9. Rahguzar, Riza. *Muhājir-i Kūchak* (The little immigrant). Tihrān: Kānūn, 1986. 56pp.

Abbās, a young boy, loses his family when Iraqis bomb the city of Khurramshahr. His nineteen-year-old brother has been wounded in the war and is in a hospital in Tihrān. Full of sorrow and hope, Abbās decides to go to Tihrān, but when he arrives, his brother is gone. Taken in by a new family, Abbās continues his search. This is a fast-paced, thought-provoking story of innocent people who are victims of war.

5–9. Rahīmī, Firiydūn. *Khāb-hā-yam Pur Az Kabutar va Bādbādak Ast* (My dreams are full of pigeons and kites). Tihrān: Kānūn, 1986. 46pp.

Raindrops, clouds in the shape of olive trees, flowers, cookies, butterflies, and a sky full of pigeons and kites—these are what Alvān sees in his dreams and what he wishes

to have in the real world. But instead there are Iraqi bombs, fire, smoke, and blood. Alvān wishes he could be taken up to the sky by all his kites and balloons, to shake the big olive tree so it would rain and the war would stop. The author's fine writing style blends the sweet and untouchable dreams of a young boy with the bitter and painful experience of war. Black-and-white illustrations add to the text.

3–5. Shāmānī, Muhammad Ali. *Bi Dunbāl-i Mīvih-yi Zindigī* (In search of the fruit of life). Tihrān: Rajā, 1985. 24pp.

When a king hears about the fruit of life that makes humans immortal, he immediately sends his men to India to search for it. Inspired by one of the stories of Masnavi of Mawlavi, the great poet and mystic of the thirteenth century, the author has created a book that children will enjoy. Beautiful illustrations complement this delightful tale.

K–7. *Zāl va Sīmurgh, Majmū'ih-yi Shānzdah Qissih Barāy-i Kūdakān* (Zāl and Sīmurgh, a collection of sixteen stories for children). Washington, D.C.: Foundation for Iranian Studies, 1983. 152pp. $6.00.

This collection includes sixteen stories published in Iran between 1966 and 1978 as individual books. *Zal va Sīmurgh* and some other stories are included in the present bibliography. There are no illustrations.

NONFICTION
English

5–9. Fox, Mary Virginia. *Iran*. Chicago: Children's Press, 1991. 128pp. $23.93. ISBN: 0-516-02727-1.

This book focuses on Persian history from the Persian Empire to the present. Religion, food, education, sports, and clothing are also discussed in the book. In the last chapter, readers are taken on a tour of the major cities. Both black-and-white and color photos complement the text. Two maps are included.

5–adult. Lengyel, Emil. *Iran*. 3rd ed. New York: Watts, 1981. 64pp. $10.40. ISBN: 0-531-02242-0.

This informative book reconstructs Persian history from the time of Cyrus the Great (550 B.C.) to the twentieth century. It also presents the historical background and splendor of the larger Iranian cities. Customs, religions, ways of life in cities and villages, food, and clothing are discussed in the book. Black-and-white photos accompany the text.

2–5. Tames, Richard. *Take a Trip to Iran.* London: Watts, 1989. 32pp. $10.90. ISBN: 0-531-10650-0.

This book has concise information about geography, history, people, religion, government, and the oil industry. A map and bright, colorful pictures accompany the simple text.

4–adult. Watson, Jane W. *Iran, Crossroad of Caravans.* Champaign, Ill.: Garrard, 1966. 112pp. $7.99. ISBN: 0-8116-6851-7.

This book presents aspects of Iranian culture from village and tribal lifestyles to poetry. Persian carpets, historical places, gardens, and Persian months are other interesting subjects discussed in this book. Two Persian short stories are also included. Both black-and-white and color photos and drawings complement the text.

Persian

3–7. Gulistān, Kāvih. *Gulāb* (Rose water). 3rd ed. Tihrān: Kānūn, 1991. unp.

The fragrance of rose water is considered a connection between people and nature. It is used both as a flavor in main dishes and desserts and as an air freshener and perfume.
Most rose water is made in the villages around Kāshān. This book describes step by step how rose water is made. Color photos accompany the text.

4–adult. _____. *Qalamkār* (Printed calico). Tihrān: Kānūn, 1973. 48pp. o.p.

Fabric printing by hand is a popular craft in Iran. In the nineteenth century, it was practiced in several cities. Now Isfahān is the only city where qalamkār fabrics are made. The book begins with the historical background of fabric printing, then describes step-by-step the procedures for making qalamkār fabrics. The easy-to-read text is accompanied by color photos.

P–5. Īmin, Līlī. *Shādimānih, Kūdakānih* (Children's joy). Washington, D.C.: Foundation for Iranian Studies, 1984. 64pp. $3.00.

A collection of Persian nursery rhymes, traditional games, and poems for children, this book can be used for special programs in libraries and schools.

4–adult. I'tisāmī, Parvīn. *Akhtar-i Charkh-i Adab* (The star of the literary world). Tihrān: Kānūn, 1986. 28pp.

This book includes four poems by Parvīn I'tisāmī, the great poet of the early twentieth century who is referred to as "the star of the literary world." The four poems, "Value of the Jewel," "Deception," "Black and White," and "Silk Workshop," like many of I'tisāmī's poems, are simple admonishing stories characterized by birds and animals. Color illustrations add to the text.

K–5. *Kalāgh Par* (Crow flies). Tihrān: Kānūn, 1986. unp.

This small collection of modern poems about nature, animals, birds, and other subjects is complemented by subtle watercolor illustrations.

4–adult. Kārgar, Dāryūsh. *Sufālgarī* (Pottery). 2nd ed. Tihrān: Kānūn, 1980. 24pp. o.p.

In this book, different procedures for making pottery, from shaping to glazing, are described. The color pictures help children visualize these different procedures as they read the text.

5–9. Qarīb Pūr, Bihrūz. *Ustād Khiymih Shab Bāzi Mīāmūzad* (The master teaches puppetry). Tihrān: Kānūn, 1984. 28pp.

Puppetry is an ancient art in Iran. Puppet shows were performed for special social events, such as weddings. This amusing story presents the historical background of traditional puppetry in Iran and illustrates, step-by-step, how to do a puppet show. The black-

and-white color illustrations help young readers understand the text.

1–adult. *Shi'r-hā-i Barā-yi Kūdakān* (Poems for children). Washington, D.C.: Foundation for Iranian Studies, 1982.

Black-and-white illustrations accompany this collection of modern Persian poems for children.

3–adult. Tāhbāz, Sīrūs. *Bāgh-i Hamīshih Bahār* (Ever spring garden). Tihrān: Kānūn, 1987. 32pp.

In Persian carpets, different colors are artistically interwoven into exquisite designs that create eternal gardens with flowers, trees, and birds. This book presents the historical background of Persian carpets and also explains the process of rug making from spinning and dyeing the wool and cotton to the steps involved in weaving. Filled with colorful, magnificent illustrations, the book gives a broad view of this glorious Persian art.

4–adult. Tavakkoli, Guli. *Arūsak-hā-yi Kāghazī* (Paper dolls). Tihrān: Kānūn, 1988. 28pp.

"Paper is paper, but it can be a thousand other things, such as a green hill, the blue sky, a pot of flowers . . . and even a village and its people." This book shows how to make paper dolls with Persian folk and tribal costumes. It also gives directions for making background scenes using scraps of colored paper to create flowers, trees, animals, sky, etc. Lovely color photographs and illustrations help children easily follow the step-by-step directions.

K–5. Yūshīj, Nīmā, and M. Āzād. *Bachi-hā Bahār* (Children, spring is here). Tihrān: Ibtikār, 1984. Book and cassette.

This collection of modern songs for children includes color illustrations in the text to accompany the good musical arrangements.

P–2. Zarrīnkilk, Nūriddīn. *Ā Avval-i Alifbāst* (The alphabet begins with A). Illus. by the author. 2 vols. Tihrān: Kānūn, 1986.

On each page, one of the thirty-two characters of the Persian alphabet is presented by a rhyming couplet that includes a word which begins with the presented letter. Elaborate and fascinating watercolor illustrations add charm and beauty to the book.

PROGRAMMING IDEAS

NURŪZ

Nurūz, or the Iranian New Year in the solar calendar, has been celebrated by Iranians for more than 2,500 years. It begins on the first day of spring (March 21), and lasts for thirteen days.

Two weeks before *Nurūz*, people begin spring housecleaning and the baking of traditional cookies and candies. They also start to grow *sabzih* (wheat or lentil seeds) and shop for new clothes and gifts.

To celebrate the New Year, Iranians decorate their homes with items to symbolize rebirth, growth, life, light, happiness, and prosperity. Traditionally, seven items, the names of which all begin with the letter S, are placed on a *sufrih* (tablecloth). These items are known as *haft sīn*. Candles, a mirror, and water are also placed on the *sufrih* to symbolize light. As a sign of growth, *sabzih*, fruit, flowers, and herbs are brought to the *sufrih*. Coins, bread, and cheese—tokens of prosperity—as well as a living goldfish in water are part of the traditional decoration. There are even colored eggs and sweets on the *sufrih*. They represent rebirth and happiness much like the same items found in Easter baskets. 'Amū Nurūz, or the symbol of spring, is supposed to bring gifts for children, much like Santa Claus does. He makes his visit on the first day of *Nurūz*. At the time of the transition of the New Year, or *tahvīl*, the members of the family sit around the *haft sīn*, light the candles, and recite the poetry of Hāfiz, a popular mystic and poet who lived in the fourteenth century. Visiting friends and relatives during the first twelve days of the New Year is also a *Nurūz* tradition.

The thirteenth day, known as *Sīzdah Bidar*, is for picnics. It is considered unlucky to stay at home, so families go to the countryside and spend the day picnicking outdoors with friends and relatives. Sprouted seeds (*sabzih*) are thrown in running water. This symbolizes the end of family quarrels and ill feelings and the beginning of peace in the coming year. This joyful day is the end of the *Nurūz* celebration.

Activities

COLORING EGGS

Eggs are colored as a symbol of rebirth and are part of the *Nurūz* decorations.

1. Hard-boil some eggs (as many as you like).
2. Color them with soft colors (lighter colors make eggs easier to paint).
3. Paint the eggs with watercolors or magic markers. Flowers, birds, butterflies, or Persian motifs are appropriate.

HAFT SĪN

Haft sīn, or "seven S's," is the major part of *Nurūz* decorations. It consists of seven items (mostly edible), the names of which begin with the letter S. They are: *sīb* (apple), *sīr* (garlic), *sirkih* (vinegar), *sumāq* (sumac), *samanū* (wheat pudding), *sinjid* (sorb, the fruit of the service tree), and *sabzih* (wheat or lentil sprouts). Figure 1 shows how the items are arranged.

Children can make a little *haft sīn* of their own. Some items are available at local stores, and a Persian or Middle Eastern store might carry items indigenous to Iran. If there is no Persian store in your area, the following sources can provide traditional items:

Asia Center
303 West Broad Street
Route 7
Falls Church, VA 22046
(703) 533-2112

International House
765-8 Rockville Pike
Rockville, MD 20852
(301) 279-2121

International Jr. Market
67114 Reseda Boulevard
Reseda, CA 91335
(818) 342-9753

MAKING *SABZIH*

Sabzih is not available in stores, but children can try to make it on their own.

1. Soak one cup of lentils or wheat in a bowl of water for three days. Change the water daily.
2. Drain the water and spread the soaked seeds in a 9-inch pie plate.
3. Cover with a piece of cheese cloth. Keep the cheese cloth damp.
4. When the sprouts are about 1/4 inch high, remove the cheese cloth and put the dish by a window.
5. Sprinkle daily with water.
6. After three to four days when the sprouts are about 2 inches high, tie a bow around the stems (see figure 2). Wheat generally grows faster than lentils.

Reading Suggestions

Burhān, Ibn-i Yūsif. *Kaiūmars.*[†]
Farjām, Farīdih. *'Amū Nurūz.*[†]

Figure 1. *Haft sīn*, or seven S's, is the major part of *Nurūz* decorations.
Illustrations: Farhang Asgari

Figure 2. *Sabzih*, one of the symbols of life, is specially grown for *Nurūz*.

Kasrā'i, Sīāvash. *After the Winter in Our Village*[†]
Yūshīj, Nimā, and M. Āzād. *Children, Spring Is Here*[†]

RUG WEAVING

Carpet and rug weaving is one of the oldest handcrafts in Iran. Carpets cover the floors of many Persian houses, and Iranian families consider buying rugs and carpets a good investment. Carpets also are used as decorations for festivals and sometimes cover the floors of mosques. Wool, cotton and silk are used to make Persian rugs. The rugs are made in many cities and villages, and each city, village, or tribe has some unique patterns of its own. These patterns are either geometrical or derived from nature, and sometimes both are combined. Leaves, trees, flowers, and birds are popular motifs. Usually the central design of the rug is framed by a wide border, shown in figure 3.

There are two types of rug weaving. The first type produces rugs with knotted piles, and the second creates flat-woven rugs with no piles called *gilīm* (see figure 4). Rug weaving, usually done by women and children, is hard and time consuming. The rugs are often made on upright looms in both houses and workshops. Persian rugs and carpets are considered the finest in the world and are exported to many other countries.

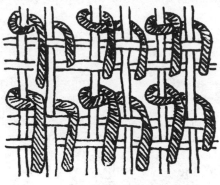

knotted piles

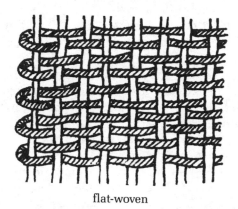

flat-woven

Figure 4. Two different styles of Persian rug construction are shown here.

Activities

RUG DESIGNING
This activity is suitable for children in grades 1 through 7.

Materials
Construction paper
Colored paper
White paper
Scissors
Glue
Crayons, markers, or watercolors

Directions
1. Use a piece of construction paper as the background of the rug (see figure 5).
2. Draw a margin design and color it.
3. Draw some Persian motifs or patterns on colored paper. A lotus, paisley, the tree of

Figure 3. A popular design found in Persian carpets

Figure 5. Flowers and paisley patterns are used in this carpet design.

Figure 6. Examples of motifs often used in Persian rugs

life, birds, and flowers can be drawn. See figure 6 for some examples.

4. Cut out the patterns or motifs. Arrange and paste them on the construction paper. (One motif can be used repeatedly.)

5. To make the fringe, use two 2-inch strips of white paper the same width as the rug. Make uniform cuts 1/8 inch apart along one edge of the paper strips. Glue the uncut edge to the back of the short ends of the rug.

RUG WEAVING
This activity is suitable for children in grades 3 through 7.

Materials
    Four pieces of wood to make the loom
    Small nails
    Thread
    Wool or polyester yarn
    Hammer

Directions
1. Make an 8-inch by 10-inch wooden frame, like a picture frame (see figure 7).
2. Pound small nails, 1/4 inch apart, along the top and the bottom of the loom.
3. Tie one end of the thread to one of the nails in one corner. Wind the thread up and down around the nails to form the warp. Secure the end of the thread by tying it to the last nail.
4. Pass the skein of yarn over and under across and through the warp threads until

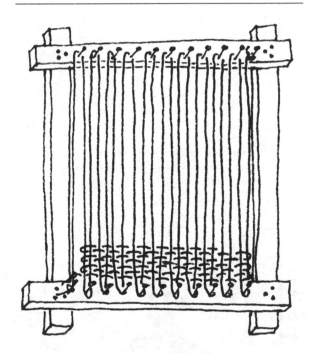

Figure 7. A simple loom made of wood and nails can be used to weave a small rug.

the row is finished. Repeat, pressing the rows together tightly to prevent gaps between the rows, or weft. Different colors of yarns can be used to create easy designs. This process is called *flat weaving* and is used in Iran to make *gilīm.*

Reading Suggestion

Tāhbāz, Sīrūs. *Bāgh-i Hamīshih Bahār* (Ever spring garden).[†]

MOSAICS

Mosaic making is one of the most popular arts in Iran. It reached its highest refinement in the seventeenth century. The famous *Masjid-i Shāh* (Shāh Mosque), known as the Blue Mosque in Isfahān, is one of the most exquisite examples of that era. The word *Kāshī*, or enamel mosaic, comes from the skilled craftsmen of Kāshān.

The procedure of mosaic making begins with a design drawn on paper. Small pieces of baked enamel tiles are then cut and sealed together according to the design and chosen colors.

Activities

BASIC MOSAIC DESIGNING
This activity is suitable for children in grades 1 through 7.

Figure 8. A pitcher is often used as a motif in mosaic designs.

Materials
A piece of white cardboard, 5 inches by 7 inches or 8 inches by 10 inches
Scissors
Glue
Crayons, oil pastels, or watercolors
Colored paper (four or more different colors)
White construction paper

Directions
1. Color the white cardboard. Aqua or turquoise make a beautiful and typically Persian background.
2. Draw a design on the white construction paper. (Paisley, a rosette, a bird, a lotus, or a pitcher are some Persian motifs; see figure 8.)
3. Cut the colored papers into small pieces about 1/4-inch square. For variety, try different geometrical shapes.
4. Arrange the pieces nicely on the design and glue them on.
5. Cut out the complete design and paste it on the colored cardboard.

ADVANCED MOSAIC DESIGN
This activity is suitable for children in grades 3 through 12.

Materials
Four pieces of 6-inch by 6-inch cardboard: one white, one blue, and two of any other color
Glue
Scissors

Directions
1. Draw a design on the white cardboard.
2. Carefully cut out the design.
3. Cut out areas of the design you wish to be colorful.
4. Use these cutout pieces of the design as patterns and trace them on the colored cardboard. Then cut out the designs.
5. Paste the white design on the blue cardboard.
6. Insert and paste appropriately the pieces of the colored cardboard that have been cut out.
7. Continue until the design is filled in. See figures 9 and 10 for finished examples.

Figure 9. An example of a design for mosaic making

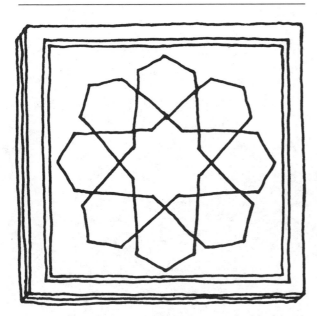

Figure 10. A simpler mosaic design suitable for grades 3 to 5

Reading Suggestion

Ibrāhīmī, Nādir. *Bārān, Āftāb va Qissih-yi Kāshī* (Rain, sunshine and the story of tile).[†]

RESOURCES FOR ADULTS

Books

Cole, Ann, Carolyn Haas, Elizabeth Heller, and Betty Weinberger. "Iran," in *Children Are Children Are Children*. Boston: Little, Brown, 1978, pp. 71–108. pbk. $15.95. ISBN: 0-316-15114-9.

Haack, Hermann. *Oriental Rugs: An Illustrated Guide.* Trans. George and Cornelia Wingfield Digby. London: Faber and Faber, 1960.

Liebetrau, Preben. *Oriental Rugs in Color.* Trans. Katherine John. New York: Macmillan, 1963. $12.95. ISBN: 0-02-571840-1.

Miller, Nina. "Iran," in *Children's Festivals from Many Lands.* New York: Friendship Press, 1964, pp. 59–61. o.p.

Moqadam, Mohammad, and Hosayn Sarshad. "Iran," in *Hi Neighbors.* Vol. 4, pp. 45–54. New York: Hastings House, 1961. o.p.

Vendors

Caspian International
P.O. Box 34902
Bethesda, MD 20814

Iran Books Inc.
8014 Old Georgetown Rd.
Bethesda, MD 20814
(301) 986-0079

Iran's House of Books
1355 Westwood Blvd., Suite 216
Los Angeles, CA 90024
(213) 478-6465

Jahan Book Company
5516 Westbard Ave.
Bethesda, MD 20816
(301) 657-1412

Ketab Corp.
6742 Van Nuys Blvd.
Van Nuys, CA 91405
(818) 908-0808

Ketab Corp.
1387 Westwood Blvd.
Los Angeles, CA 90024
(213) 477-7477

Persian Book Mart
P.O. Box 241574
Memphis, TN 38124
(901) 452-6908

Publishers

Foundation for Iranian Studies
4343 Montgomery Ave., Suite 200
Bethesda, MD 20814
(301) 657-1990

Mage Publisher
1032 29th Street NW
Washington, DC 20007
(800) 962-0922

Mazda Publishers
P.O. Box 2603
Costa Mesa, CA 92626
(714) 751-5252

Vartan Publishers
P.O. Box 4621
Glendale, CA 91202
(818) 507-1687

Selected Bibliography

This basic compilation of materials for adults includes general and culture-specific considerations for promoting cultural diversity with literature for young people. Many of the sources listed have extensive bibliographies, appendixes, and special sections that will give additional references and resources. You may also want to review the introductions to the chapters of this book for other titles of professional interest.

Allen, Adela Artola. *Library Services for Hispanic Children: A Guide for Public and School Librarians.* Phoenix, Ariz.: Oryx Press, 1987.

Austin, Mary C., and Esther Jenkins. *Promoting World Understanding through Literature, K–8.* Englewood, Colo.: Libraries Unlimited, 1983.

Banks, James, and C. A. Banks, eds. *Multicultural Education: Issues and Perspectives.* New York: Allyn and Bacon, 1989.

Beilke, Patricia F., and Frank J. Sciara. *Selecting Materials for and about Hispanic and East Asian Children and Young People.* Hamden, Conn.: Shoe String Press, Library Professional Publications, 1986.

Booklist. Chicago: American Library Association Monthly.
   This review periodical regularly features special lists of materials for children and young adults about various cultures.

Carlson, Ruth. *Emerging Humanity: Multi-ethnic Literature for Children and Adolescents.* Dubuque, Iowa: William C. Brown, 1972.

Davis, Enid. *A Comprehensive Guide to Children's Literature with a Jewish Theme.* New York: Schocken, 1981.

Duran, Daniel. *Latino Materials: A Multimedia Guide for Children and Young Adults.* New York: Neal Schuman, 1979.

Heath, Alan. *Windows on the World: Multicultural Festivals for Schools and Libraries.* Englewood, Colo.: Libraries Unlimited, 1991.

Human and Anti-Human Values in Children's Books: New Guidelines for Parents, Educators and Librarians. New York: Council on Interracial Books for Children, 1976.

Issues in Children's Book Selection: A School Library Journal/Library Journal Anthology. New York: Bowker, 1973.

Jenkins, Esther, and Mary C. Austin. *Literature for Children About Asians and Asian-Americans.* Westport, Conn.: Greenwood Press, 1987.

Johnson, Dianne. *Telling Tales: The Pedagogy and Promise of African American Literature for Youth.* Westport, Conn.: Greenwood Press, 1990.

Keating, Charlotte. *Building Bridges of Understanding between Cultures.* Tucson, Ariz.: Palo Verde, 1971.

Klein, Gillian. *Reading into Racism: Bias in Children's Literature and Learning Materials.* London: Routledge, 1985.

Kruse, Ginny Moore, and Kathleen T. Horning. *Multicultural Children's and Young Adult Literature: A Selected Listing of Books Published between 1980–88.* Madison, Wis.: Cooperative Children's Book Center, Univ. of Wisconsin-Madison, 1989.

Kulpers, Barbara. *American Indian Reference Books for Children and Young Adults.* Englewood, Colo.: Libraries Unlimited, 1991.

MacCann, Donnarae, and Gloria Woodard, eds. *The Black American in Books for Children: Readings in Racism*. 2d ed. Metuchen, N.J.: Scarecrow Press, 1985.

_____. *Cultural Conformity in Books for Children: Further Readings in Racism*. Metuchen, N.J.: Scarecrow Press, 1977.

Pilger, Mary Anne. *Multicultural Projects Index: Things to Make and Do to Celebrate Festivals, Cultures, and Holidays around the World*. Englewood, Colo.: Libraries Unlimited, 1991.

Povsic, Frances. *Eastern Europe in Children's Literature: An Annotated Bibliography of English-Language Books*. Bibliographies and Indexes in World Literature: Series no. 8. Westport, Conn.: Greenwood Press, 1986.

Preiswerk, Roy, ed. *The Slant of the Pen: Racism in Children's Books*. Geneva: World Council of Churches, 1980.

Schon, Isabel. *Books in Spanish for Children and Young Adults: An Annotated Guide*. Series I (1978), Series II (1983), Series III (1985), Series V (1989). Metuchen, N.J.: Scarecrow Press.

_____. *A Hispanic Heritage: A Guide to Juvenile Books about Hispanic People and Cultures*. Metuchen, N.J.: Scarecrow Press, 1980.

Sims, Rudine. *Shadow and Substance: Afro-American Experience in Contemporary Children's Fiction*. Urbana, Ill.: National Council of Teachers of English, 1982.

About the Authors

Julie Corsaro is a school librarian at Edgewood Junior High School in Highland Park, Ill. She is an active member of the American Arab Anti-Discrimination Committee (ADC) and recently served as an intern at the International Youth Library in Munich.

Oralia Garza de Cortes is youth services librarian at the Terrazas Branch of the Austin (Tex.) Public Library.

Enid Davis has been a children's librarian and a public library administrator in Santa Clara County (Calif.) for the past twenty years. She is currently the founder of the University of Folk and Fairy Tales, a storytelling, instructional, and lecturing operation for audiences of all ages. For more information, call (415) 948-5971.

Shahla Sohail Ghadrboland has an MLS degree from Syracuse University and is currently a children's librarian at the Enoch Pratt Library in Baltimore, Md. She is involved in the development of cultural activities for a local Persian school and began a mobile Persian book collection for children.

Elaine Goley is Youth Materials Selection Specialist at the Houston Public Library.

Carla D. Hayden is currently the First Deputy Commissioner/Chief Librarian for the Chicago Public Library. She has also been an assistant professor in the School of Library and Information Science at the University of Pittsburgh. Her interest in multiculturalism in literature for youth has been a primary focus throughout her professional career.

Ginny Lee is a former school librarian in Hayward, Calif. She received her MLS degree from the University of Chicago, and has been a children's librarian with the Chicago Public Library and a school librarian in Colorado. Ms. Lee lived in China for three years and majored in Chinese as an undergraduate.

Suzanne Lo received her MLS degree from the University of California-Berkeley. She is Branch Head Librarian of the Oakland Public Library's Asian Branch. Ms. Lo is a contributor to *Our Family, Our Friends, Our World: An Annotated Guide to Multicultural Books for Children and Young Adults* (Bowker, 1991) and past president of the California chapter of the Chinese American Librarians Association.

Susan Ma is a Senior Librarian at the San Jose (Calif.) Public Library. She has been a children's librarian for fourteen years and has worked at selecting materials in fourteen Asian languages. Ms. Ma is currently president of the California Chapter of the Chinese American Library Association.

Martha Ruff received her MLS degree from the University of Chicago. Ms. Ruff is a board member of the Association of Black Storytellers (ABS). She is a performing storyteller and recently served on the Caldecott Award Committee.

Louise Yarian Zwick received her MLIS degree from the University of California-Berkeley. She is the former branch manager and children's librarian at the Stanaker Branch of the Houston Public Library.

Index by Culture

ASIAN MATERIALS

HISPANIC MATERIALS

Hofsinde, Robert (Gray Wolf). *Indian Costumes* 133
   Indian Sign Language 133
Hughs, Jill. *Aztecs* 133
The Indian Texans 133
Kulpers, Barbara. *American Indian Reference Books for Children and Young Adults* 155
Lepthien, Emilie U. *The Choctaw* 133
   The Seminole 133–34
Mangurian, David. *Children of the Incas* 134
Marsh, Jessie. *Indian Folk Tales from Coast to Coast* 138
May, Robin. *Plains Indians of North America* 134
McDermott, Gerald. *Arrow to the Sun* 138
McIntyre, Loren. *The Incredible Incas and Their Timeless Land* 134
McKissack, Patricia. *The Apaches* 134
   Aztec Indians 134
   The Maya 134
Morrison, Marion. *Indians of the Andes* 134–35
Nabokov, Peter, editor. *Native American Testimony* 135
Newman, Sandra C. *Indian Basket Weaving* 140
O'Dell, Scott. *Black Star, Bright Dawn* 130
   Island of the Blue Dolphins 130
   Streams to the River, River to the Sea 130
Ortiz, Simon. *The People Shall Continue,* 130
Osinski, Alice. *The Nez Perce* 135
   The Sioux 135
Porter, Frank W. *The Nanticoke* 135
Rohmer, Harriet, adapter. *The Legend of Food Moutain* 138
Smith, J. H. *Eskimos* 135
Sneve, Virginia Driving Hawk. *Jimmy Yellow Hawk* 130
Speare, Elizabeth George. *The Sign of the Beaver* 130
Stuart, Gene S. *The Mighty Aztecs* 135
Tall Bull, Henry, and Tom Weist. *Cheyenne Legends of Creation* 138–39
   The Rolling Head 139
Tannenbaum, Beulah and Harold E. *Science of the Early American Indians* 135–36
Turnbaugh, Sarah P., and William Turnbaugh. *Indian Baskets* 140
Weiss, Harvey. *Shelters* 136
Wood, Marion. *Spirits, Heroes and Hunters from North American Mythology* 139

PERSIAN MATERIALS

Āmilī, Hamīd. *Khālih Sūskih* 143
Āzād, M. *Qissih-yi Tawqī* 143–44
   Zāl va Sīmurgh 144
Āzar Yazdī, Mihdī. *Qissih-hā-yi Khūb Barā-yi Bachih-hā-yi khūb* 144
Bahār, Mihrdād. *Bastūr* 144

Bātmānglīj, Muhammad, and Najmīyih Bātmānglīj. *Afsanih-yi Zal* 144
Bihrangī, Samad. *Uldūz va Arūsak-i-sukhangū* 144
Burhān, Ibn-i Yūsif. *Kaiumars, Nukhustīn Shāh-i Jahān* 145
Cole, Ann, Carolyn Haas, Elizabeth Heller, and Betty Weinberger. "Iran," in *Children Are Children* 153
Davīdam-u-Davīdam 145
Farjām, Faridih. *'Amū Nurūz* 145
   Mihmān-hā-yi Nākhāndih 145
Fox, Mary Virginia. *Iran* 146
Gulistān, Kāvih. *Gūlab* 147
   Qalamkār 147
Haack, Hermann. *Oriental Rugs* 153
Ibrahīmī Nādir. *Bārān, Āftāb va Qissih-yi Kāshī* 145
Imin, Līlī. *Shādimānih, Kūdakānih* 147
I'tisāmī, Parvīn. *Akhtar-i Charkh-i Adab* 147
Kalāgh Par 147
Kārgar, Dāryūsh. *Sufālgarī* 147
Kashkūlī, Mahdukht. *Rasm-i Mā Sahm-i Mā* 145
Kasrā'ī Sīāvash. *Ba'd Az Zimistān Dar Ābādī-yi Mā* 145
Lengyel, Emil. *Iran* 146–47
Liebetrau, Preben. *Oriental Rugs in Color* 153
Lutfī, Kiānūsh. *Gandum-u Kī Mīkhurih?* 145–46
   Yikī Būd Yikī Nabūd 145
Malikī, Kiānā. *Kadū-yi Qil Qilzan* 146
Mehdevi, Anne. *Parveen* 143
Miller, Nina. "Iran," in *Children's Festivals from Many Lands* 153
Moqadam, Mohammad, and Hosayn Sarshad. "Iran," in *Hi Neighbors* 153
Mūradī Kirmānī, Hūshang. *Qissih-hā-yi Majid* 146
Picard, Barbara Leonie. *Tales from Ancient Persia* 143
Qarīb Pūr, Bihrūz. *Ustād Khiymih Shab Bāzi Mīāmūzad* 147–48
Rahguzar, Rizā. *Muhājir-i Kūchak* 146
Rahīmī, Firiydūn. *Khāb-hā-yam Pur Az Kabutar va Bādbādak Ast* 146
Scott, Sally. *The Magic Horse* 143
Shamani, Muhammad Ali. *Bi Dunbāl-i Mīvih-yi Zindigī* 146
Shi'r-hā-i Barā-yi Kūdakān 148
Stanley, Diane. *Fortune* 143
Tāhbāz, Sīrus. *Bāgh-i Hamīshih Bahār* 148
Tames, Richard. *Take a Trip to Iran* 147
Tavakkoli, Gulī. *Arūsak-hā-yi Kāghazī* 148
Walkstein, Diane. *The Red Lion* 143
Watson, Jane W. *Iran* 147
Yūshīj, Nīmā, and M. Āzad. *Bachi-hā Bahār* 148
Zāl va Sāmurgh, Majmū'ih-yi Shānzdah Qissih Barāy-i Kūdakān 146
Zarrīnkilk, Nūrīddīn. *Ā Avval-i Alifbāst* 148